THE SELECTED LETTERS OF

D. H. LAWRENCE

Great Letters Series

LOUIS KRONENBERGER
GENERAL EDITOR

THE SELECTED LETTERS OF JOHN KEATS
EDITED BY LIONEL TRILLING

THE SELECTED LETTERS OF WILLIAM COWPER
EDITED BY MARK VAN DOREN

THE SELECTED LETTERS OF HENRY ADAMS
EDITED BY NEWTON ARVIN

THE SELECTED LETTERS OF THOMAS GRAY
EDITED BY JOSEPH WOOD KRUTCH

THE SELECTED LETTERS OF LORD BYRON
EDITED BY JACQUES BARZUN

THE SELECTED LETTERS OF GUSTAVE FLAUBERT
EDITED BY FRANCIS STEEGMULLER

THE SELECTED LETTERS OF CHARLES LAMB
EDITED BY T. S. MATTHEWS

THE SELECTED LETTERS OF ANTON CHEKHOV
EDITED BY LILLIAN HELLMAN

THE SELECTED LETTERS OF HENRY JAMES
EDITED BY LEON EDEL

THE SELECTED LETTERS OF D. H. LAWRENCE
EDITED BY DIANA TRILLING

OTHER TITLES IN PREPARATION

THE SELECTED LETTERS OF WILLIAM JAMES
EDITED BY ELIZABETH HARDWICK

THE SELECTED LETTERS OF T. E. LAWRENCE
EDITED BY IRVING HOWE

THE SELECTED LETTERS OF MARK TWAIN
EDITED BY ROBERT LOWELL

THE SELECTED LETTERS OF JOSEPH CONRAD
EDITED BY GRAHAM GREENE

THE SELECTED LETTERS OF CHARLES DICKENS
EDITED BY FREDERICK DUPEE

THE SELECTED LETTERS OF MARY WORTLEY MONTAGU
EDITED BY LOUIS KRONENBERGER

THE
SELECTED LETTERS OF
D. H. LAWRENCE

EDITED WITH AN INTRODUCTION BY
DIANA TRILLING

NEW YORK
FARRAR, STRAUS AND CUDAHY, INC.

PREFACE

IN MAKING this selection of Lawrence's correspondence I have used only letters which have already been published in one place or another and have made no attempt to investigate the still-unpublished material in libraries and private collections. A thorough research into the letters which have not yet seen publication will of course be necessary for a definitive edition of Lawrence's correspondence but that would constitute a very different kind of enterprise from the one I have undertaken with this volume.

By far the largest number of letters in this selection is drawn from *The Letters of D. H. Lawrence,* edited with an introduction by Aldous Huxley, The Viking Press, New York: 1932; Wm. Heinemann, London: 1932. I wish to acknowledge my profound indebtedness to Mr. Huxley and my gratitude to the Viking Press for permission to borrow so copiously from that collection. Were it not for Mr. Huxley's magnificent effort in gathering these letters in the years immediately following Lawrence's death, there is no doubt that much of this correspondence might have been destroyed or hopelessly scattered, which would have been an irreparable loss not alone to literary study but to literature itself.

The source of all letters other than those taken from the Huxley *Letters* is indicated in footnotes; it can therefore be understood that where no source is mentioned, the letter comes from Mr. Huxley's volume. The other sources I have used are as follows:

Amy Lowell by S. Foster Damon, Houghton Mifflin, Boston and New York: 1935

[v]

D. H. Lawrence's Letters to Bertrand Russell, edited with an introduction by Harry T. Moore, Gotham Book Mart, New York: 1948

D. H. Lawrence: Reminiscences and Correspondence by Earl and Achsah Brewster, Martin Secker, London: 1934

Early Life of D. H. Lawrence by Ada Lawrence and G. Stuart Gelder, Martin Secker, London: 1932

Eight Letters by D. H. Lawrence to Rachel Annand Taylor, with a foreword by Majl Ewing, Pasadena, California: 1956

I Will Send Address: New Letters of D. H. Lawrence by Mark Schorer, *London Magazine,* February 1956, Vol. 3, No. 2

Letters to S. S. Koteliansky, Encounter, December 1953, Vol. 1, No. 3

Lorenzo in Taos by Mabel Dodge Luhan, Martin Secker, London: 1933

"Not I, But the Wind . . ." by Frieda Lawrence, Wm. Heinemann, London: 1935

The Intelligent Heart by Harry T. Moore, Farrar, Straus and Young, New York: 1954

Lorenzo in Taos was published in America by Alfred A. Knopf in 1932. *"Not I, But the Wind . . ."* was published in America by the Viking Press in 1934. I list the English editions of these two books because it was with the English editions that I happened to work. Since it was impossible for me to consult the original letters, the texts which I employ precisely folow the texts in the publications which were my sources, even including apparent errors. For permission to quote from the books and articles which I list here I am personally as well as formally indebted to the Viking Press, which controls American publication rights on all Lawrence correspondence. I am also very grateful to the authors, editors and publishers who made this material publicly available.

My largest personal debt of gratitude is owed to Mr. Harry T.

Moore. Not only has Mr. Moore's admirable biography of Lawrence, *The Intelligent Heart*, provided some of the most interesting documents in this selection and served as my constant handbook for biographical information about Lawrence, but Mr. Moore has himself been generous and helpful quite beyond the call of ordinary scholarly comradeship. The acknowledgments in my footnotes—where information comes directly from Mr. Moore, his initials, H. T. M., appear in parentheses—can give no adequate measure of the amount of knowledge and time he has put at my disposal, patiently answering countless questions about the correct dating of letters and the possible identification of persons mentioned by Lawrence in his correspondence. Mr. Moore also called my attention to the privately published *Eight Letters of D. H. Lawrence to Rachel Annand Taylor*, which I am certain I should not otherwise have heard of, and lent me his copy of this little publication. In order to further my intention of presenting the letters in as complete a form as possible, Mr. Moore laboriously dug through his files to provide the salutations and subscriptions which he had omitted in printing the previously unpublished letters in *The Intelligent Heart*. And he painstakingly read proof on this volume to insure as much accuracy as his large scholarship had within its gift. Since I have no personal acquaintance with Mr. Moore, I am the more moved by such an exhibition of kindness.

I also want to thank the following persons for various courtesies they have shown me in the preparation of this volume: Lady Cynthia Asquith and the late Mr. J. Middleton Murry, Mr. Marshall Best of the Viking Press, Mr. Irving Kristol and Mr. Stephen Spender of *Encounter*, Mr. Leo Lerman, Mr. Donald Gallup of the Yale University Library, Mr. Laurence Pollinger, executor of the Estate of D. H. Lawrence, Mr. Mark Schorer, Miss Frances Steloff of the Gotham Book Mart. I am especially appreciative of the detailed assistance given me by Mr. Louis Kronenberger, the general editor of this series.

D.T.

CONTENTS

A LETTER OF INTRODUCTION

Dearest Norman:*

When I saw you the other day, you asked me how my Lawrence introduction was going, whether I had finished it yet,
and you forced me to the unhappy admission that it was going
not at all, despite a hundred beginnings and the absolute need
to be done with it this summer. Your response was what I
should have foreseen it would be, one of those generational
leers of yours: you knew all about me and my generation—oh,
this statistical urgency of yours!—what made us comfortable
and what strained us, what constituted a subject-matter and
what put a block in the road. You immediately knew what was
standing in my way: I was afraid to write about Lawrence
because he used to be so important to me, as to most of my
friends, and I used to think his ideas were *true.* Now I didn't
think so any more and I was afraid to confront the reasons.

Well, for the moment I offered no dissent because—it's probably a mistake for me to confess this to you—it had seemed to
me, too, that my inability to get the job done was a "resistance,"
a refusal of self-knowledge, and it would be fairly clear that
what I would be resisting in an essay on Lawrence would be an
assessment of my present-day feelings about him and the dis-
closure of whatever changes had taken place in me since I first
read him with the sense that he was *my* author. He's not at all
my author any more, that's sure. It doesn't occur to me to pick
him up for pleasure, to learn something that would make my

---

* Norman Podhoretz was born in 1930 and graduated from Columbia College
in 1950. A literary critic, he has contributed to many periodicals including
Commentary, The New Yorker, Partisan Review, Scrutiny, and the *New Leader*
where he launched a notable series of articles on the younger generation, since
when he has come to be thought of as spokesman for his literary age group.

life nicer or bigger although there never was an author who consciously undertook to make life so large. When I read Lawrence today it is to add to my knowledge of him, not to my imagination of me, and this change might certainly have its disconcerting personal implications.

But then, what do you read Lawrence for, Norman, you who were so barely born the year he died? To learn about you? I doubt it. The situation is as archeological for you as it is for me; there are always these unfathomable reaches of History which you in some subtle fashion put between yourself and anything that happened before this very instant. I'm talking not only of you, of course, or of the things you've written, but of an anxiety about time which seems to me to be common among your literary contemporaries: you all have this sense of time as a kind of cultural bulldozer laying total waste to the land with each flip of the calendar, you're as sensitive to the shifts in decades as we were to the passage of a century. For all of you an examination of yourselves as you were yesterday is like an ad-venture into a lost civilization. It's what accounts of course for your shared precocity, the speed and thoroughness with which you leave your yesterdays behind you. But it's also what ac-counts for your *schmerz,* the big hole at the center of your present which you wait for the future to fill. You like to blame this emptiness on your immediate culture rather than on a defect in your historical connection. Your refusal of any but your strictly contemporary experience, a refusal which is im-plicit in your compulsive historicity—this is the way it was in the '20s, this is the way it was in the '30s—is resistance in its essence, a rejection of the very idea of self-knowledge whose core, after all, is a recognition that the human circumstance is not one's own invention.

But to get back to my difficulties with Lawrence. It was surely quite possible that I was reluctant to retrace my experience of so personally involving an author. It had also occurred to me that perhaps I had talked myself out: it always makes an interesting speculation why an author is suddenly revived; in the last year or two Lawrence has strangely reappeared in our conversational lives, people seem to be clumsily edging up to the notion that perhaps here is a man who still has something to say to us. But now I know this isn't the explanation either, I've discovered what has really been troubling me. It's not that I hesitate to re-examine Lawrence's ideas—and we of course mean his sexual ideas—and I find I have more things I'd like to say than there are people to listen. But they're of a random personal kind that balks at the conventions of a formal literary essay, it's the literariness that stops me, the orderliness of presentation and the pedagogic attitude conventionally required of an introduction. I've actually written of Lawrence only once before but I become claustrophobic at the thought of plowing over the same old ground again, about how Lawrence was born in 1885 and died of tuberculosis in 1930 and how he was the son of a coal-miner father and a school-teacher mother and how he loved his mother too much and it made him nervous and about how he was a poet and therefore mustn't be read literally, but a poet without an esthetic other than his doctrine, his doctrine *was* his esthetic, and about how his doctrine had been distorted by people who haven't bothered to read him thoroughly and about how his doctrine has been misread even by people who have read him more or less thoroughly because it assaults their most precious assumptions etc. etc. It isn't that the old ground is no longer fertile; there's not an inch of it but would yield. And I don't ignore the requirements of conscience in writing about Lawrence, the need for a special sanity and balance of the sort we like to think is pedagogic and which does of course finally rest on one's willingness to school oneself in what Lawrence actually wrote and intended: there are so many and such assorted irresponsibilities Lawrence has suffered. But surely one can be as responsible outside as within the established forms, just as one can often best comprehend an object by the full indulgence of one's subjectivity, Lawrence in his travel writing

[xiii]

being a classic instance. I'm all at once impatient of an objectivity which adds up to little more than submitting to a convention of literary address and moderating one's voice. I especially want to take Lawrence, who is always written about so grimly, out of the study into the living room where I can be easy and unsolemn, or I want to write a letter, this letter. Lawrence needs to be gossiped about, he was that kind of man and writer; at least he peculiarly needs to be come at with as much human immediacy as one can manage.

There's the matter of Frieda Lawrence, for instance. She was a Lawrence *fact,* a human fact of the greatest significance in Lawrence's literary career. How can one write about the author of these letters and ignore the wife who was so consistently at his shoulder when he was writing most of them? It's absurd the way criticism and even biography are willing to explore every influence that touches a writer except the woman he marries. I remember how careful I was myself, in my introduction to the *Viking Portable Lawrence,* not to say anything that would offend Frieda or that could be construed as an invasion of her privacy; but that was because she was still alive. Expectably, she took offense anyway, I was told: it angered her that I had written of Lawrence that a decade and a half after his death he was even less read and appreciated than in his lifetime—so small a scrap of truth to undo such a substantial effort of propriety! But now that Frieda is dead that limitation is removed and I can deal with her as with any other of Lawrence's compositions and as his composer too, which she naturally was, as Lawrence well knew and said quite simply. Why are Lawrence's letters so wonderful, the best in modern literature and second only to Keats' in the whole history of English literature, except that they are so absolutely personal, so close to home, so miraculously without an eye to posthumous publication? If we don't hesitate to read a man's mail, if we don't hesitate to read letters even as personal as these of Lawrence, why should we scruple to read such a public statement as his choice of a wife? I want to start with Frieda and throw her out as an institutional piety; instead I'll embrace her for the big, significant, soft, silly reality she actually was. It's no accident that a man marries the woman he marries and if he's a writer, sooner or later he'll somehow explain his choice in his books. But sometimes it's easier, and it should always be thought more respectable, to get at the books through the wife than at the wife through the books.

I'll begin with Frieda, then, and tell you what I think of her but you must keep in mind that I *really* know nothing about her, I've never even known anyone who met her. I think Frieda was a bit of a swamp, and this, dear Norman, is literary criticism, impressionistic to-be-sure, but literary criticism nonetheless, whatever its high savor of gossip; it has directly to do with the kind of writer Lawrence was. She had a swampy mind and spirit, she had no intellect, no real intelligence, yet she had wits; she was shrewd like so many Continental and so few American women, she had her own kind of innocence but it was not of the sort which is so continuing and inexplicable a fact of our American ineptitude. No American woman, no matter how gifted in masochism—and we make a female specialty of it in this country, it's part of our pioneer heritage—could have been married to Lawrence without going mad; perhaps even a Frenchwoman married to Lawrence would have gone mad. It took a German woman like Frieda to stay entirely sane and make a successful career of the lunacy of her marriage.

Now we must remember that in a way she had been bred for her fate, unlike our Bennington girls, the ones who look to art and lunacy for their personal salvation. For our poor girls, the lunatic life of art has only a negative force, it's the obverse of the mental-health culture in which they have been reared. But Frieda, being German, had a large cultural support when she chose Lawrence. Lunacy *was* mental health in post-war Germany and so far as Frieda is concerned it doesn't make the least bit of difference that she was statistically pre-war, almost forty and long removed from Germany by the time the war ended;

[xv]

she seems to me to have been entirely typical of Germany in the years after the first war—being an aristocrat, she was no doubt ahead of herself; the upper classes, especially in Europe, always move in advance of their national culture, they can afford to take more chances. To make a successful life on the slippery edge of madness was the progressive thing for someone of Frieda's background to do, like wandering around with a knapsack or painting wooden bowls. Essentially there was a good deal of the *wandervogel* in Frieda throughout her life and Lawrence liked it in her although it also made trouble between them as it would no doubt have gone on to make trouble for Lady Chatterley and Mellors if the book hadn't ended when it did: you'll remember Constance Chatterley and her sister had had German, not English, young womanhoods. Was it Frieda or was it Lawrence—I think it was Frieda—who said she had been in a sleep when Lawrence found her, the wife of a Nottingham professor of languages, pouring tea while her three children romped on the lawn? She had whiled away some of the tedium of faculty life with an inconsequential adultery or two, but we can guess that it wasn't sex that had impelled her to her infidelities any more than it was sex speaking when she invited Lawrence to stay the night in the absence of Professor Weekley —not sex, that is, in primary terms. Do I do Frieda an injustice? —I always have this impression that it was art or, rather, creativeness that was the great imperative for her; sex was just a secondary gain in the life of self-expression. Lawrence brought Frieda into the full tumultuous tide of creative living, eventually he made her famous, which was its own immaculate pleasure, but right from the start he gave her the creative status which Weekley couldn't provide, he made her the woman behind his genius which is so much more what women seem to want than being geniuses themselves. We have it in Frieda's own words in her foolish memoir of her husband where she says with the catastrophic naïveté which is her style, "I had always regarded Lawrence's genius as given to me. I felt deeply responsible for what he wrote." More revealing than the remark itself is its context, an account of Lawrence's relation with Mabel Dodge Luhan; it seems that Mabel and Lawrence wanted to do a book together, it was to be about Mabel, and Frieda explains her position: "I did not want this. I had always regarded Lawrence's genius as given to me." It's from passages like this that I draw my impression that for Frieda art rather outranked sex. But Lawrence could have been a bad artist and it would have been all the same to Frieda so long as he was for self-expression in the largest possible quantity; she had no taste, as we mean the exercise of artistic judgment. But then neither had Lawrence; Lawrence never thought of art in terms of taste any more than he thought of art in terms of permanence. The value for Lawrence of a created work lay not in its lastingness or in its conformity to esthetic standard but in its rightness at the moment and for its creator, in its usefulness as a form of personal communication. He cared just as much about his painting as about his writing and he wasn't a very good painter; and he could devote himself to embroidery and the decoration of little boxes with the same casual gravity he gave to his major literary efforts. Is it funny that I use the word "casual" of Lawrence? It's the accurate word. Certainly there was never a writer who took himself so solemnly as a human being but so unsolemnly as an artist.

I don't for a moment mean that Lawrence was unsolemn about the content of his books or even about their method. He was always the subject of his books and he regarded himself as the most serious subject in the world. And he was a very conscious artist, he was anything but the primitive some of his critics have made him out to be; nothing could have been more intellectualized than his theory of the unconscious source of art. But he never "saw himself" as an artist, only as a person and workman; although his extraordinary gifts were recognized unusually early in his career, it never occurred to him to suppose they earned him any privilege in society. Writing was simply the way he made his living as someone else made his by carpentry or ditch-digging and he did it as competently and quietly as if ours were a world in which as much status accrued to a carpenter as to a literary celebrity. Because he attracted to himself a group of followers for whom he was prophet and savior, and manifestly enjoyed the role, we tend to accuse him of playing artist to the philistines. But this is a mistake, he never bullied people with his artistic superiority, only with his messianism; he never asked or claimed a superior social or personal place on the basis of his talents or their recognition. As an artist he was the most unassuming man who ever lived. It is also a mistake to think of Lawrence, as we are likely to, as one of those instances of unacknowledged or unrewarded genius whose recollection is supposed to fortify the rising artist against a life of failure. Lawrence suffered enormous hardship; he was ill, he was poor, he had great trouble with the press, he was persecuted by the law, he was accused of being a German spy in the war, with alarming regularity his best friends became his public enemies. But there have been few serious let alone revolutionary artists whose right to special critical notice was won so fast and surely. He stopped teaching with the publication of his first novel, *The White Peacock,* which, incidentally, had been taken by the first publisher who saw it, and never again attempted to earn his living except by writing—in any writer's life this implies a large demand on society and a considerable victory if it is managed even meagerly. And despite the hostility which he generated every step of his way, the sheer power of his gift imposed itself unusually early, demanded and received its acknowledgment no matter how grudging or unsympathetic. From the very beginning he was always thought of as a genius and, after all, that isn't the common way we mask our dislikes.

But I have wandered too far from Frieda and her first marriage and Professor Weekley. Poor Professor Weekley: I gather he was something of a scholar, he wrote a series of books on etymology, but I'm afraid this doesn't make him the less dim. As he comes through the letters and biographies he seems to have been a person of low emotional intensity and high self-conscious principle who, having once laid successful claim to a woman of spirit, felt he owed it to himself never again to settle for less. I can scarcely suppose he was quite as awful as Lawrence pictures him in the letter to Amy Lowell where he describes Frieda's interview with him when she returned to England in 1914, two years after the elopement. It's a brilliant letter but somehow Lawrence's effort to make Weekley into the very image of castrated middle-class respectability, calling Frieda a prostitute and refusing her all communication with her children, doesn't ring entirely true for me; I have an idea that Lawrence is projecting into Weekley an aspect of his own judgment on Frieda and himself. Lawrence had been miserable about his equivocal situation with Frieda in the two years between the elopement and their marriage; whenever he thought people mistakenly assumed they were married, he hurried to set the record straight. He had wanted this married woman and he had had the courage to take what he wanted, perhaps it was even an important condition of his love for Frieda that she was already another man's wife and a mother; he overrode Frieda's hesitations in fine style and got her to run off with him. But he hated living with her without marriage, it shocked him and he expected others to be shocked. The worst of which I seem to be able to accuse Weekley in the scene Lawrence recreates is a certain hamming and an inadequate imagination in supposing he could outmatch Lawrence by taking a high moral line: this was Lawrence's game and was there anyone to beat him at it? I didn't guess it from Lawrence's reports of Weekley, actually I learned it from Harry Moore's biography, but I suppose I should have been able to figure out that Weekley wanted Frieda the more, not the less, because she had left him for Lawrence: twenty years later, when Lawrence died, Weekley asked her to come back to him and I find this touching, it quite rounds out my image of him, that he had held on to Frieda all these years as the test of his manliness. It's like something in a Lawrence novel, isn't it, but Weekley was precisely like someone in a Lawrence novel, one of those men who need a woman like Frieda to validate their masculinity. Lawrence needed a woman like Frieda himself, to validate his masculinity too, which not only identifies him with Weekley but also with all his other Weekley characters, including Clifford Chatterley, all the frightened insufficient men in his novels who depend on women for their strength. This of course is the confusing thing about Lawrence and his books. Everybody knows Lawrence was representing an image of himself in the gamekeeper Mellors in *Lady Chatterley's Lover*. But Lawrence was not only Mellors in that novel, he was Clifford Chatterley as well. Lawrence is not only the heroes in his fiction but the villains too, which is what licenses the cruelty in his books. This is what licenses Lawrence's quite extreme cruelty to Clifford Chatterley: Chatterley is himself.

I'm convinced Frieda was the best possible, indeed the only possible wife for Lawrence. She had a lot of strength, she was *there,* yet she was sufficiently amorphous to mold herself to any notion of femaleness Lawrence needed to impress upon her. She must have been an awful nuisance the way he couldn't even write a letter without her telling him where she agreed and disagreed and adding her own postscripts à la Lawrence, and it's embarrassing how she tried to ape his style. *His* style, of all things for a German lady to ape! But he loved it, of course, when they were newly together—he was twenty-seven when they eloped, she was thirty-three and she must have been still open and sweet-looking then; she aged badly, from the pictures one gathers she became both sharp and overblown, a bit witchlike—and it was very shrewd of him to have chosen her, very therapeutic. Do you remember his remark about how he believed in art, not for art's sake, but for his own sake? "One sheds one's sicknesses in books, repeats and presents again one's emoto be totally assimilated into the sexual experience, he feared to give the sexual emotions any autonomy unless they were sanctified by love. It was a conflict so strong and so deeply rooted in his own personal history that it was impossible of resolution and it accounts, in my opinion, for our inability ever finally to understand what Lawrence is driving toward in his fiction, our inability ever to parse either his plots or his characters and finally say, with any conviction of accuracy, just what it is he *approves* in the relations between his heroes and heroines. We know of what Lawrence disapproves, we know he disapproves of all assertions of will and all sexual behavior which has mere sensation as its goal. But even here he is ambiguous, flagrantly so at times. In the character of Mellors, for example, it's impossible to distinguish what Lawrence would call an assertion of will from what he presents to us as an expression of the gamekeeper's inviolable mesculinity and wholly admirable pride. And surely it is difficult to rid Mellors' exercises in sensuality of the charge that they are efforts—and why not, indeed?— to achieve new sensations, new thrills. It's striking that Lawrence never tells us what Mellors and Constance Chatterley actually do on their big sensual excursion; this is the one sexual scene in *Lady Chatterley's Lover* where Lawrence himself did the expurgating. We can conjecture that he drew back at this point as much because he realized he was violating a cardinal tenet of his own faith—his injunction against sensation-seeking—as because of his puritanism.

Whoever has read Lawrence with any thoroughness and tried to grasp his sexual doctrine must at last ask himself, what did Lawrence *really* want of the relationship between a man and a woman, not in metaphoric terms—in the realm of metaphor we accept the fact that we are expected to make our own interpretations and that we may be mistaken—but in didactic terms. (This is another of the contradictions in Lawrence: so much a poet, he yet insists that we read him as a preacher.) Does he want sex without love? Obviously not. Does he want love without sex? Obviously not. Does he want sex and love together? Well, yes and no. Certainly he wants them in conjunction more than he wants them separate, and yet when he puts them in conjunction he is at once and quite automatically driven to attack the quality either of the love or of the sex. The answer is, I'm afraid, that he wants neither sex nor love but some combined transcendence of both, a transcendence that has its source and fulfillment only in phantasy. This transcendence he calls marriage. "Your most vital necessity in this life," he wrote Dunlop, the friendly consul at Spezia, "is that you shall love your wife completely and implicitly and in entire nakedness of body and spirit. . . . You asked me once what my message was . . . this that I tell you is my message as far as I've got any." And you recall that little story he wrote called "Love" in which the girl refuses adoration, appreciation, caressing, anything we commonly think of as love-making. She doesn't want her sweetheart to touch her and yet it's not that she is averse to sexuality, it's just that she wants no demonstrations either of physical or spiritual courtship, all she wants is marriage. Marriage was Lawrence's message. But no marriage on land or sea, Norman; no marriage you or I have ever known, no marriage he had ever known. Lawrence spoke about marriage as he spoke about a return to the dark gods of an earlier civilization than our Hebraic-Christian civilization, as a metaphor against loneliness. His message makes no reasonable sense: when was there ever an entire nakedness of body and spirit between a man and a woman, it's rather dreadful to contemplate. But of course his message makes sense as poetry, as an overleap of the imagination in order to dramatize the insufficiency of our ordinary civilized sexual relationships.

I read Lawrence today and I'm utterly confounded by the effect he had on me and my friends when we first read him: we thought his metaphors were translatable into a program for practical conduct! We knew he addressed himself to us not on behalf of a new way of acting but a new way of being. We understood, of course—after all, we weren't stupid—that his sociology, his politics, his anthropology, his religion were all of them directed only to the quality of being which Lawrence hoped to produce; we never read *The Plumed Serpent* as a defense of Hitler or Mussolini, we knew he didn't mean us to run around like Aztecs or Incas or whatever they were. Yet in the sexual sphere we seemed to find in his books a literal sanction which literally is not there—the sanction for a free, even an experimental sexuality, and we recognized neither the contradictions in his doctrine nor its abstraction from reality. Since Lawrence's morality had to do with the kind of person one is and since all his thinking had as its object the discovery of a better way of being, both of which preoccupations are of course wholly in line with the concerns of the romantic poets, we read Lawrence like the last of the romantics, a bit on the mystical side but still the most intense and personal of the romantic idealists, the one who imposed on us the heaviest burden of self-consciousness and self-realization, as it used to be called. In our effort to meet his high challenge to self-awareness, we failed to perceive that there is no world for Lawrence's people, that they are isolated in their intensity, and that he doesn't permit *us* to live in the actual world—this and his profound sexual puritanism, the fact that he licenses sex only as a sacrament.

You're wiser in your generation, Norman, than we were about Lawrence; no, not wiser, keener. Having been born in the years of the economic depression gives you a keener nose for reality and a quicker instinct to protect practise against theory, which is also why you're less generous than we were. You're more acute in your reading of Lawrence because you're less generous in your imagination of heroism; transcendence worries you, perhaps a little too much. You immediately smell out Lawrence's remoteness from actual life and his restrictiveness, you know that if you take him literally he would pull you after himself into some unwholesome morass and that he doesn't

[xxix]

represent the romantic ideal of freedom. Steven, for instance, says that after a bout of Lawrence he always turns to Colette: we would have scorned such an idea, thought it frivolous, but Steven is right of course and we were wrong: as a sexual writer, Colette is exactly the indicated antidote to Lawrence. And yet I wonder. I wonder if this reality principle of yours doesn't define a weakness as much as a strength. At least we *hoped* ourselves capable of ultimate emotion, ultimate vision, ultimate experience and, measuring our capacity, we were willing to make mistakes; we didn't enter maturity, like you who, born in the depression, still remain determinists of every kind except economic, all set to accept whatever limitations on our being and call them our fate. We didn't invoke reality *only* as a negative force, *only* as a restriction of possibility; there were *some* times when we supposed reality was on our side. Dear Norman, there surely is much to be said for a view of life, like Lawrence's, which not only refuses the simple on the sole ground that it is less than the complex but which also insists that we make our own conditions and that our fate can be grand. I keep thinking of your English contemporaries, those angry young men as they are so inaccurately called, who are so full of self-pity and envy and not at all angry, really, because it takes pride to be angry and they have no pride. What a poor spectacle their protest makes alongside that of Lawrence whose pride and rage were like a banner! I'm glad that we in our country have not yet produced a counterpart of this English thing, it reassures me that we're still a going concern over here. But I'd be more reassured if we weren't nowadays *quite* so wry about transcendence, in the degree that we are supposed to be worldly. There's much to be said for challenging fate instead of ducking behind it.

I speak of my impression that Lawrence may be due for a revival, people seem to be talking about him again. If this is true, it will be amusing to see what his newest readers will do with him. Obviously they won't look to Lawrence for sexual permission, as we did; anyway, nobody looks to literature for his sexual morality any more, this is all provided in nursery school, by the white mice. Perhaps what we'll have next is Lawrence as a domestic poet, a poet of the domestic self, a mystic of the hearth; but then I can't imagine what we'll do with his child-lessness—do you suppose our society will ever again be able to accept a prophet of marriage who is not also a prophet of parenthood? (But I'll tell you something about the childless Lawrence. He was opposed to birth control in marriage, it's in a letter to Frieda when they first went to Germany together and she was worried about becoming pregnant.) It seems to me there are a variety of aspects in which Lawrence can be made sympathetic to the contemporary young reader: he was all for religion, after all, even though he wasn't theological; and he was against practical politics, once he discovered what a fool he made of himself when he came near them; and he was a great do-it-yourself man, always puttering about painting walls and building furniture. And we mustn't forget his instinct for community, this is Lawrence strictly in our mood of the '50s, all for communities of the like-minded and utterly unable to sustain a real friendship. On the surface, Lawrence's Rananim, the ideal community to which he was always proposing that he and Frieda and a few chosen souls should take off, may seem a far cry from the PTA but the more I think about Lawrence the more I come to see how similar his societal instinct was to that of our present-day run of progressive young fathers and mothers: it was an instinct to work shoulder-to-shoulder with other in-dividuals in a common cause, it was not an instinct to personal relationship of a kind which nourishes the capacity for feeling. I used to be sorry for Lawrence because of his friends, I thought he had a more than normally developed impulse for friendship as an overflow of his genius and that he had simply not had the good fortune to meet people who were properly responsive; I supposed it was because they were frustrated by their inability to meet the requirements of friendship with Lawrence that the people who had known him best turned sour and wrote those nasty memoirs. Now I assign a good portion of the responsibility for Lawrence's aborted relationships to Lawrence himself, for choosing his intimates as he did, with full knowledge of their weaknesses, and then moving in on them at the points where they were most vulnerable. After all, Lawrence was never blind to the kind of man Middleton Murry really was, he knew that Murry's dealings with Katherine Mansfield revealed the basic pattern of his character; Lawrence didn't have to go on with him as he did, inviting Murry's self-abnegations just so he could assert his contempt of them. And the same with Mabel Luhan: from their first contact, Mabel had shown her hand. Her invitation to Lawrence to visit her in Taos was patently the communication of a woman any sensible man runs a mile from, enclosing strong Indian medicine to draw Lawrence to America and assuring him she was willing him in her direction. But instead of answering no thank you very much, I'm busy in Europe, Lawrence acted coy, he was flattered and he stimulated Mabel to persist until she had thoroughly entangled him and then, when he was living on her hospitality, he behaved abominably; he criticized everything she did—the way she dressed, the way she ran her house, the way she treated her husband—all the while paying himself out to her on a long sexual line which he was jolly sure was firmly in Frieda's keeping! Or there was his relation with Lady Ottoline Morrell, who was generous to him and to whom he showed but poor gratitude. It isn't that one minds his having caricatured Lady Ottoline as Hermione in *Women in Love*, that's the way some writers have to work and I suppose a good book is worth a friendship. But surely it was unforgivable of him to tell her it was all her fault, the fault of her will, that Maria Nys had attempted suicide. Who was he to accuse other people of assertions of will who himself had all but driven Bertrand Russell to suicide and who would have done the same to E. M. Forster too, except that Forster, with his quiet sanity, skittered right away from under?

No, it would be my opinion that, the memoirs apart, Lawrence got rather better than he deserved from his friends. No one tried to bludgeon *him* out of his sanity, his friends gave him money or tried to get it for him, they gave him their houses to live in, they listened to him and tried to understand what he was talking about. And if this was because he was a great man and perhaps their only path to immortality, this still doesn't absolve Lawrence from the duty of appreciating them for their appreciation of him. Recently I was reading H. D.'s tribute to Freud, it's an awful little book, and I was thinking how foolish it was of Freud to let himself be taken in by H.D. as he seemed to have been—until I suddenly realized, not how foolish, but how nice it was of Freud to have accepted H. D. so generously, despite her apparent sloppy-mindedness and inconsequentiality; of course there was vanity in his acceptance of her discipleship, but even more there was a genuine kindliness in his accepting her just because she had this discipleship to give. There would seem to have been but two places where neither the biographical record as we now have it nor the correspondence indicates a misuse on Lawrence's part of the friendships that were offered him, with the Aldous Huxleys and with Lady Cynthia Asquith. The Huxleys were wonderfully kind to Lawrence in his last years when he was very ill; there's nothing in the correspondence to suggest that this was a martyrdom they endured, we gather that Lawrence showed himself at his best with them, which was very good indeed, perhaps because Huxley had the rare distinction among Lawrence's friends of truly understanding Lawrence's writings; certainly Huxley's introduction to the Lawrence letters is still the best single piece of Lawrence criticism that has been written. As for Lady Cynthia, she was a special instance. Although we're told that Lawrence was a chameleon in his responses to people, giving them pretty much what they expected of him, Lady Cynthia would seem to have been the only person in Lawrence's life who expected of him and received an almost wholly consistent temperateness. Moore says in his biography that Lawrence was in love with her but he gives no evidence apart from the letters which for some reason don't convey that impression to me. Yet it's perfectly easy for me to believe that Lawrence loved Lady Cynthia dearly as the sole representative of her class who never apologized to him for it, either explicity or implicitly. She held her social place with a lovely quiet and assurance. If Lawrence was a snob he was also an artist, with a fine feel for the real thing. Lady Cynthia was probably closest to the real thing Lawrence ever met in his long search for the distinction which would validate the differences in social class.

Certainly Lawrence's letters to Lady Cynthia have a particular charm and sincerity. Much of the time Lawrence wrote insincerely to his friends; this is one of the unexpected things about him, that someone who could be so outrageous could also be so careful to put up a good front. This is a wholesomeness in Lawrence, his insincerity, and when the front breaks down we have reason to worry for him. But with Lady Cynthia we have the impression that the front and his true feelings are in a unique alignment, we feel this is how he might have been had the circumstances of his life not pushed him quite so hard. There are moments of course when he is sharp even with her, as when he writes for help with passports and other legal troubles, but the sharpness is a matter of direct response to the situation in which he finds himself, he's not making an unhappy symbol of Lady Cynthia and he is never assertive. Sometimes he teases her, as when he writes after the birth of a new baby, and we realize how seldom he could tease or be teased. Always he writes to her in his best domestic vein: "We live awfully cheaply. I know these things interest you more than eternal truths. . . ."

and he goes on to report that his house costs 60 francs a month, the maid 25. Is it too elaborate to put it that Lady Cynthia seems to compare to Frieda as Colette compares to Lawrence, representing his release from the ultimate confrontations which were so sympathetic to Frieda's Germanic temperament? But then of course it would never have done for Lawrence to have married Lady Cynthia; married to her he would not have become Lawrence.

Frieda was the girl for Lawrence. "Be definite, my dear; be detailed, be business-like," Lawrence wrote to Frieda in 1912; it was when they were about to start life together. "In our marriage, let us be business-like. The love is there—then let the common-sense match it." It is one of Lawrence's most appealing qualities, his gift for the business-like and an important reason to read his letters because they remind us that however remote from reality was the world in which Lawrence preached his doctrine he knew better than most of us how to live in a world where people have to buy and cook their food, pack their luggage, make trains, mail books and correct proofs. I know nothing more magical in the history of literature than the sensible, unfretful confidence with which Lawrence dispatched his precious copiless manuscripts from whatever out-of-the-way spot in which he had chosen to settle in his eternal wanderings, with apparently no thought that they might be lost, and if you assign this poise to a deficient sense of reality, you're wrong; in the practical matters of mailing things or making trains or dealing with agents and publishers, Lawrence was nothing if not realistic, he had the superlative good sense to know that in the long run caution is a mockery of wisdom: of all writers who have ever lived, he was most sparing of his business energies and beautifully business-like. And he was right, of course: he didn't lose his manuscripts and his mail did arrive at its destination and so did he and Frieda arrive at theirs. I daresay if it had been up to Frieda to make the arrangements, things would have been different: Frieda was the kind of person who instinctively misses a train, she never learned Lawrence's sense about living. So devoted to the creative, she had no way of dealing with the ordinary, whether it was eating a meal or making a dress, except by exalting it into a poetic principle, a process in which the ordinary inevitably loses its charm and becomes a mere artistic commonplace. Frieda would have thought she had to show herself superior to the business of life; Lawrence proved he was its equal. This was a great amiability in his nature, a genuine good humor.

But then everyone speaks of Lawrence's good spirits, his gaiety and bounce, the wonderful companion he could be, his ability to make one see and hear more than one thought possible; we have constantly to correct the image pressed on us by his books, and even by many of the letters, of irascibility and over-intensity, our sense of a man so finely drawn that life is an unbearable exacerbation of the nerves. There is always the report that it was a privilege to know him even slightly: Rebecca West, for instance, who spent only a few hours in his company, remembers the occasion as a rare experience of enhancement; she too tells us how he made her see and feel more than anyone she had ever met—he had just arrived in the Italian town where she visited with him and even on his way from the railroad station had already caught its essence; he was writing about it in his hotel room a few minutes later and then they went for a walk together and Lawrence made this small excursion into a memorable adventure, sharing with her his own quick response to the countryside, his extraordinary feeling for nature. This is what gives the letters their grace, is it not? this is what gave Lawrence his grace as a human being—the immediacy with which he saw life and the directness with which he shares his experience. It may have been a half-mad life and surely he was a sick man long before his body finally gave over to the tuberculosis that had threatened it for so many years. But for all the sickness, he never wrote a line, not the merest business note, that didn't intend to quicken life and make it more splendid.

Affectionately,

D.T.

Westport, Connecticut, September 1957.

CORRESPONDENTS

The following is a list of the persons to whom Lawrence addressed the letters in this selection:

ASQUITH, LADY CYNTHIA (1887–   )—Daughter of the 11th Earl of Wemyss. Wife of the Hon. Herbert Asquith, lawyer and son of the Prime Minister. Novelist and biographer; 1918–37, secretary to Sir James Barrie. Author of a memoir, *Remember and Be Glad*, 1952.

BRAMBLE, HELEN W.—Associated with *Forum*, an American magazine.

BRETT, THE HON. DOROTHY (1883–   )—Painter. Daughter of Viscount Esher and sister of the Ranee of Sarawak. Author of a Lawrence memoir, *Lawrence and Brett*, 1933.

BREWSTER, MRS. ACHSAH—American painter resident in Capri. Wife of Earl and mother of Harwood. Author, with Earl Brewster, of a Lawrence memoir, *D. H. Lawrence: Reminiscences and Correspondence*, 1934.

BREWSTER, EARL—American painter resident in Capri. Husband of Achsah and father of Harwood. Author, with Achsah Brewster, of a Lawrence memoir, *D. H. Lawrence: Reminiscences and Correspondence*, 1934.

BREWSTER, HARWOOD—Daughter of Earl and Achsah Brewster. Born 1912.

BROWN, CURTIS—Literary agent.

BURROW, DR. TRIGANT (1875–1950)—American psychiatrist and psychoanalyst.

BYNNER, WITTER (1881–   )—American poet resident in New Mexico. Author of a Lawrence memoir, *Journey with Genius*, 1951.

CAMPBELL, (CHARLES HENRY) GORDON; later LORD GLENAVY (1885–   )—Irish lawyer resident in London. Friend of the Murrys.

CARSWELL, CATHERINE; formerly MRS. H. P. M. JACKSON (1879–1946)—Critic and novelist. Wife of Donald, mother of John Patrick (J. P.). Author of *Life of Robert Burns* and a Lawrence memoir, *The Savage Pilgrimage*, 1932.

CARSWELL, DONALD (1882–1940)—Lawyer. Husband of Catherine.

CHAMBERS, J. D.—Youngest brother of Jessie Chambers, the Miriam of *Sons and Lovers*.

CLARKE, MRS. W. E.—See Ada Lawrence.

CLARKE, JACK—Elder son of Ada Lawrence Clarke and nephew of Lawrence. Died in a German prison camp in World War II.

COLLINGS, ERNEST—Artist, a mail acquaintance of Lawrence.

COOPER, GERTRUDE—Childhood neighbor and friend of Lawrence.

CROSBY, CARESSE—Wife of Harry Crosby. Co-owner, with her husband, of the Black Sun Press in Paris, publishers of *The Escaped Cock* and other works of Lawrence.

CROSBY, HARRY—See Caresse Crosby.

D., T. D. (THOMAS DACRE DUNLOP, later SIR THOMAS)—Member of the consular service, later Inspector-General of consular establishments, Foreign Office. English consul at Spezia during Lawrence's stay there in early 1914.

DAVIES, RHYS—Anglo-Welsh novelist and short story writer, author of *The Withered Root* and other books.

EAMES, MARIAN (MRS. HAMILTON EAMES)—An American acquaintance, daughter of Mrs. Witt of Taos.

ERNST, MORRIS L.—New York lawyer, author of numerous books on social and political questions.

FORSTER, E. M. (1879–   )—English novelist and short story writer, author of *A Passage to India* and other books.

GARDINER, ROLF—Social reformer and work-camp leader.

GARNETT, EDWARD (1868–1937)—Critic and literary adviser to publishers. Husband of Constance, well-known translator of Russian authors, and father of David (Bunny) who was later the author of *Lady into Fox* and other books.

GLENAVY, LADY (BEATRICE, MRS. GORDON CAMPBELL) —Wife of Gordon Campbell.

GRAY, CECIL—English composer and biographer of Philip Heseltine (the composer, Peter Warlock).

HAWK, A. D.—Landlord of the Lawrences in New Mexico. Father of William Hawk.

HAWK, WILLIAM—Son of A. D. Hawk, husband of Rachel. Neighbor of the Lawrences in New Mexico.

HEINEMANN, WILLIAM—Lawrence's first publisher in England.

HENRY, MRS. NANCY—Associated with the Oxford University Press, publishers of Lawrence's *Movements in European History*.

HOPKIN, MRS. SALLIE A.—Wife of William E. Hopkin, mother of Enid (later Mrs. Hilton).

HOPKIN, WILLIAM E. (1852–1951)—Nottingham resident and historian. Lifelong friend of Lawrence and his family. Husband of Sally, father of Enid.

HUXLEY, ALDOUS (1894–   )—English writer, author of *Point Counterpoint* and other books. Editor, *The Letters of D. H. Lawrence*, 1932.

HUXLEY, MRS. JULIETTE—Wife of Julian Huxley, well-known biologist and brother of Aldous Huxley.

HUXLEY, MARIA (1900 [?]–1955)—Wife of Aldous Huxley.

JAFFE, DR. ELSE—Elder sister of Frieda Lawrence. Political economist, student of Max Weber. Wife of Dr. Edgar Jaffe, professor of political economy at Munich. Later Lawrence's German translator.

JOHNSON, WILLARD (SPUD or SPOODLE)—Friend of Witter Bynner. Editor, *The Laughing Horse*, a small American periodical.

KOTELIANSKY, S. S. (1880–1955)—Russian economist and literary translator in exile in England.

LAWRENCE, FRIEDA; *Geb.* VON RICHTHOFEN (1879–1956) —Wife of D. H. Lawrence, former wife of Ernest Weekley, professor of modern languages at the University of Nottingham. After Lawrence's death, wife of Angelo Ravagli. Author of a Lawrence memoir, *"Not I, But the Wind ...",* 1935.

LAWRENCE, ADA (1887–1948)—Younger sister of Lawrence, wife of W. E. Clarke. Author of a Lawrence memoir, *Young Lorenzo,* 1932, and, with Stuart Gelder, of *Early Life of D. H. Lawrence,* 1932.

LOWELL, AMY (1874–1925)—American poet who had become acquainted with Lawrence on a trip to England.

LUHAN, MABEL DODGE (1879–   )—Wealthy Buffalo-born member of the international artistic world. Formerly a well-known hostess in New York and Florence, later resident in Taos, New Mexico, where she married her fourth husband, Tony Luhan, a full-blooded Pueblo Indian. Author of a series of reminiscences, *Intimate Memories,* and of a Lawrence memoir, *Lorenzo in Taos,* 1933.

MANSFIELD, KATHERINE (1888–1923)—Short story writer, author of *The Dove's Nest* and other volumes. Wife of J. Middleton Murry. Died of tuberculosis in France.

MARSH, EDWARD; later SIR EDWARD (1872–1953)—Of the Colonial Service; at various times Private Secretary to Winston Churchill and Mr. Asquith. Editor, *Georgian Poetry,* an annual anthology.

McLEOD, A. W.—Teacher at the Davidson Road School at Croydon where Lawrence also taught as a young man.

MONROE, HARRIET—Editor, *Poetry,* an American magazine.

MORRELL, LADY OTTOLINE (1873–1938)—Daughter of Lt. Gen. Arthur Cavendish-Bentinck, half-sister of the 6th Duke of Portland, wife of Philip Morrell.

MORRELL, PHILIP—Liberal M. P., husband of Lady Ottoline Morrell. Several times raised questions in the House of Commons about the suppression of Lawrence's books.

MORRISON, MRS. NELLY—In whose house in Florence the Lawrences stayed in 1921.

MURRY, JOHN (JACK) MIDDLETON (1889–1957)—English journalist, critic and editor. Husband of Katherine Mansfield with whom he edited *Rhythm* and the *Blue Review*, literary periodicals. Later, editor of the *Athenaeum* and of the *Adelphi*. Author of a Lawrence biography, *Son of Woman*, 1931, and of *Reminiscences of D. H. Lawrence*, 1933.

ORIOLI, GIUSÈPPE (PINO)—Bookseller in Florence. Publisher of *Lady Chatterley's Lover* in its first unexpurgated edition.

PINKER, J. B.—Literary agent.

RUSSELL, BERTRAND; later EARL RUSSELL (1872–   )—English mathematician and philosopher.

PEARN, NANCY—English literary agent in the offices of Curtis Brown.

RICHTHOFEN, BARONIN VON—Mother of Frieda Lawrence. Wife of Baron Friedrich von Richthofen, an army officer and an official in the German Civil Service.

SKINNER, MOLLIE L.—A West Australian nurse and writer. Co-author, with Lawrence, of *The Boy in the Bush*.

SECKER, MARTIN—Lawrence's chief publisher in England after 1921.

STERNE, MABEL DODGE—See Mabel Dodge Luhan.

STIEGLITZ, ALFRED—New York photographer and authority on modern painting.

TAYLOR, MRS. RACHEL ANNAND—Born in Aberdeen, 1876. Poet; later, a cultural historian.

WILSON, CHARLES—A miner, secretary of the Miners' Association at Willington.

THE SELECTED LETTERS OF

D. H. LAWRENCE

To WILLIAM HEINEMANN

12, Colworth Road, Addiscombe, Croydon.
December 15th, 1909.

Dear Sir,

I have just received the accompanying letter from Mr. Ford Madox Hueffer.[1] I hasten to forward it to you, and in doing so to offer you the novel[2] of which he speaks.

It is my first. I have as yet published nothing but a scrap of verse. At the moment I feel a trifle startled and somewhat elated by Mr. Hueffer's letter, but already a grain of doubt is germinating in me.

I hope you will allow me to send you the MSS. Of course I am willing to fulfil all Mr. Hueffer's injunctions. I know nothing of the publishing of books.

Yours sincerely,
D. H. LAWRENCE.

To W. E. HOPKIN

20, Dulverton Rd., Leicester, 24 Aug., 1910.

Dear Mr. Hopkin,

I am very sorry that I cannot be at home to tea and talk with you to-morrow. Mother is laid-up here, and I must certainly

[1] Later Ford Madox Ford. Novelist, editor of the *English Review*.
[2] *The White Peacock.*

stay with her until Saturday. She came for a holiday with my Aunt, and whilst here a tumour or something has developed in her abdomen. The doctor looks grave and says it is serious: I hope not. But you will understand, will you not, why I cannot keep my promise for to-morrow. I am disappointed. I seem to have lost touch altogether with the old "progressive" clique: in Croydon the Socialists are so stupid, and the Fabians so flat. It would have been jolly to talk with you about things. I'll say my millionth damn!

Give my regards to Mrs. Hopkin and to Enid.[3]

Yours very sincerely,

D. H. LAWRENCE.

To RACHEL ANNAND TAYLOR[4]

12, Colworth Road, Addiscombe, Croydon.
30th Sept., 1910.

Dear Mrs. Taylor,

Our 'English Association'—vague, middle-class Croydonians, mostly ladies, lingering remnants of the Pre-Raphaelites—asked me to give a paper on 'A Living Poet.'

"I will give you," I said, "Rachel Annand Taylor."

"Excuse me," they said, "but how do you spell it."

I have got the Fiammetta (*I* can't even spell *her*) sequence. I admire them, and wish to goodness I had your art.

"This is deep Hell to be expressionless." I have to devote myself to prose. Please, if you are bold enough, persuade somebody to buy my novel "The White Peacock"—which Heinemann will publish directly.—(a bit of advertisement.)

But to come to the point. I have only got Fiammetta (esoteric creature): if I can't borrow 'Rose and Vine' I'll buy it (this is poverty, believe me); but isn't there another, earlier volume? Shall I need it?—would you lend it to me?

3 Enid Hopkin, daughter of W. E. Hopkin.
4 From *Eight Letters by D. H. Lawrence to Rachel Annand Taylor.*

Those old ladies would love me to describe you to them, but I won't. I will keep you vaguely in upper air, as a poetess should be.

You said you would ask me to come and see you. Why did you not?—But do not answer that pertinent question. I always shrink more from receiving explanations than from making them.

I have not been into any literary society—indeed, not in London at all, for months and months. I am not a success, and to be a failure wearies me.

Do you dislike my informalities (euphemism!)?

Yours sincerely,

D. H. LAWRENCE.

Do you remember meeting me at the Rhys'?[5]

"Where are the knights that rode away—"

To RACHEL ANNAND TAYLOR[6]

12, Colworth Road, Addiscombe, Croydon.

26 Oct., 1910.

Dear Mrs. Taylor,

I have received this morning a copy of "Rose & Vine" from Adrian Berrington. Was it to him you introduced me at your rooms? I am much obliged to him for the loan of the book.

I like "Rose & Vine"—but not so much as Fiammetta. The former are very choice and charming and curious and careful. But they are rather like the clothes a woman makes before her first baby is born: they have never been worn; they "cleave not to the mould." One longs for touch of harshness.—And I don't like your arrangement of vowel sounds: it is not emotional enough—too intellectual. One can get good Swinburnian consonant music by taking thought, but never Shakespearean vowel-loveliness, in which the emotion of the piece flows.

5 Ernest Rhys, first editor of Everyman's Library.
6 From *Eight Letters by D. H. Lawrence to Rachel Annand Taylor.*

[5]

I like the first two pieces best: that, I suppose, is commonplace to say. I would never have written "The Appeal to the Artist"— it is arrogant.

Forgive me if I'm stupid. I like Fiammetta better: I like The Doubt—& the Epilogue, very much.

But why do you persist in separating soul & body? I can't tell, in myself, or in anybody, one from the other.

I have been a long time answering your other letter. I've been rather tired this week. Next week, I think, I shall go home again.

You are better, are you? The beeches in the country are feathered orange like buff-orpington hens. You should go & see them.

Auf wiedersehen,
D. H. LAWRENCE.

To RACHEL ANNAND TAYLOR[7]

Lynn Croft Eastwood Notts, 3 Dec. 1910.

Dear Mrs. Taylor,

I did not know where you were. I am glad you wrote to me.

I have been at home now ten days. My mother is very near the end. Today I have been to Leicester. I did not get home till half past nine. Then I ran upstairs. Oh she was very bad. The pains had been again.

"Oh my dear" I said, "is it the pains?"

"Not pain now—oh the weariness" she moaned, so that I could hardly hear her. I wish she could die tonight.

My sister[8] and I do all the nursing. My sister is only 22. I sit upstairs hours and hours till I wonder if ever it were true that I was at London. I seem to have died since, & that is an old life, dreamy.

I will tell you. My mother was a clever, ironical, delicately

---

[7] From *Eight Letters by D. H. Lawrence to Rachel Annand Taylor.*
[8] Ada.

moulded woman of good, old burgher descent. She married below her. My father was dark, ruddy, with a fine laugh. He is a coal miner. He was one of the sanguine temperament, warm & hearty, but unstable: he lacked principle, as my mother would have said. He deceived her & lied to her. She despised him—he drank.

Their marriage life has been one carnal, bloody fight. I was born hating my father: as early as ever I can remember. I shivered with horror when he touched me. He was very bad before I was born.

This has been a kind of bond between me and my mother. We have loved each other, almost with a husband & wife love, as well as filial & maternal. We knew each other by instinct. She said to my aunt—about me:

"But it has been different with him. He has seemed to be part of me."—And that is the real case. We have been like one, so sensitive to each other that we never needed words. It has been rather terrible & has made me, in some respects, abnormal.

I think this peculiar fusion of soul (don't think me high-falutin) never comes twice in a life-time—it doesn't seem natural. When it comes it seems to distribute one's consciousness far abroad from oneself, & one understands! I think no one has got 'Understanding' except through love. Now my mother is nearly dead, and I don't quite know how I am.

I have been to Leicester today, I have met a girl who has always been warm for me—like a sunny happy day—and I've gone & asked her to marry me: in the train, quite unpremeditated, between Rothley & Quorn—she lives at Quorn. When I think of her I feel happy with a sort of warm radiation—she is big & dark and handsome. There were five other people in the carriage. Then when I think of my mother:—if you've ever put your hand round the bowl of a champagne glass and squeezed it & wondered how near it is to crushing-in & the wine all going through your fingers—that's how my heart feels—like the champagne glass. There is no hostility between the warm

[7]

happiness & the crush of misery: but one is concentrated in my chest, & one is diffuse—a suffusion, vague.

Muriel* is the girl I have broken with. She loves me to madness, & demands the soul of me. I have been cruel to her, & wronged her, but I did not know.

Nobody can have the soul of me. My mother has had it, & nobody can have it again. Nobody can come into my very self again, and breathe me like an atmosphere. Don't say I am hasty this time—I know. Louie[1]—whom I wish I could marry the day after the funeral—she would never demand to drink me up & have me. She loves me—but it is a fine, warm, healthy, natural love—not like Jane Eyre, who is Muriel, but like—say Rhoda Fleming or a commoner Anna Karénin. She will never plunge her hands through my blood & feel for my soul, & make me set my teeth & shiver & fight away. Ugh—I have done well—& cruelly—tonight.

I look at my father—he is like a cinder. It is very terrible, mismarriage.

They sent me yesterday one copy of the Peacock for my mother. She just looked at it. It will not be out till spring.

I will tell you next time about that meeting when I gave a paper on you. It was *most* exciting. I worked my audience up to red heat—& I laughed.

Are you any better?—you don't say so. Tell me you are getting strong, & then you & I will not re-act so alarmingly—at least, you on me.

Goodnight,

D. H. LAWRENCE.

---

* Jessie Chambers, the Miriam of *Sons and Lovers*.
[1] Louisa Burrows, later one of the prototypes for Ursula in *The Rainbow*. Daughter of Alfred Burrows, wood-carver, the original of Ursula's father in the same novel.

To W. E. HOPKIN
                    Davidson Rd. Boys' School, South Norwood, S.E.
                                            20 Feby., 1911.

Dear Mr. Hopkin,

I had a letter from Ada[2] this morning telling me that Hall's are kicking up a bit of dust over the representation of Alice.[3] In my thinking, she ought to be flattered. She's shown as highly moral and salted with wit enough to save even the insipid Sodom of Eastwood—*sauf votre respect*—that is.

However, if they really feel that their noble chapel-going dignity is impaired, I wish you would assure them that I will contrive to have, in the next impression, the name changed to Margaret Undine Widmerpuddle, or any such fantasy they shall choose, far away from the sound of Hall or Gall. I suppose it's ————,[4] snuffing idiot. I'll have a whack at him, one day—so let him beware.

The book's going moderately, but the shekels are not deluging me yet. Alas, no!

I'm afraid my sister is having a rough time with father. I wish he were in——no, I won't say it aloud. Is one never to have five minutes' peace?

Apologise to Mrs. Hopkin on my behalf, please, because I have not answered her letter. I will do so. Congratulate Miss Potter[5] for me, and tell her I shall want her to speak up for me on the Judgment Day. And, I exhort you, try to keep Enid[6] away from this deadly contamination of pen and ink. *Est et silentio tuta merces*—I don't know whether the quotation's correct, but it means that the "reward is for faithful silence." I wish I merited it.

Try and soothe off the virtuous indignation of the Halls, I beg you. I don't want the publishers to be annoyed: it is they

2 Lawrence's sister.
3 Alice Hall had been represented as Alice Gall in *The White Peacock.*
4 Probably White Holditch, husband of Alice Hall. (H. T. M.)
5 Unidentified.
6 Enid Hopkin.

who are responsible, you see. I can get the name changed without much trouble, myself. Really, if many more perverse things happen, I shall betake myself to Job's muck-heap, putting a potsherd in my pocket, and advising one or two of my prosperous friends in Uz and suchlike places of my intention. In short, I'm fed up.

My regards to Mrs. Hopkin. Thanks for puffing me in the Rag.[7]

Yours,

D. H. LAWRENCE.

I was very young when I wrote the *Peacock*—I began it at twenty. Let that be my apology.

To ADA LAWRENCE[8]

12, Colworth Road, Addiscombe, Croydon.

April 9, 1911.

I am sorry more than I can tell to find you going through the torment of religious unbelief: it is so hard to bear, especially now. However, it seems to me like this: Jehovah is the Jew's idea of God, not ours. Christ was infinitely good, but mortal as we. There still remains a God, but not a personal God: a vast, shimmering impulse which waves onwards towards some end, I don't know what—taking no regard for the little individual, but taking regard for humanity. When we die, like rain-drops falling back again into the sea, we fall back into the big, shimmering sea of unorganised life which we call God. We are lost as individuals, yet we count in the whole. It requires a lot of pain and courage to come to discover one's own creed, and quite as much to continue in lonely faith. Would you like a book or two of philosophy? or will you merely battle out your own ideas? I would still go to chapel if it did me any good. I shall go

---

7 Probably the *Eastwood and Kimberley Advertiser*. (H. T. M.)
8 From *Early Life of D. H. Lawrence*.

myself, when I am married. Whatever name one gives Him in worship we all strive towards the same God, so we be generous hearted: Christians, Buddhists, Mrs. Dax,⁹ me, we all stretch our hands in the same direction. What does it matter the name we cry? It is a fine thing to establish one's own religion in one's heart, not to be dependent on tradition and second-hand ideals. Life will seem to you, later, not a lesser, but a greater thing. This which is a great torment now will be a noble thing to you later on. Let us talk, if you feel like it, when I come home.

To MARTIN SECKER
12, Colworth Road, Addiscombe, Croydon.
12 June, 1911.

Dear Sir,

I am very much flattered by your offer to publish a volume of my short stories: to tell the truth, I sit in doubt and wonder because of it.

There have appeared in print, in the English *Review,* two and two only of my tales. Because nobody wanted the things, I have not troubled to write any. So that, at present, I have two good stories published, three very decent ones lying in the hands of the editor of the English *Review,* another good one at home, and several slight things sketched out and neglected. If these would be any good towards an autumn volume, I should be at the top of happiness. If they are not enough—I am in the midst of a novel, and bejungled in work, alas!

My second novel is promised to Wm. Heinemann. It is written, but I will not publish it, because it is erotic: in spite of which Mr. Heinemann would take it. But I am afraid for my tender reputation. Therefore, I stick at my third book like a broody hen at her eggs, lest my chickens hatch in a winter of public forgetfulness.

---

9 Mrs. Alice Dax, an Eastwood resident of advanced social ideas, was a strong influence in Lawrence's young manhood.

Of course I am sensible to the honour you do me—only wish I could make more satisfactory return.

Yours sincerely,

D. H. LAWRENCE.

To EDWARD GARNETT

16, Colworth Rd., Addiscombe, Croydon.

18 Dec., 1911.

Dear Garnett,

Your letter concerning the Siegmund[1] book is very exciting. I will tell you just what Hueffer said, then you will see the attitude his kind will take up.

"The book," he said, "is a rotten work of genius. It has no construction or form—it is execrably bad art, being all variations on a theme. Also it is erotic—not that I, personally, mind that, but an erotic work *must* be good art, which this is not."

I sent it to our friend with the monocle. He wrote to me, after three months: "I have read part of the book. I don't care for it, but we will publish it."

I wrote back to him: "No, I won't have the book published. Return it to me."

That is about fifteen months ago. I wrote to Hueffer saying: "The novel called *The Saga of Siegmund* I have determined not to publish." He replied to me: "You are quite right not to publish that book—it would damage your reputation perhaps permanently."

When I was last up to Heinemann's, two months ago, I asked Atkinson[2] to send me the MS. He promised to do so, and said: "I have never finished it. It's your handwriting, you know,"— a sweet smile. "Perfectly legible, but so *tedious*"—a sweet smile.

That's all the criticism he ever ventured.

---

[1] *The Saga of Siegmund,* later published as *The Trespasser.*

[2] An editor at Heinemann. Probably Atkinson is "our friend with the monocle" referred to earlier in the letter though it may have been Heinemann himself.

Is Hueffer's opinion worth anything, do you think? Is the book *so* erotic? I don't want to be talked about in an "Ann Veronica" fashion.

If you offer the thing to Duckworth, do not, I beg you, ask for an advance on royalties. Do not present me as a beggar. Do not tell him I am poor. Heinemann owes me £50 in February— I have enough money to tide me over till he pays—and that fifty will, at home, last me six months. I do not want an advance —let me be presented to Duckworth as a respectable person.

Atkinson has not yet said anything about the poems. I told him I preferred to publish about 25 of the best, impersonal pieces. He has not answered at all. I shall be glad when I have no more dealings with that firm.

You would get my yesterday's letter before you left the Cearne³ to-day——?

We will, then, discuss the book on Wednesday. I shall change the title. Shall I call it *The Livanters*—is that a correct noun from the verb "To Livant"? To me, it doesn't look an ugly word, nor a disreputable one.

Yours sincerely,

D. H. LAWRENCE.

To A. W. McLEOD⁴

Compton House, St. Peter's Road, Bournemouth.

24th Jan. 1912.

My dear Mac,

I was very glad to hear from you—but is it *such* a fag to write? Whom has ————— assaulted, how bad is it—and what is to

---

³ Country home of the Garnetts.

⁴ Although an excerpt from this letter appears in Harry T. Moore's *The Intelligent Heart*, it has not hitherto been published in full. It appears here through the kindness of Mr. Moore. The deleted names were withheld by Mr. McLeod, who died in 1956. As this book goes through the press, news is received that fifty unpublished letters from Lawrence to Mr. McLeod, written between 1908 and 1912, have been discovered in a house in Croydon, where Lawrence and McLeod taught together in the Davidson Road School. In the American edition of the Huxley *Letters*, Mr. McLeod's initials are incorrectly given as A. D.

be the result? Where is —————— now? Why won't your cold get better? Do be careful. Don't go my way and get chesty. It is the very devil in the end.

Implore Miss Mason to put in her letters the school *news*: to tell me how —————— is behaving, and how —————— has come to Hades etc. She at least has some length about her: you and the rest are stumpy correspondents.

I am getting very well I think. I've had a fierce and fiendish cold which lingers—but notwithstanding all, I get fatter— "fatter" is the term, I think—in preference to "more corpulent."

How can I, in a far-off land, tell you interesting things— unless I become geographical? Of me, there is nothing to say. But you are the Davidson chronicler, and a jolly bad one.

Atkinson has left Heinemann, and it was rumoured Walter de la Mare was to take his place. With Atkinson my verses are left also—I wrote Heinemann—William is away—they were indefinite concerning the poems—and tried to soft-sawder me into not giving the second, love-novel which they practically refused, to Duckworth. But to Duckworth it shall go, if I can revise it to my taste. It is to be called "The Trespasser," so we'll know how to speak of it. I do very little work—just the revising of this novel—no creative work.

I'm writing in the billiard room where a little Finn, whose 21st is today, is playing billiards with an old gent from South Africa. I live in constant dread of a cue in my ear and a ball in my eye. Also Scriven and I were celebrating our acquaintance— with Scotch—in his room till the small hours—So I'm dull as cold tea.

The old ladies continue to mother me—the younger ones— shall we say, to sister me. The men are very amiable, but nearly teetotallers now. There was one chap here last week, with whom I had fine sport. He was mad with his wife on Friday, so he went out with me to Poole Harbour. There he went on the razzle. I had a fiendish time. He kept it up when we got back here: walked away with a baby in a pram in Christchurch

Rd—tried to board and drive off with a private motor car—nearly had a fight in the Central Hotel, and got us turned out. We were four, arm in arm, swaying up the main street here [,] people dodging out of the way like hares. It was hot. In the end, I had to throw all the drinks they kept forcing on me on to the floor, lest I got as drunk as they.

Then, when at last, after superhuman struggles, I got him home—he was a big, well-built Yorkshire man of 35—plenty of cash—had been in the army—*I*—*I* had to stand the racket from Mrs. Jenkinson, whom I like, who is young and pretty and has travelled a good bit—and who sits at my table. I wished most heartily on Friday evening that I was over Lethe's soothing stream.

But now I am forgiven. It is raining today—the weather is so-so—it has never been cold. I can scarcely say when I shall be back in Croydon—if ever. But I'll tell you later. I don't think I want to return to Davidson—but we'll let that dog lie, also.

I wish I could see you. I suppose you don't feel like taking a trip down here on Sunday?—only five bob. I should love it.

With fond affection to thee—and regards to all the world.

D. H. LAWRENCE.

To EDWARD GARNETT

Queen's Square, Eastwood, Notts.
12 Feb., 1912.

Dear Garnett,

I saw L————[5] yesterday—she was rather ikey (adj.—to be cocky, to put on airs, to be aggressively superior). She had decided beforehand that she had made herself too cheap to me, therefore she thought she would become all at once expensive and desirable. Consequently she offended me at every verse end—thank God. If she'd been wistful, tender and passionate, I should have been a goner. I took her to the castle, where was

[5] Louie. (Louisa Burrows)

an exhibition from the Art School—wonderfully good stuff. She stared at the naked men till I had to go into another room—she gave me a disquisition on texture in modelling—why clay lives or does not live;—sarked me for saying a certain old fellow I met was a bore: could not remember, oh no, had not the ghost of a notion when we had last visited the castle together, though she knew perfectly: thought me a fool for saying the shadow of the town seen faintly coloured through a fog was startling—and so on. I took her to a café, and over tea and toast told her for the fourth time. When she began to giggle, I asked her coolly for the joke: when she began to cry, I wanted a cup of tea. It's awfully funny. I had a sort of cloud over my mind—a real sensation of darkness which lifted and trembled slightly. I seemed to be a sort of impersonal creature, without heart or liver, staring out of a black cloud. It's an awfully funny phenomenon. I saw her off by the 5.8 train, perfectly calm. She was more angry and disgusted than anything, thank God.

The sequel—which startled *me*—I will tell you personally some time. It shall not be committed to paper.

I have another rendezvous to-day—and one I've had to put off. But I can't tell you those things via the post.

I send you these sketches. I think they're not bad. Would the *Saturday* or the *Nation* look at them? I'm awfully sorry to trouble you so—really. The colliery one apropos the strike, might go down.

The weather here is livid—I loathe it. In May I go to Germany. God speed the day.

Don't smite the trembling edifice of my character in Miss Whale's[6] eyes—and give her my regards.

D. H. LAWRENCE.

---

[6] Secretary at Duckworth. (H. T. M.)

To EDWARD GARNETT

13, Queen's Square, Eastwood, Notts.
8th March, 1912.

My dear Garnett,

It is good news from the *Forum*! I have altered the story much to my satisfaction. What do you think? I enclose also the duplicate. Will the title do? Shall you send the duplicate to the *English* and ask Harrison to publish it simultaneously with the *Forum*? You know better than I.

I enclose a story I wrote three years back, and had forgotten. It is on the same theme, and I thought it might interest you—it is really curious. But before it was ever submitted to a publisher I would like thoroughly to revise it.

I had a letter from Duckworth, which I shall answer now "yes." But he says the title *Trespasser* is not particularly strong, and will I find another? I have cudgelled my brains into smithereens, and can find nothing. God help us.

What do you mean by Miss Cook's[7] M.S., by the way? Has she sent you something?

I had two shocks this morning, by the post. One of the men who taught in the school at Croydon with me, has died suddenly of pneumonia. And ————[8] my very old friend, the Don Juanish fellow I told you of—went and got married three months back, without telling a soul—and now boasts a son: "Jimmy, a very fine lad." He writes me eight pages, closely packed, this morning. The girl is living at home, with "Jimmy" in Stourbridge. The managers asked ———— ———— to resign his post, because of the blot on the scrutcheon. He said he'd "see them fizzled first." In the end, he was removed to a little headship on the Stafford-Derby border—has been there six weeks—alone—doing fearfully hard work. Don Juan in hell, what ho! He implores me to go and stay a week with him. I

---

[7] Probably Miss Helen Corke, writer and close friend of Lawrence in his Croydon years. (H. T. M.)
[8] Name withheld for obvious reasons.

suppose I'll have to. This has upset me—one never knows what'll happen. You know ———— has already got one illegitimate child. It's a lovely story, the end of it: the beginning was damnable. She was only nineteen, and he only twenty. Her father, great Christian, turned her out. ———— wouldn't acknowledge the kid, but had to pay, whether or not. That's five years back. Last October, I am told, the girl got married. Before the wedding—two days or so—she went to ————'s home with the child, and showed it to Georgie's father and mother.

"I've come, Mr. ————, for you to own this child. Who's the father of that?" pushing forward the small girl.

"Eh bless her, it's just like him," cried old Mrs. ————, and she kissed the kid with tears.

"Well, Lizzie," said ———— to the girl, "if our George-Henry says that isn't his'n he's a liar. It's the spit and image of him."

Whereupon Lizzie went away satisfied, got married to a collier, and lives in Cordy Lane. She, with one or two others, will rejoice over George's final nabbing. Isn't it awful?

All this, by the way, is quite verbal truth.

Vale!

D. H. LAWRENCE.

To EDWARD GARNETT

Queen's Square, Eastwood, Notts.
17 April, 1912.

Dear Garnett,

Did I answer your last letter? I can't for my life remember. Why do you take so much trouble for me?—if I am not eternally grateful, I am a swine.

It is huge to think of Iden Payne acting me on the stage: you are like a genius of *Arabian Nights,* to get me through. Of course I will alter and improve whatever I can, and Mr. Payne

has fullest liberty to do entirely as he pleases with the play—*
you know that. And of course I don't expect to get money by
it. But it's ripping to think of my being acted.

I shall be in London next week, I think—from Thursday to
Sunday—then I can see Walter de la Mare, and Harrison,[1] who
want to jaw me, and you who don't want to jaw me. Mrs.
—————[2] will be in town also. She is ripping—she's the finest
woman I've ever met—you must above all things meet her . . .
she is the daughter of Baron von Richthofen, of the ancient and
famous house of Richthofen—but she's splendid, she is really.
How damnably I mix things up. Mrs. ————— is perfectly
unconventional, but really good—in the best sense. I'll bet
you've never met anybody like her, by a long chalk. You *must*
see her next week. I wonder if she'd come to the Cearne, if you
asked us. Oh, but she is the woman of a lifetime.

I shall love to see you again. Don't be grumpy.

Yours,

D. H. LAWRENCE.

To EDWARD GARNETT

Hotel Rheinischer Hof, Trier, 9 May, 1912.

Dear Garnett,

I've not had any letters since I've been here—since Friday,
that is—so I don't know what is taking place. Write to me, I
beg you—I am staying in Trier till next Monday or Tuesday—
then, for a week or two, my address will be c/o Frau Karl Krenkow, Waldbröl, Rheinprovinz.

Of course I've been in Metz with Mrs. —————'s[3] people.
There's such a hell of a stir up. Nothing is settled yet. —————[4]

---

* Probably *A Collier's Friday Night*. (H. T. M.)
1 Austin Harrison, successor of Hueffer at the *English Review*.
2 Weekley. (Frieda, later Mrs. Lawrence)
3 Weekley
4 Weekley. (Ernest, husband of Frieda, professor of modern languages at the
University of Nottingham and author of many books on etymology)

knows everything. Oh Lord, what a mess to be in—and this after eight weeks of acquaintance! But I don't care a damn what it all costs. I'll tell you how things work out. At present all is vague.

I had to quit Metz because the damn fools wanted to arrest me as a spy. Mrs. ———[5] and I were lying on the grass near some water—talking—and I was moving round an old emerald ring on her finger, when we heard a faint murmur in the rear— a German policeman. There was such a to-do. It needed all the fiery little Baron von Richthofen's influence—and he *is* rather influential in Metz—to rescue me. They vow I am an English officer—*I*—*I!!* The damn fools. So behold me, fleeing eighty miles away, to Trier. Mrs. ———[5] is coming on Saturday. Oh Lord, it's easier to write history than to make it, even in such a mild way as mine.

Tell me if my literary affairs are shifting at all. Regards to Miss Whale.

Yours,

D. H. LAWRENCE.

Isn't it all funny!

To FRIEDA LAWRENCE[6]

Waldbröl-Mittwoch.[7]

I have had all your three letters quite safely. We are coming on quickly now. Do tell me if you can what is E...'s[8] final decision. He will get the divorce, I think, because of his thinking you ought to marry me. That is the result of *my* letter to him. I will crow my little crow, in opposition to you. And then after six months, we will be married—will you? Soon we will go to Munich. But give us a little time. Let us get solid before we

---

5 Weekley.
6 From *"Not I, But the Wind..."*
7 The date of this letter is May 1912, probably May 15.
8 Ernest. (Weekley)

set up together. Waldbröl restores me to my decent sanity. Is Metz still bad for you—no? It will be better for me to stay here —shall I say till the end of next week? We must decide what we are going to do, very definitely. If I am to come to Munich next week, what are we going to live on? Can we scramble enough together to last us till my payments come in? I am not going to tell my people anything till you have the divorce. If we can go decently over the first three or four months—financially—I think I shall be able to keep us going for the rest. Never mind about the infant. If it should come, we will be glad, and stir ourselves to provide for it—and if it should not come, ever—I shall be sorry. I do not believe, when people love each other, in interfering there. It is wicked, according to my feeling. I want you to have children to me—I don't care how soon. I never thought I should have that definite desire. But you see, we must have a more or less stable foundation if we are going to run the risk of the responsibility of children—not the risk of children, but the risk of responsibility.

I think after a little while, I shall write to E . . . again. Perhaps he would correspond better with me.

Can't you feel how certainly I love you and how certainly we shall be married? Only let us wait just a short time, to get strong again. Two shaken, rather sick people together would be a bad start. A little waiting, let us have, because I love you. Or does the waiting make you worse?—no, not when it is only a time of preparation. Do you know, like the old knights, I seem to want a certain time to prepare myself—a sort of vigil with myself. Because it is a great thing for me to marry you, not a quick, passionate coming together. I know in my heart "here's my marriage." It feels rather terrible—because it is a great thing in my life—it is *my* life—I am a bit awe-inspired—I want to get used to it. If you think it is fear and indecision, you wrong me. It is *you* who would hurry, who are undecided. It's the very strength and inevitability of the oncoming thing that makes me wait, to get in harmony with it. Dear God, I am marrying you, now, don't you see. It's a far greater thing than ever I knew. Give me till next week-end, at least. If you love me, you will understand.

If I seem merely frightened and reluctant to you—you must forgive me.

I try, I will always try, when I write to you, to write the truth as near the mark as I can get it. It frets me, for fear you are disappointed in me, and for fear you are too much hurt. But you are strong when necessary.

You have got all myself—I don't even flirt—it would bore me very much—unless I got tipsy. It's a funny thing, to feel one's passion—sex desire—no longer a sort of wandering thing, but steady, and calm. I think, when one loves, one's very sex passion becomes calm, a steady sort of force, instead of a storm. Passion, that nearly drives one mad, is far away from real love. I am realizing things that I never thought to realize. Look at that poem I sent you—I would never write that to you. I shall love you all my life. That also is a new idea to me. But I believe it.

Auf Wiedersehen,

D. H. LAWRENCE.

To FRIEDA LAWRENCE[1]

Adr Herrn Karl Krenkow, Waldbröl-Rheinprovinz.
14 May 1912.

Yes, I got your letter later in the day—and your letter and E . . .'s[2] and yours to Garnett, this morning. In E . . .'s, as in mine to E . . . , see the men combining in their freemasonry against you. It is very strange.

I will send your letter to Garnett. I enclose one of his to me. It will make you laugh.

With correcting proofs, and reading E . . .'s letter, I feel rather detached. Things are coming straight. When you got in London, and had to face that judge, it would make you ill. We

1 From *"Not I, But the Wind . . ."*
2 Ernest. (Weekley)

are not callous enough to stand against the public, the whole mass of the world's disapprobation, in a sort of criminal dock. It destroys us, though we deny it. We are all off the balance. We are like spring scales that have been knocked about. We had better be still awhile, let ourselves come to rest.

Things are working out to their final state now. I did not do wrong in writing to E . . . Do not write to my sister yet. When all is a "fait accompli" then we will tell her, because then it will be useless for her to do other than to accept.

I am very well, but, like you, I feel shaky. Shall we not leave our meeting till we are better? Here, in a little while, I shall be solid again. And if you must go to England, will you go to Munich first—so far? No, I don't want to be left alone in Munich. Let us have firm ground where we next go. Quakiness and uncertainty are the death of us. See, tell me exactly what you are going to do. Is the divorce coming off? Are you going to England at all? Are we going finally to pitch our camp in Munich? Are we going to have enough money to get along with? Have you settled anything definite with E . . . ?—One *must* be detached, impersonal, cold, and logical, when one is arranging affairs. We do not want another fleet of horrors attacking us when we are on a rather flimsy raft—lodging in a borrowed flat on borrowed money.

Look, my dear, now that the suspense is going over, we can wait even a bit religiously for one another. My next coming to you is solemn, intrinsically—I am solemn over it—not sad, oh no—but it is my marriage, after all, and a great thing—not a thing to be snatched and clumsily handled. I will not come to you unless it is safely, and firmly. When I have come, things shall not put us apart again. So we must wait and watch for the hour. Henceforth, dignity in our movements and our arrangements—no shufflings and underhandedness. And we must settle the money business. I will write to the publishers, if necessary, for a sub. I have got about £30 due in August—£24 due —and £25 more I am owed. Can we wait, or not, for that?

[23]

Now I shall do as I like, because you are not certain. Even if I stay in Waldbröl a month, I won't come till our affair is welded firm. I can wait a month—a year almost—for a sure thing. But an unsure thing is a horror to me.

I love you—and I am in earnest about it—and we are going to make a great—or, at least, a good life together. I'm not going to risk fret and harassment, which would spoil our intimacy, because of a hasty forcing of affairs.

Don't think I love you less, in being like this. You will think so, but it isn't true. The best man in me loves you. And I dread anything dragging our love down.

Be definite, my dear; be detailed, be businesslike. In our marriage, let us be businesslike. The love is there—then let the common-sense match it.

Auf Wiedersehen,
D. H. LAWRENCE.

This poetry will come in next month's *English*. I'm afraid you won't like it.

D. H. L.

And I love you, and I am sorry it is so hard. But it is only a little while—then we will have a *dead cert*.

To EDWARD GARNETT
bei Herr Karl Krenkow, Waldbröl, Rheinprovinz.[3]

Dear Garnett,

I suppose I shall have to keep on amusing you, though I myself am anything but amused. I tell you, making history is no joke. But I won't die in the attempt, if I can help it.

Now that title—the readers at Duckworth's ought to have altered it, for *I* did not know that *A Game of Forfeits* was finally settled upon. As for *Author of the White Peacock*—now would

---

3 The date of this letter is almost certainly May 21, 1912. (H. T. M.)

you expect me to think of it? I wonder you can be so heartless. I've not signed any agreement with Messrs. Duckworth—I suppose it doesn't matter. And supposing I actually haven't a penny in the world—at present I've about four quid—would your chief give me a sub—£10? But for the Lord's sake, don't ask him yet—I'd rather anything. Always, somewhere, I shall find *some* woman who'll give me bed and board. Thank God for the women.

F—that is Mrs. ———— [4]her name is Frieda—"The Peaceful" —let me call her F.—she has gone to Munich—hundreds of miles away—and I am eating my heart out, and revising my immortal Heinemann novel, *Paul Morel*,[5] in this tiny village stuck up in the Rhineland. If you wouldn't make it a laughing matter—I'd open my poor heart to you—a rare museum. But you are too "narquois!" I left F. in Trier—200 miles from here —a week ago. Oh there has been *such* a to-do.

To live, one must hurt people so. One has to make up one's mind, it must be so. Of course my people at home wonder what I'm up to—I shall tell them all later, but nothing now—and they too are hurt. And F. is making herself ill. Now she's gone to München, to her sister. The Richthofens are an astonishing family—three girls—women—the eldest[6] a Doctor of Social Economics—a Professor too—then Frieda—then the youngest[7] —28—very beautiful, rather splendid in her deliberate worldliness. They are a rare family—father a fierce old aristocrat— mother utterly non-moral, very kind. You should know them.

I am going to Munich directly—perhaps Saturday. The soles of my feet burn as I wait. Here, the slow oxen go down the main street, drawing the wagons, under my window—the country is all still, and oxen plough and harrow. In the Gasthaus, the Lutheran choir practises in one room, we drink in the next.

4 Weekley.
5 Later published as *Sons and Lovers*.
6 Else.
7 Johanna. ("Nusch")

My cousin ———[8] is newly married—and wishes she weren't. She's getting in love with me. Why is it women *will* fall in love with me? And I haven't an eye for a girl, damn it. I just remain in a state of suspense, till I can go to Munich.

Frieda sort of clings to the idea of you, as the only man in England who would be a refuge. She wanted to write to you—so I send you her letter. Don't be wise and cryptic. After all, Frieda isn't in any book, and I'm not, and life hurts—and sometimes rejoices one. But—you see—in life one's own flesh and blood goes through the mill—and F.'s eyes are tired now. I hope I can go to Munich on Saturday—it is 15 hours' journey from this God-forsaken little hole. But people are wonderfully good to me. The Rhineland is nice—we were at Bonn and on the Drachenfels on Sunday—so magical. But it will always be to me a land of exile—and slow, slow cattle drawing the wagons. Those slow, buff oxen, with their immense heads that seem always asleep, nearly drive me mad as they step tinkling down the street. After them, I could hug the dog in the milk-cart, that lifts his paw quickly and daintily over the shaft, and sits down panting.

Is it Tuesday?—I never know how the days go. Miss Whale is quite right when she says I'm good—I *am* good. Give her my love. Only the women have eyes for goodness—and *they* wear green moral spectacles, most of 'em.

Vale!

D. H. LAWRENCE.

To MRS. S. A. HOPKIN

bei Professor Alf. Weber, Icking, bei München.

2 June, 1912.

Dear Mrs. Hopkin,

Although I haven't heard from you, I'll get a letter off to you, because to people I like, I always want to tell my good news.

---

8 Hannah Krenkow. (H. T. M.)

When I came to Germany I came with Mrs. ———[9] went to
Metz with her. Her husband knows all about it—but I don't
think he will give her a divorce—only a separation. I wish he'd
divorce her, so we could be married. But that's as it is.

I came down from the Rhineland to Munich last Friday
week. Frieda met me there, in Munich. She had been living
with her sister in a village down the Isar Valley, next village to
this. We stayed in Munich a night, then went down to Beuerberg for eight days. Beuerberg is about 40 kilometres from
Munich, up the Isar, near the Alps. This is the Bavarian Tyrol.
We stayed in the Gasthaus zur Post. In the morning we used
to have breakfast under the thick horse-chestnut trees, and the
red and white flowers fell on us. The garden was on a ledge,
high over the river, above the weir, where the timber rafts
floated down. The Loisach—that's the river—is pale jade green,
because it comes from glaciers. It is fearfully cold and swift.
The people were all such queer Bavarians. Across from the inn,
across a square full of horse-chestnut trees, was the church and
the convent, so peaceful, all whitewashed, except for the
minaret of the church, which has a black hat. Every day, we
went out for a long, long time. There are flowers so many they
would make you cry for joy—Alpine flowers. By the river, great
hosts of globe flowers, that we call bachelor's buttons—pale gold
great bubbles—then primulas, like mauve cowslips, somewhat—
and queer marsh violets, and orchids, and lots of bell-flowers,
like large, tangled, dark-purple harebells, and stuff like lark-
spur, very rich, and lucerne, so pink, and in the woods, lilies of
the valley—oh, flowers, great wild mad profusion of them,
everywhere. One day we went to a queer old play done by the
peasants—this is the Ober-Ammergau country. One day we
went into the mountains, and sat, putting Frieda's rings on our
toes, holding our feet under the pale green water of a lake, to
see how they looked. Then we go to Wolfratshausen where

9 Weekley.

[27]

Frieda's sister has a house—like a chalet—on the hill above the white village.

Now Frieda and I are living alone in Professor Weber's[1] flat. It is the top storey of this villa—quite small—four rooms beside kitchen. But there's a balcony, where we sit out, and have meals, and I write. Down below, is the road where the bullock wagons go slowly. Across the road the peasant women work in the wheat. Then the pale, milk-green river runs between the woods and the plain—then beyond, the mountains, range beyond range, and their tops glittering with snow.

I've just had to run into the kitchen—a jolly little place— wondering what Frieda was up to. She'd only banged her head on the cupboard. So we stood and looked out. Over the hills was a great lid of black cloud, and the mountains nearest went up and down in a solid blue-black. Through, was a wonderful gold space, with a tangle of pale, wonderful mountains, peaks pale gold with snow, and farther and farther away—such a silent, glowing confusion, brilliant with snow. Now the thunder is going at it, and the rain is here.

I love Frieda so much, I don't like to talk about it. I never knew what love was before. She wanted me to write to you. I want you and her to be friends always. Sometime perhaps she— perhaps we—shall need you. Then you'll be good to us, won't you?

The world is wonderful and beautiful and good beyond one's wildest imagination. Never, never, never could one conceive what love is, beforehand, never. Life *can* be great—quite god-like. It *can* be so. God be thanked I have proved it.

You might write to us here. Our week of honeymoon is over. Lord, it was lovely. But this—do I like this better?—I like it so much. Don't tell anybody. This is only for the good to know. Write to us.

D. H. LAWRENCE.

1 Alfred Weber, brother of Max Weber, noted social scientist.

To EDWARD GARNETT
                    Icking, bei München, Sunday, 4 Aug., 1912.
Dear Garnett,

What can have become of you, that we have not heard from you for so long? And we ask Bunny[2] (so he will have it)—but he knows nothing of you. He's awfully like you, in a thousand ways—his walk, his touch of mischief and wickedness, and nice things besides. But he hasn't got your appetite for tragedy with the bleeding brow: perhaps he'll get it later: some female or other will create the want for it in him. (F. reads my letters.)

We are awfully fond of him. I reckon he's a lucky dog. But I'd rather have a dog lucky and adorable, like him, than unlucky and lugubrious like myself. You should see him swim in the Isar, that is effervescent and pale green, where the current is fearfully strong. He simply smashes his way through the water, while F. sits on the bank bursting with admiration, and I am green with envy. By Jove, I reckon his parents have done joyously well for that young man. Oh, but you should see him dance Mordkin passion dances, with great orange and yellow and red and dark green scarves of F.'s, and his legs and arms bare; while I sit on the sofa and do the music, and burst with laughter, and F. stands out on the balcony in the dark, scared. Such a prancing whirl of legs and arms and raving colours you never saw: and F. shrieks when he brandishes the murderous knife in my music-making face; and somebody calls in German from below: "Go and trample somewhere else," and at last he falls panting. Oh, the delightful Bunny!—it is incredible that he is also so much like you. He should have come and stayed with us last night, but didn't turn up. I suppose he's on the razzle in München.

We are going away from here. Oh, I must tell you how the Baroness von Richthofen[3] "schimpfed" me on Friday night. She

2 David Garnett, son of Edward and Constance.
3 Mother of Frieda Lawrence.

suddenly whirled in here on her way from the Tyrol to Constance, stayed an hour, and spent that hour abusing me like a
washerwoman—in German, of course. I sat and gasped. "Who
was I, did I think, that a Baroness should clean my boots and
empty my slops: she, the daughter of a high-born and highly
cultured gentleman"—at the highly-cultured I wanted to say
"I don't think!" "No decent man, no man with common sense
of decency, could expect to have a woman, the wife of a clever
professor, living with him like a barmaid, and he not even able
to keep her in shoes." So she went on. Then in München, to
Else, her eldest daughter, says I am a lovable and trustworthy
person. You see, I saw her off gracefully from the station.

We are going away to-morrow morning, early. F. is just
holding forth—reciting, I call it—that everybody in the world
is a rotter, except herself. Why I am a rotter at the present
moment, it will be interesting to hear later. I have at last nailed
F.'s nose to my wagon. At last, I think, she can't leave me—at
least for the present: despite the loss of her children. I am sick
to death of the bother. It's the rotten outsiders who plant
nettles in paradise. But, thank God, we are going away: walking
to Mayrhofen, about 10 miles from Innsbruck—stopping there
for a week or two—perhaps Bunny will come—then going on
down into Italian Switzerland, where we shall spend the winter,
probably on Lake Garda, or Maggiore. We've got £23 between
us, at present. We shall have to live cheap as mice, but I think
we shall manage.

I had a letter from ———[4] *re* a story. His is a wishy-washy
noodle, God help me. My stories are too "steaming" for him.
I sent him 3 more, and asked him to forward to you at the
Cearne all the MS. of mine he doesn't want. Heinemann is
hesitating over the poetry. He—or rather de la Mare, wants to
know, do I think of publishing a book of German sketches such
as those of which the *Westminster Gazette* has accepted three—

[4] Probably either Hueffer or Austin Harrison, his successor at the *English
Review*. (H. T. M.)

and would I let W. H. have the rejection thereof. I s'll say yes (a lie). Won't somebody in America have my stories now the *Trespasser* is out there? I am going to write six short stories. I must try and make running money. I am going to write *Paul Morel*[5] over again—it'll take me three months. But Duckworth won't bring it out till Jan., will he? Write me to "Haus Vogelnest," Wolfratshausen, bei München, if you don't get an address from me. I hope you are well, and all that. I've thought of a new novel—purely of the common people—fearfully interesting.

> *Vale!*
> D. H. LAWRENCE.

To MRS. S. A. HOPKIN

> *Mayrhofen 138, in Zillertal, Tirol, Austria.*
> *19 Aug., 1912.*

You know that it is not forgetfulness makes us not write to you. You know you are one of the very, very few who will take us into your heart, together. So, if the months go by without your hearing, I know you will understand—I know you will be sticking by us, and we shall be depending on you. I wanted my sister[6] to come and talk with you, but she wouldn't; you see, it is harder for her, she is young, and doesn't understand quite. And she is going to marry Eddie Clarke in the spring, is going to become a hard, respectable married woman— I think the thought of me is very bitter to her—and she won't speak of me to anybody. Only she, of all my people, knows. And I told Jessie[7] to leave her a chance of ridding herself of my influence: nobody else. Mrs. ———[8] writes me—I told her I was with another woman—but no details. I am sorry for her, she is so ill.

Things have been hard, and worth it. There has been some

---

5 Later published as *Sons and Lovers.*
6 Ada.
7 Jessie Chambers, the Miriam of *Sons and Lovers.*
8 Dax (H. T. M.)

sickening misery. . . . F. is to see the children, and stay with them, next Easter. It has been rather ghastly, that part of the affair. If only one didn't hurt so many people.

For ourselves, Frieda and I have struggled through some bad times into a wonderful naked intimacy, all kindled with warmth, that I know at last is love. I think I ought not to blame women, as I have done, but myself, for taking my love to the wrong woman, before now. Let every man find, keep on trying till he finds, the woman who can take him and whose love he can take, then who will grumble about men or about women. But the thing must be two-sided. At any rate, and whatever happens, I do love, and I am loved. I have given and I have taken—and that is eternal. Oh, if only people could marry properly; I believe in marriage.

Perhaps Frieda will have to come to London to see her husband, in the autumn. Then she might want you to help her. Would you go to London, if she needed you?

We think of spending the winter in Italy, somewhere on Lake Garda. We shall be awfully poor, but don't mind so long as we can manage. It is ————⁹ and the children that are the trouble. You see he loves Frieda madly, and can't let go.

We walked from the Isarthal down here—or at least, quite a long way—F. and I—with our German shoulder-bags on our backs. We made tea and our meals by the rivers. Crossing the mountains, we got stranded one night. I found a lovely little wooden chapel, quite forsaken, and lit the candles, and looked at the hundreds of Ex Voto pictures—so strange. Then I found F. had gone. But she came back to the shrine, saying we were at the top of the pass and there was a hay-hut in the Alpine meadow. There we slept that night. In the dawn, the peaks were round us, and we were, as it seemed, in a pot, with a green high meadow for a bottom.

Here we are lodging awhile in a farmhouse. A mountain

⁹ Weekley.

stream rushes by just outside. It is icy and clear. We go out all day with our rucksacks—make fires, boil eggs, and eat the lovely fresh gruyère cheese that they make here. We are almost pure vegetarians. We go quite long ways up the valleys. The peaks of the mountains are covered with eternal snow. Water comes falling from a fearful height, and the cows, in the summer meadows, tinkle their bells. Sometimes F. undresses and lies in the sun—sometimes we bathe together—and we *can* be happy, nobody knows how happy.

There are millions of different bells: tiny harebells, big, black-purple mountain harebells, pale blue, hairy, strange creatures, blue and white Canterbury bells—then there's a great blue gentian, and flowers like monkey-musk. The Alpine roses are just over—and I believe we could find the edelweiss if we tried. Sometimes we drink with the mountain peasants in the Gasthaus, and dance a little. And how we love each other—God only knows.

We shall be moving on soon, walking south, by the Brenner, to Italy. If you write, address us at "Haus Vogelnest"—Wolfratshausen—bei München. F., with me, sends love.

Yours,
D. H. LAWRENCE.

To A. W. McLEOD

Villa Igéa, Villa di Gargnano,
Lago di Garda, Italy, Friday, 6th Oct., 1912.

Dear Mac,

Your books came to-day, your letter long ago. Now I am afraid I put you to a lot of trouble and expense, and feel quite guilty. But thanks a thousand times. And F. thanks you too.

I have read *Anna of the Five Towns* to-day, because it is stormy weather. For five months I have scarcely seen a word of English print, and to read it makes me feel fearfully queer. I don't know where I am. I am so used to the people going by outside, talking or singing some foreign language, always Italian now: but to-day, to be in Hanley, and to read almost my own dialect, makes me feel quite ill. I hate England and its hopelessness. I hate Bennett's resignation. Tragedy ought really to be a great kick at misery. But *Anna of the Five Towns* seems like an acceptance—so does all the modern stuff since Flaubert. I hate it. I want to wash again quickly, wash off England, the oldness and grubbiness and despair.

To-day it is so stormy. The lake is dark, and with white lambs all over it. The steamer rocks as she goes by. There are no sails stealing past. The vines are yellow and red, and fig trees are in flame on the mountains. I can't bear to be in England when I am in Italy. It makes me feel so soiled. Yesterday F. and I went down along the lake towards Maderno. We climbed down from a little olive wood, and swam. It was evening, so weird, and a great black cloud trailing over the lake. And tiny little lights of villages out, so low down, right across the water. Then great lightnings split out.—No, I don't believe England need be so grubby. What does it matter if one is poor, and risks one's livelihood, and reputation. One *can* have the necessary things, life, and love, and clean warmth. Why is England so shabby?

The Italians here sing. They are very poor, they buy twopenn'orth of butter and a penn'orth of cheese. But they are healthy and they lounge about in the little square where the boats come up and nets are mended, like kings. And they go by the window proudly, and they don't hurry or fret. And the women walk straight and look calm. And the men adore children—they are glad of their children even if they're poor. I think they haven't many ideas, but they look well, and they have strong blood.

I go in a little place to drink wine near Bogliaco. It is the living-room of the house. The father, sturdy as these Italians are, gets up from table and bows to me. The family is having supper. He brings me red wine to another table, then sits down again, and the mother ladles him soup from the bowl. He has his shirt-sleeves rolled up and his shirt collar open. Then he nods and "click-clicks" to the small baby, that the mother, young and proud, is feeding with soup from a big spoon. The grandfather, white-moustached, sits a bit effaced by the father. A little girl eats soup. The grandmother by the big, open fire sits and quietly scolds another little girl. It reminds me so of home when I was a boy. They are all so warm with life. The father reaches his thick brown hand to play with the baby—the mother looks quickly away, catching my eye. Then he gets up to wait on me, and thinks my bad Italian can't understand that a quarter litre of wine is 15 centesimi (1¼d.) when I give him thirty. He doesn't understand tips. And the huge lot of figs for 20 centesimi.

Why can't you ever come? You could if you wanted to, at Christmas. Why not? We should love to have you, and it costs little. Why do you say I sark you about your letters?—I don't, they *are* delightful. I think I am going to Salo to-morrow and cen get you some views of the lake there. I haven't got the proofs of my poems yet. It takes so long. Perhaps I will send you the MS. of *Paul Morel*—I shall alter the title—when it's done.

Thanks—*je te serre la main.*

D. H. LAWRENCE.

To ERNEST COLLINGS

Villa Igéa, Villa di Gargnano (Brescia),
Lago di Garda, Italy, 14 Nov., 1912.

Dear Mr. Collings,

Call me "Sir" if you will. I assure you I am a man. My name is David Herbert Lawrence. My age is 27 years. I was, but am no more, thank God—a school teacher—I dreamed last night I was teaching again—that's the only bad dream that ever afflicts my sturdy conscience.

How queer to think of *A Still Afternoon in School*. It's the first thing I ever had published. Ford Madox Hueffer discovered I was a genius—don't be alarmed, Hueffer would discover *anything* if he wanted to—published me some verse and a story or two, sent me to Wm. Heinemann with *The White Peacock,* and left me to paddle my own canoe. I very nearly wrecked it and did for myself. Edward Garnett, like a good angel, fished me out. Now I am living here on my paltry literary earnings. You should look up, in back *English Reviews, Odour of Chrysanthemums*—a story full of my childhood's atmosphere—and the glamorous enough "Fragment of Stained Glass." Excuse my cheek.

I can see all the poetry at the *back* of your verse—but there isn't much inside the lines. It's the rhythm and the sound that don't penetrate the blood—only now and then. I don't like the crackly little lines, nor the "thou wouldest" style, nor "mighty hills" and garlands and voices of birds and caskets—none of that. I can remember a few things, that nearly made poems in themselves.

> "We met again, and for a short laughing
> Did play with words; till suddenly
> I knew—didst thou?"

And then all the rest is inconsequent to me.

> "The coverings of the doorway
> Are flung open:
> Superb thou standest, wild-eyed, eager girl,
> Letting fall thy gown to feel the little
> Winds of the morning soothe thy breasts and
> shoulders."

Then you go on "Walk the earth in gladness"—but that girl isn't going to *walk the earth.*

The first stanza of "Adventure" is so nice, and I love

> "Now—go thy way.
> Ah, through the open door

Is there an almond tree
Aflame with blossom!
A little longer stay—
Why do tears blind me?
Nay, but go thy way."

That's a little poem, sufficient in itself. Then you go off to the "Love did turn to hate" business. And fancy anybody saying "Boy, whither away?" Then I like

"I think you must have died last night,
For in my dreams you came to me——"

then the rest isn't good. Do them in better form—put them in blank verse or something. Your rhythms aren't a bit good.

Forgive me if I'm nasty. That's what I say to myself, what I say to you.

I think we might get on well together. I'm quite nice really, though nobody will tell you so. If we can't meet in Italy, we may in England. Fools, to think your Sappho drawings improper. You'd think men were born in trousers that grew on them like skin. Our clothes consume us, like Heracles' garment.

Excuse this horrid bit of paper. And thanks so much for letting me read the poems. I suppose you are between 30 and 40 years of age? Do you mind your papers being squashed into this envelope?

Yours sincerely,
D. H. LAWRENCE.

To EDWARD GARNETT

Villa Igéa, Villa di Gargnano (Brescia),
Lago di Garda, Italy, 14 Nov., 1912.

Dear Garnett,

Your letter has just come. I hasten to tell you I sent the MS. of the *Paul Morel* novel to Duckworth registered, yesterday.

And I want to defend it, quick. I wrote it again, pruning it and shaping it and filling it in. I tell you it has got form—*form:* haven't I made it patiently, out of sweat as well as blood. It follows this idea: a woman of character and refinement goes into the lower class, and has no satisfaction in her own life. She has had a passion for her husband, so the children are born of passion, and have heaps of vitality. But as her sons grow up she selects them as lovers—first the eldest, then the second. These sons are *urged* into life by their reciprocal love of their mother—urged on and on. But when they come to manhood, they can't love, because their mother is the strongest power in their lives, and holds them. It's rather like Goethe and his mother and Frau von Stein and Christiana—As soon as the young men come into contact with women, there's a split. William gives his sex to a fribble, and his mother holds his soul. But the split kills him, because he doesn't know where he is. The next son gets a woman who fights for his soul—fights his mother. The son loves the mother—all the sons hate and are jealous of the father. The battle goes on between the mother and the girl, with the son as object. The mother gradually proves stronger, because of the tie of blood. The son decides to leave his soul in his mother's hands, and, like his elder brother, go for passion. He gets passion. Then the split begins to tell again. But, almost unconsciously, the mother realises what is the matter, and begins to die. The son casts off his mistress, attends to his mother dying. He is left in the end naked of everything, with the drift towards death.

It is a great tragedy, and I tell you I have written a great book. It's the tragedy of thousands of young men in England—it may even be Bunny's tragedy. I think it was Ruskin's, and men like him.—Now tell me if I haven't worked out my theme, like life, but always my theme. Read my novel. It's a great novel. If *you* can't see the development—which is slow, like growth—I can.

As for the *Fight for Barbara*—I don't know much about plays.

If ever you have time, you might tell me where you find fault with the *Fight for Barbara. The Merry Go Round* and the other are candidly impromptus. I *know* they want doing again—re-casting. I should like to have them again, now, before I really set to work on my next novel—which I have conceived—and I should like to try re-casting and re-forming them. If you have time, send them me.

I should like to dedicate the *Paul Morel* to you—may I? But not unless you think it's really a good work. "To Edward Garnett, in Gratitude." But you can put it better.

You are miserable about your play. Somehow or other your work riles folk. Why does it? But it makes them furious. Nevertheless, I shall see the day when a volume of your plays is in all the libraries. I can't understand why the dreary weeklies haven't read your *Jeanne* and installed it as a "historical document of great value." You know they hate you as a creator, all the critics: but why they shouldn't sigh with relief at finding you—in their own conceptions—a wonderfully subtle renderer and commentator of history, I don't know.

Pinker[1] wrote me the other day, wanting to place me a novel with one of the leading publishers. Would he be any good for other stuff? It costs so many stamps, I don't reply to all these people.

Have I made those naked scenes in *Paul Morel* tame enough? You cut them if you like. Yet they are so clean—and I *have* patiently and laboriously constructed that novel.

It is a marvellous moonlight night. The mountains have shoulder-capes of snow. I have been far away into the hills to-day, and got great handfuls of wild Christmas roses. This is one of the most beautiful countries in the world. You must come. The sunshine is marvellous, on the dark blue water, the ruddy mountains' feet, and the snow.

F. and I keep struggling forward. It is not easy, but I won't

[1] J. B. Pinker, literary agent.

complain. I suppose, if in the end I can't make enough money by writing, I shall have to go back to teaching. At any rate I can do that, so matters are never hopeless with me.

When you have time, do tell me about the *Fight for Barbara*. You think it couldn't be any use for the stage? I think the new generation is rather different from the old. I think they will read me more gratefully. But there, one can only go on.

It's funny, there is no *war* here—except "Tripoli." Everybody sings Tripoli. The soldiers howl all the night through and bang tambourines when the wounded come home.—And the Italian papers are full of Servia and Turkey—but what has England got to do with it?

It's awfully good of you to send me a paper. But you'll see, one day I can help you, or Bunny. And I will.

You sound so miserable. It's the damned work. I wish you were here for awhile. If you get run down, do come quickly. *Don't* let yourself become ill. This is such a beastly dangerous time. And you could work here, and live cheap as dirt with us.

Don't mind if I am impertinent. Living here alone one gets so different—sort of *ex cathedra*.

D. H. LAWRENCE.

To ELSE JAFFE[2]

Villa Igéa, Villa di Gargnano,
Lago di Garda, 14 Dec., 1912.

Dear Else,

I was not cross with your letter. I think you want to do the best for Frieda. I do also. But I think you ask us to throw away a real apple for a gilt one. Nowadays it costs more courage to assert one's desire and need, than it does to renounce. If Frieda and the children could live happily together, I should say "Go" because the happiness of two out of three is sufficient. But if she would only be sacrificing her life, I would not let her go if I

---

[2] From *"Not I, But the Wind..."*

could keep her. Because if she brings to the children a sacrifice, that is a curse to them. If I had a prayer, I think it would be "Lord, let no one ever sacrifice living stuff to me—because I am burdened enough."

Whatever the children may miss now, they will preserve their inner liberty, and their independent pride will be strong when they come of age. But if Frieda gave all up to go and live with them, that would sap their strength because they would have to support her life when they grew up. They would not be free to live of themselves—they would first have to live *for her,* to pay back. It is like somebody giving a present that was never asked for, and putting the recipient under the obligation of making restitution, often more than he could afford.

So we must go on, and never let go the children, but will, will and will to have them and have what we think good. That's all one can do. You say: "Lawrence kommt mir vor wie ein Held"—I hope he may "gehen dir aus" similarly. He doesn't feel at all heroic, but only in the devil of a mess.

Don't mind how I write, will you?

Yours sincerely,

D. H. LAWRENCE.

To EDWARD GARNETT

Villa Igéa, Villa di Gargnano,
Lago di Garda (Brescia), 12 Jan., 1913.

Dear Garnett,

I am going to send you a new play I have written. It is neither a comedy nor a tragedy—just ordinary. It is quite objective, as far as that term goes, and though no doubt, like most of my stuff, it wants weeding out a bit, yet I think the whole thing is there, laid out properly, planned and progressive. If you don't think so, I am disappointed.

I enjoy so much writing my plays—they come so quick and exciting from the pen—that you mustn't growl at me if you think them waste of time. At any rate, they'll be stuff for shaping later on, when I'm more of a workman. And I look at the future, and it behoves me to keep on trying to earn money somehow. The divorce will come off, I think, for sure. Then Frieda and I must see to ourselves, and I must see to the money part. I *do* think this play might have a chance on the stage. It'll bear cutting, but I don't think it lacks the stuff for the theatre.—I am afraid of being a nuisance. Do you feel, with me, a bit like the old man of the seas? If I weren't so scared of having no money at all, I'd tell you to shovel all my stuff on to Pinker, get rid of the bother of me, and leave me to transact with him. The thought of you pedgilling away at the novel frets me. Why can't I do those things?—I can't. I could do hack work, to a certain amount. But apply my creative self where it doesn't want to be applied, makes me feel I should burst or go cracked. I couldn't have done any more at that novel—at least for six months. I must go on producing, producing, and the stuff must come more and more to shape each year. But trim and garnish my stuff I cannot—it must go. The plays I can re-write and re-create: I shall love it, when I want to do it. But I don't want to do it yet.

I'm simmering a new work[4] that I shall not tell you about, because it may not come off. But the thought of it fills me with a curious pleasure—venomous, almost. I want to get it off my chest.

We had a good time with Harold[5]—you may congratulate us all.

It is rainy weather for three days, so that we are amazed and indignant. It has been *so* sunny all the time.

And again, about my getting some work. I shall never go into a big school to teach again. I'll be the proverbial poor poet in the garret first—and I must say I loathe the fellow. I've no sympathy with starvers, Gissings or Chattertons. I might get a

---

4 *The Sisters,* later *Women in Love.*
5 Harold Hobson, son of J. A. Hobson, the economist.

little country school. But I don't want to bury Frieda alive. Wherever I go with her, we shall have to fall into the intelligent, as it were, upper classes. I could get along with anybody, by myself, because, as Frieda says, I am common, and as you say, ⅕th Cockney. I find a servant maid more interesting as a rule than a Violet ————⁶ or a Grace ————.⁷ After all, I was brought up among them. But Frieda is a lady, and I hate her when she talks to the common people. She is not a bit stick-up, really more humble than I am, but she makes the *de haut en bas* of class distinction felt—even with my sister. It is as she was bred and fed, and can't be otherwise. So, that really cuts out a country school. I mustn't take her to England to bury her alive. We had six months without anybody at all. One needs *some* people, to keep healthy and well aired. I ought to live near London. Perhaps I could get some publishers' reading to do. We could manage on £200 a year. It ought not to be impossible. You must help me a bit, with advice.

If we come to England at Easter, there is not long here. Frieda wants to see her children then, but I don't know. I never thanked you for the American copy of the *Trespasser*. It is ugly. Have a bit of patience with me. You won't come out and see us? When do the poems appear?—I shall want a dozen copies, I owe so many people a remembrance. But I can pay for them. Frieda sends her regards.

Yrs.,
D. H. LAWRENCE.

To A. W. McLEOD

Villa Igéa, Villa di Gargnano,
Lago di Garda (Brescia), 17 Jan., 1913.

Dear Mac,

It's high time I wrote and thanked you for the notes and book. It's a delightful little Burns. And Henley was awfully

---

⁶ Probably Violet Hunt, wife of Hueffer. (H. T. M.)
⁷ Not identified.

good, but made me rather wild. Frieda and I have had high times, arguing over Andrew Lang and Henley and Lockhart. As for the book, my novel on the subject, I wonder if I shall ever get it done. I have written 80 pages of a new novel: a most curious work, which gives me great joy to write, but which, I am afraid, will give most folk extreme annoyance to read, if it doesn't bore them.

We've got a theatre here, and last night I went to see *Amletto*. Do you recognise our old friend? Now he was, really, the most amazing creature you can imagine: rather short, rather stout, with not much neck, and about forty years old: a bit after the Caruso type of Italian: the Croton type. I almost fell out of my little box trying to suppress my laughter. Because being one of the chief persons in the audience, and of course, the only Englishman, and ranking here as quite a swell—they acted particularly for me. I sat in my box No. 8, and felt a bigger farce than the stage. Poor Amletto—when he came forward whispering—'Essere—o non essere,' I thought my ears would fall off. When the gravedigger holds up a skull and says 'Ecco, Signore! Questo cranio è quel——" I almost protested. Hamlet addressed as Signore!—No—it was too much. I saw *Ghosts* and gulped it down—it was rather good. I have seen a D'Annunzio play, and rather enjoyed it—fearful melodrama. But they are only peasants, the players, and they play farces: and the queen is always the old servant woman, born for the part; and the king is always the contadino, or the weedy, weedy, old father— also born for the part. And Hamlet is usually the villain in some 'amour'—and poor Amletto, if I hadn't known what it was all about, I should have thought he had murdered some madam '*à la* Crippen' and it was *her* father's ghost chasing him: whilst he dallied between a bad and murderous conscience, a slinking desire to avoid everybody, and a wicked hankering after 'Ofaylia'—that's what she sounds like. I am muddled.

It's nasty weather—a beastly wind from the Po that has

brought the snow right down the mountains, not many yards above us. I object. I came here for sunshine, and insist on having it.

I got the blues thinking of the future, so I left off and made some marmalade. It's amazing how it cheers one up to shred oranges or scrub the floor.

Did H. H.[8] send you the pictures all right? He's a lazy devil. If they've not come, drop him a p.c. and ask if he's posted them to the wrong address. Write me a letter soon: it is nice to feel one's folk in England. Tell F. T.[9] I'll write him soon. My love to everybody.

D. H. LAWRENCE.

To ERNEST COLLINGS

Villa Igéa, Villa di Gargnano,
Lago di Garda (Brescia), 17 Jan., 1913.

Dear Collings,

Your letters are as good as a visit from somebody nice. I love people who can write reams and reams about themselves: it seems generous. And the points are interesting. What a rum chap you are! Are you a celibate? (Don't answer if you don't want to—I'm a married man, or ought to be.) Your work seems too—too—one-sided (I've only seen a tiny bit of it, as you know) —as if it were *afraid* of the female element—which makes me think you are more or less a Galahad—which is not, I believe, good for your art. It is hopeless for me to try to do anything without I have a woman at the back of me. And you seem a bit like that—not hopeless—but too uncertain. Böcklin—or somebody like him—daren't sit in a café except with his back to the wall. I daren't sit in the world without a woman behind me. And you give me that feeling a bit: as if you were uneasy of what is behind you. Excuse me if I am wrong. But a woman that

---

8 Harold Hobson.
9 Philip F. T. Smith, headmaster at Davidson Road School. (H. T. M.)

I love sort of keeps me in direct communication with the un-known, in which otherwise I am a bit lost.

Don't ever mind what I say. I am a great bosher, and full of fancies that interest me. Only these are my speculations over the two drawings. I think I prefer the Sphinx one. And then, when it comes to the actual *head,* in both cases, one is dissatis-fied. It is as if the head were not the inevitable consequence, the core and clinching point of the rest of the picture. They seem to me too fretful for the inevitability of the land which bears them. The more or less of wonder in the *Sappho* I liked better. Why is the body, so often, with you, a strange mass of earth, and yet the head is so fretful? I should have thought your conception needed a little more of fate in the faces of your figures, to be expressed: fate solid and inscrutable. But I know nothing about it. Only what have you done with your body, that your head seems so lost and lonely and dissatisfied?

My great religion is a belief in the blood, the flesh, as being wiser than the intellect. We can go wrong in our minds. But what our blood feels and believes and says, is always true. The intellect is only a bit and a bridle. What do I care about knowledge. All I want is to answer to my blood, direct, without fribbling intervention of mind, or moral, or what-not. I con-ceive a man's body as a kind of flame, like a candle flame, for-ever upright and yet flowing: and the intellect is just the light that is shed on to the things around. And I am not so much concerned with the things around—which is really mind—but with the mystery of the flame forever flowing, coming God knows how from out of practically nowhere, and being *itself,* whatever there is around it, that it lights up. We have got so ridiculously mindful, that we never know that we ourselves are anything—we think there are only the objects we shine upon. And there the poor flame goes on burning ignored, to produce this light. And instead of chasing the mystery in the fugitive, half-lighted things outside us, we ought to look at ourselves, and say 'My God, I am myself!' That is why I like to live in

Italy. The people are so unconscious. They only feel and want: they don't know. We know too much. No, we only *think* we know such a lot. A flame isn't a flame because it lights up two, or twenty objects on a table. It's a flame because it is itself. And we have forgotten ourselves. We are Hamlet without the Prince of Denmark. We cannot *be*. 'To be or not to be'—it is the question with us now, by Jove. And nearly every English-man says 'Not to be.' So he goes in for Humanitarianism and suchlike forms of not-being. The real way of living is to answer to one's wants. Not 'I want to light up with my intelligence as many things as possible' but 'For the living of my full flame—I want that liberty, I want that woman, I want that pound of peaches, I want to go to sleep, I want to go to the pub and have a good time, I want to look a beastly swell to-day, I want to kiss that girl, I want to insult that man.' Instead of that, all these wants, which are there whether-or-not, are utterly ignored, and we talk about some sort of ideas. I'm like Carlyle, who, they say, wrote 50 volumes on the value of silence.

Send me some more drawings, if ever you have any quite to spare. I liked your photograph, but it wasn't very much of a revelation of you. I like immensely to hear about your art. Write me when you feel you can write a lot.

Yours,

D. H. LAWRENCE.

To EDWARD GARNETT

Villa Igéa, Villa di Gargnano,

Lago di Garda (Brescia), 11 March, 1913.

Dear Garnett,

I am anxious down to my vitals about the poems. I thought my friends in the field—de la Mare and so on—would review them decently for me. God help us. I've got the pip horribly at present. I don't mind if Duckworth crosses out a hundred shady pages in *Sons and Lovers*. It's got to sell, I've got to live.

I'm a damned curse unto myself. I've written rather more than half of a most fascinating (to me) novel. But nobody will ever dare to publish it. I feel I could knock my head against the wall. Yet I love and adore this new book. It's all crude as yet, like one of Tony's[1] clumsy prehistorical beasts—most cumbersome and floundering—but I think it's great—so new, so really a stratum deeper than I think anybody has ever gone, in a novel. But there, you see, it's my latest. It is all analytical—quite unlike *Sons and Lovers*, not a bit visualised. But nobody will publish it. I wish I had never been born. But I'm going to stick at it, get it done, and then write another, shorter, absolutely impeccable—as far as morals go—novel. It is an oath I have vowed—if I have to grind my teeth to stumps, I'll do it—or else what am I going to live on, and keep Frieda on withal? Don't you mind about this tirade.

I think we shall give this place up at the end of this month. Frieda wants to come to England. We might have Mrs. Anthony's[2] rooms, down in Ashdown Forest, mightn't we—at least for a time? Then she would have our rent—at least, some of it—and be richer.

She is up at San Gaudenzio, perched on the brim of the mountain over the lake, in a farmstead of olives and vines, a situation beautiful as a dream. We are going up there this afternoon. I don't think 30 lire a month much for her room, do you? It's only 24/– a calendar month—and the folk *are* nice.

I have also got some friends who have a small grammar school in the Isle of Man, at Ramsey. I'm sure I could get a bit of teaching there, and I think Ramsey wouldn't be a bad place to live in, for the summer.

We have written to your brother Robert Garnett.

Thank Bunny for his letters—he sounds a bit unhooked—manhood comes hard to him, evidently. He's like me, I suppose.

---

1 H. T. M. believes this refers to Mrs. Anthony. (see below)
2 An artist-friend of the Garnetts (maiden name Antonia Cyriax) who, under the name of Mrs. Anthony, was hiding in Italy from her unbalanced husband.

I had a devil of a time getting a bit weaned from my mother, at the age of 22. She suffered, and I suffered, and it seemed all for nothing, just waste cruelty. It's funny. I suppose it is the final breaking away to independence.

Forgive me if I am impertinent.

Ask Duckworth to send me £50, will you? That must take me on five months or so, and then if there's any more due, I can draw, and if there isn't, I must wait.

I had rather not come to England this summer. But it is a case of Frieda's children. We wouldn't trouble you at the Cearne for very long—at the most not more than a fortnight. Does it seem an imposition? We can do all our own work, get in food and cook. And we shouldn't come before about the middle of April.

It's very sunny and pretty. Frieda has gone boating on the lake with some Germans. I didn't want to go—have had a damned cold.

I wish somebody would give my poems a lift.

A rivederla,

D. H. LAWRENCE.

I enclose Bunny an orchid. I find lovely flowers for him, and lose them again.

The novel is *not* about Frieda and me, nor about a Baroness neither.

To EDWARD GARNETT

Villa Jaffé, Irschenhausen,
(Post) Ebenhausen, bei München, Friday, 17.4.13.

Dear Garnett,

I am sorry the poems only sold 100.—Frieda is very cross. Don't you think Duckworth's printers or somebody are very slow? If one wants things to go like hot cakes, the cakes should be hot, surely. But the poems hung fire for months—*Sons and*

Lovers does likewise. The interest—what of it there may be—goes lukewarm. It's no good—if *Hamlet* and *Oedipus* were published now, they wouldn't sell more than 100 copies, unless they were pushed: I know that Duckworth will have to wait till my name is made, for his money. I can understand he is a bit diffident about putting me forward. But he needn't be afraid. I *know* I can write bigger stuff than any man in England. And I have to write what I can write. And I write for men like David[3] and Harold[4]—they will read me, soon. My stuff is what they want: when they know what they want. You wait.

Bliss Carman[5] was very nice. I have half a mind to write to him. Shall I?

We—or rather Frieda—had a letter from Harold this morning.

I am only doing *reviews* for the *Blue Monthly*,[6] or whatever it is.

Shall I send some poems, and a story, for the *Forum*?

I have written 180 pages of my newest novel, *The Sisters*. It is a queer novel, which seems to have come by itself. I will send it to you. You may dislike it—it hasn't got hard outlines—and of course it's only first draft—but it is pretty neat, for me, in composition. Then I've got 200 pages of a novel which I'm saving—which is very lumbering—which I'll call, provisionally, *The Insurrection of Miss Houghton*.[7] That I shan't send you yet, but it is, to me, fearfully exciting. It lies next my heart, for the present. But I am finishing *The Sisters*. It will only have 300 pages. It was meant to be for the *jeunes filles,* but already it has fallen from grace. I can only write what I feel pretty strongly about: and that, at present, is the relation between men and women. After all, it is *the* problem of to-day,

---

3 David (Bunny) Garnett.
4 Harold Hobson.
5 Canadian poet.
6 The *Blue Review,* edited by J. Middleton Murry and Katherine Mansfield with whom Lawrence became acquainted in the summer of 1913.
7 Later published as *The Lost Girl.*

the establishment of a new relation, or the readjustment of the old one, between men and women. In a month *The Sisters* will be finished (D.V.).

It is queer, but nobody seems to want, or to love, *two* people together. Heaps of folk love me alone—if I were alone—and of course all the world adores Frieda—when I'm not there. But together we seem to be a pest. I suppose married *(sic)* people ought to be sufficient to themselves. It's poverty which is so out of place.

I want to go back to Italy. I *have* suffered from the tightness, the *domesticity* of Germany. It is our domesticity which leads to our conformity, which chokes us. The very agricultural landscape here, and the distinct paths, stifles me. The very oxen are dull and featureless, and the folk seem like tables of figures. I have longed for Italy again, I can tell you.

I think these letters of ours are typical. Frieda sprawls so large I must squeeze myself small. I am very contractible. But aren't you writing a book about Dostoievsky? Those things crack my brains. How does it go? You *are* a pessimist really. We have *not* mentioned Mrs. G. to anybody, I believe. Tell David to write to me here.

D. H. LAWRENCE.

To J. M. MURRY

28, Percy Avenue, Kingsgate, Broadstairs.
(About July 15th, 1913.)[8]

Dear Murry,

Oh, but why didn't you come and let us lend you a pound. I think that when times have been so rough, you *shouldn't* bring about a disappointment on yourselves, just for the money. That seems to me wrong. We could just as well lend you five pounds as have it in the bank—if you want it. I consider now that your not coming on Sunday was a piece of obtuseness on

---

[8] The date of this letter is probably July 22 or 23. (H. T. M.)

your part. You are one of the people who *should* have a sense
of proportionate values; you ought to know when it's worth
while to let yourself borrow money, and when it isn't. Because
you *must* save your soul and Mrs. Murry's* soul from any
further hurts, for the present, or any disappointments, or any
dreary stretches of misery.

When Marsh¹ said on Sunday, because we couldn't understand why you hadn't come: "I suppose they hadn't the money
for the railway tickets," I thought it was stupid, because you
seemed so rich, because you can earn so much more than I can.
I had no idea.

So now I think you'd better come down for the week-end.
Come on Saturday and stay till Monday morning. We can put
you up. Don't on any account bring chickens or any such like
rubbish. We can get them down here. Though perhaps they
are cheaper in town. Bring one if you like.

Come for the week-end, and bathe. We've got a tent in a
little bay on the foreshore, and great waves come and pitch
one high up, so I feel like Horace, about to smite my cranium
on the sky. I can only swim a little bit and am a clown in the
water, but it's jolly. So you come, and bathe on Saturday. It'll
be high tide then about 5.0. And bathe on Sunday, and bathe
on Monday morning. Then you'll feel much jollier.

I am not poor, you know. But I didn't know you were really
stony. Only I have to watch it, because Frieda doesn't care.

Regards to you both,

D. H. LAWRENCE.

Let us know by what train you'll come on Saturday.
What a shame for Mrs. Murry to have had such a chase. I
put in a sovereign. Will she give Monty² half a sovereign if she
can—if not give me the money back when you like.—D.H.L.

* Although Murry and Katherine Mansfield were not married until 1918, they
were commonly known as the Murrys.
1 Edward Marsh, editor of an annual anthology, *Georgian Poetry*.
2 Montague Weekley, son of Frieda Lawrence. (H. T. M.)

To EDWARD MARSH

Fiascherino, Lerici, Golfo della Spezia, Italy.
14 Ottobre, 1913.

Dear Marsh,

Don't think that it is because your last letter offended me at
all, that I don't write. In reality, I quite agreed with what you
said. I know my verse is often strained and mal-formed.
Whether it gets better I don't know. I don't write much verse
now. I've got to earn my living by prose. One day I'll copy you
out some of my later things, if you'd care to see them.

We've been on the move since God knows when. That is why
I haven't written. When we left Bavaria, I walked across
Switzerland to Italy. Switzerland is rather banal. Then we
have prospected here and there to find a spot for the winter.
Now we are settled in Fiascherino. It is an hour's walk from
San Terenzo, Shelley's place. We've got a little pink cottage
among vines and olives. I also just caught a flea, and am in a
rage because it leapt from my fingers out into the infinite.
What a glorious flying jump a flea can take! The full moon
shines on the sea, which moves about all glittering among black
rocks. I go down and bathe and enjoy myself. You never saw
such clear, buoyant water. Also I don't swim more than a
dozen yards, so am always trying to follow the starry Shelley
and set amid the waves. I don't work much, and don't want to
work. If I'd got the smallest income I should be delighted to
loaf for ever. But now I watch the servant, Felice, and my heart
goes down plump. She is delighted to serve such grand and
glorious people as we are. She is sixty, very wrinkled, but full
of gusto. She strides up to the little arbour they call the Belve-
dere—it is impossible to think it only means Bellevue—bearing
the soup-tureen as if she were the Queen of Sheba taking spice
to Solomon: barefoot, she comes, with her petticoats kilted up,
and a gleam of triumph in her eye. Think if I couldn't afford
to pay her wages. I would take my last bathe. Don't mind my

[53]

lapsing into pounds shillings and pence. If I die rich, I shall order my tombstone to be a big gold sovereign, with me for king—Fidei Defensor, etc., round the rim. I caught the flea, by the way. One can be so keen on the chase. Figs are falling with ripeness in the garden. I am trying drying some—you dip them in boiling water. But I am in such a rage that the bright and shiny flies hover so thick about them when they are spread out, that they can't really get enough sun to dry them: always clouded with shadow.

How did you like your walk in Spain? I try to think of you, but can't quite see you. I suppose it would be rather fine. How did you like Lascelles Abercrombie?[3] You will introduce me to him when there is an opportunity, will you not? Davies[4] says he'll come here in the spring. I can see his one eating, gnawing anxiety is to write. God help us, when a poet must hunt his muse like Tartarin de Tarascon the one remaining hare. We take ourselves too seriously, *nous autres poètes*.

Write me a letter, and tell me all that is happening in the world of rhyme, will you? If anything good comes, let me know and I'll try to get it. Remember me to Gibson,[5] if you see him. Tell Davies he ought to come before spring, but we'll be glad to see him then if he can't get before. I have to go to Tellaro for the letters—it is a little sea-robbers' nest still inaccessible—and I feel so disgusted when, after hunting down the post-master— to-day he was helping the priest to tack up trimmings in the church—I get only a broad smile and a wave of the hand that implies a vacuum in space, and a "niente, signore, niente oggi, niente, niente." It is nearly half an hour's walk too. So when the post-master is forced to follow at my heels up the cobbly track humbly to deliver me my letter, I am justified.

Many greetings from us to you.

D. H. LAWRENCE.

3 English poet.
4 W. H. Davies, "vagabond" poet.
5 W. W. Gibson, English poet.

To LADY CYNTHIA ASQUITH

Lerici, per Fiascherino, Golfo della Spezia, Italy.
23rd October, 1913.

Dear Mrs. Asquith,

I have been wanting to write to you for such a long time.[6] But we have been "on the way" here. It is ages since we left Bavaria. Frieda went to her people in Baden Baden, which I didn't want to do. So I walked across Switzerland—and am cured of that little country forever. The only excitement in it is that you can throw a stone a frightfully long way down—that is forbidden by law. As for mountains—if I stick my little finger over my head, I can see it shining against the sky and call it Monte Rosa. No, I can't do with mountains at close quarters— they are always in the way, and they are so stupid, never moving and never doing anything but obtrude themselves.

Then I got to beastly Milano, with its imitation hedgehog of a cathedral, and its hateful town Italians, all socks and purple cravats and hats over the ear, did for me.

But we've got an adorable place here, a beautiful palazzino in large grounds, that descend in terraces to the sea—that's the Italian for it. I call it a little pink four-roomed cottage in a big vine garden, on the edge of a rocky bay. Frieda calls it a pink-washed sepulchre, because it is—or was—so dirty inside. Lord, what a time we've had, scrubbing it. It was no use calling on Elide, the girl. She had never seen a scrubbing brush used. So I tied my braces around my waist and went for it. Lord, to see the dark floor flushing crimson, the dawn of deep red bricks rise from out this night of filth, was enough to make one burst forth into hymns and psalms. "Ah," cries Elide, "l'aria e la pulizia—air and cleanliness are the two most important things in this life." She might as well have said nectar and ambrosia, for all she knew of 'em.

---

[6] Lawrence had been introduced to the Asquiths by Edward Marsh in July 1913.

But the Italians don't consider their houses, like we do, as being their extended persons. In England my house is my outer cuticle, as a snail has a shell. Here it is a hole into which I creep out of the rain and the dark. When they eat, the Capitano and his wife—the place belongs to them, she inherited it, but they let it and live in town—they fling all their scraps and "bouts de vin" on the floor unceremoniously, and the cats and the flies do the war dance about them.

It's a lovely position—among the vines, a little pink house just above a rocky bay of the Mediterranean. One goes down in a towel to bathe. And the water is warm and buoyant—it *is* jolly. I wish you could try it too.

We live awfully cheaply—I know these things interest you more than eternal truths—house, 60 francs a month, maid 25, and vegetables in abundance, cheap as dirt. And in the morning one wakes and sees the pines all dark and mixed up with perfect rose of dawn, and all day long the olives shimmer in the sun, and fishing boats and strange sails like Corsican ships come out of nowhere on a pale blue sea, and then at evening all the sea is milky gold and scarlet with sundown. It is very pretty.

Did you make your dash to Venice—and did it stink? Lord, but how Italy can stink. We have to fetch letters from Tellaro—twenty-five minutes upstairs and downstairs on the sea-edge, an inaccessible little sea-robbers' place—and my dear heart, but it *is* dirty.

I hope you are pretty well—are you? But isn't it a bit much, to go dashing to Venice and back in a week? Why don't you go to Margate again? I think it makes an awful difference, when one is happy in a place. How is the jonquil[7] with the golden smile. Is Mr. Asquith making heaps of money at the bar? I believe I'm going to get about £150 this winter, which will be rolling wealth for us here.

We heard from Eddie Marsh yesterday—such a heavy acorn

7 This may refer to the Asquiths' small son John.

fell on my head at this moment—now that is an omen. Are you any good at soothsaying? He is fearfully warm and generous, I think. I think I was wrong to feel injured because my verse wasn't well enough dished-up to please him.

The Mediterranean can get *very* cross. To-day the wind is the Maestrale—and the sea is showing its teeth in an unbecoming fashion.

I'm going to have a play published.[8] The black hen has just come home. She went lost. Elide is waving her hands with joy. A very decent play. They won't give me any copies or I'd send you one. But you must read it.

My regards to Mr. Asquith and to the Jonquil and to you.

Yours sincerely,
D. H. LAWRENCE.

To A. W. McLEOD

Lerici, per Fiascherino, Golfo della Spezia, Italy.
Sunday, 27.10.13.

Dear Mac,

Your letter, with the cutting, came yesterday, and to-day the books. You are a decent chap. Frieda wanted to read *Ann Veronica.* I have read it, and found it rather trashy. I love *Tristram Shandy.* But the book on *Art and Ritual* pleases me most just now. I am just in the mood for it. It just fascinates me to see art coming out of religious yearning—one's presentation of what one wants to feel again, deeply. But I haven't got far in. As for the divorce, it is curious how at first it upsets me and then goes off, and matters no more. I have found that one has such a living social self. I am sure every man feels first, that he is a servant—be it martyr or what—of society. And if he feels that he has trespassed against society, and it is adverse to him, he suffers. Then the individual self comes up and says, "You fool."

8 *The Widowing of Mrs. Holroyd.*

[57]

Now again, only the sea—it is rather dark to-day, with heavy waves—and the olives matter to me. London is all smoke a long way off. But yesterday I was awfully grateful to you for your sane and decent letter. You must continue to believe in me—I don't mean in my talent only—because I depend on you a bit. One doesn't know, till one is a bit at odds with the world, how much one's friends who believe in one rather generously, mean to one. I felt you had gone off from me a bit, because of *Sons and Lovers.* But one sheds one's sicknesses in books—repeats and presents again one's emotions, to be master of them.

I did send some verse the other day to the *English,* but I think Harrison doesn't want to publish my poetry—he wants my prose more. He has got three soldier stories, which he is going to publish in a sort of series—perhaps four—so he says—which will make a book afterwards. I hope they'll go all right. I have been so much upset, what with moving and Frieda's troubling about the children—you know she has three—and what not, that I haven't been able to work. It is no joke to do as Frieda and I have done—and my very soul feels tired. But here it is going to pick up again and I am going to work like a brick.

It is very warm and beautiful here—and we bathe in a warm, bright sea. This afternoon we have been making a visit to the contadini laggiù. They have the only other house on the bay—and a lot of garden and vines going up in terraces. The kitchen is the top room in the house—and wherever you sit, if you look at the window, you see the sea moving. It is very queer. I have never been in such a house. They are awfully nice people. I want you to come here, if you can—either at Christmas or Easter. It is so beautiful. Perhaps we shall keep the cottage too for next winter. Do try and come.

I should like an Ernest Dowson, if you would lend me him. I will send him back carefully. I only know one or two things of his and he interests me.

You didn't tell me very much news. Write to me again and let me know about folk.

Frieda is going to write to you.

Love,
D. H. LAWRENCE.

How are you and what are you doing and what do you think of things nowadays?

If your mother happens to have a recipe for marrow jam—Frieda wants to make some with pumpkins—send it when you write, will you?—D.H.L.

To J. M. MURRY

Lerici, per Fiascherino, Golfo della Spezia, Italy.

Thursday (1913).

Dear Murry,

I'm going to answer your letter immediately, and frankly.

When you say you won't take Katherine's[9] money, it means you don't trust her love for you. When you say she needs little luxuries, and you couldn't bear to deprive her of them, it means you don't respect either yourself or her sufficiently to do it.

It looks to me as if you two, far from growing nearer, are snapping the bonds that hold you together, one after another. I suppose you must both of you consult your own hearts, honestly. She must see if she really wants *you*, wants to keep you and to have no other man all her life. It means forfeiting something. But the only principle I can see in this life, is that one *must* forfeit the less for the greater. Only one must be thoroughly honest about it.

She must say, "Could I live in a little place in Italy, with Jack, and be lonely, have rather a bare life, but be happy?" If

---

9 Katherine Mansfield.

she could, then take her money. If she doesn't want to, don't try. But don't beat about the bush. In the way you go on, you are inevitably coming apart. She is perhaps beginning to be unsatisfied with you. And you can't make her more satisfied by being unselfish. You must say, "How can I make myself most healthy, strong, and satisfactory to myself and to her?" If by being lazy for six months, then be lazy, and take her money. It doesn't matter if she misses her luxuries: she won't die of it. What luxuries do you mean?

If she doesn't want to stake her whole life and being on you, then go to your University abroad for a while, alone. I warn you, it'll be hellish barren.

Or else you can gradually come apart in London, and then flounder till you get your feet again, severally, but be clear about it. It lies between you and Katherine, nowhere else.

Of course you can't dream of living long without work. Couldn't you get the *Westminster* to give you *two* columns a week, abroad? You must *try*. You must stick to criticism. You ought also to plan a book, either on some literary point, or some man. I should like to write a book on English heroines. You ought to do something of that sort, but not so cheap. Don't try a novel—try essays—like Walter Pater or somebody of that style. But you *can* do something *good* in that line; something concerning *literature* rather than life. And you must rest, and you and Katherine must heal, and come together, before you do *any serious* work of any sort. It's the split in the love that drains you. You see, while she doesn't really love you, and is not satisfied, *you* show to frightful disadvantage. But it would be a pity not to let your mind flower—it might, under decent circumstances, produce beautiful delicate things, in perception and appreciation. And she has a right to provide the conditions. But not if you don't trust yourself nor her nor anybody, but go on slopping, and pandering to her smaller side. If you work yourself sterile to get her chocolates, she will most justly detest you—she is *perfectly* right. She doesn't want you to sacrifice herself to you, you fool. Be more natural, and positive, and stick to your own guts. You spread them on a tray for her to throw to the cats.

If you want things to come right—if you are ill and exhausted, then take her money to the last penny, and let her do her own housework. Then she'll know you love her. You can't blame her if she's not satisfied with you. If I haven't had enough dinner, you can't blame *me*. But, you fool, you squander yourself, not for *her*, but to provide her with petty luxuries she doesn't really want. You insult her. A woman unsatisfied must have luxuries. But a woman who loves a man would sleep on a board.

It strikes me you've got off your lines, somewhere you've not been man enough: you've felt it rested with your honour to give her a place to be proud of. It rested with your honour to give her a man to be satisfied with—and satisfaction is never accomplished even physically unless the man is strongly and surely himself, and doesn't depend on anything but his own *being* to make a woman love him. You've tried to satisfy Katherine with what you could earn for her, give her: and she will only be satisfied with what you *are*.

And you don't know what you are. You've never come to it. You've always been dodging round, getting Rhythms and flats and doing criticism for money. You are a fool to work so hard for Katherine—she hates you for it—and quite right. You want to be strong in the possession of your own soul. Perhaps you will only come to that when this affair of you and her has gone crash. I should be sorry to think that—I don't believe it. You must save yourself, and your self-respect, by making it complete between Katherine and you—if you devour her money till she walks in rags, if you are both outcast. Make her certain—don't pander to her—stick to *yourself*—do what you *want* to do—don't *consider* her—she hates and loathes being considered. You insult her in saying you wouldn't take her money.

The University idea is a bad one. It would further disintegrate you.

If you are disintegrated, then get integrated again. Don't be a coward. If you are disintegrated your first duty is to yourself, and you may use Katherine—her money and everything—to get right again. You're not well, man. Then have the courage to get well. If you are strong again, and a bit complete, *she'll* be satisfied with you. She'll love you hard enough. But don't you see, at this rate, you distrain on her day by day and month by month. I've done it myself.

Take your rest—do *nothing* if you like for a while—though I'd do a *bit*. Get better, first and foremost—use anybody's money, to do so. Get better—and do things you like. Get yourself into condition. It drains and wearies Katherine to have you like this. What a fool you are, what a fool. Don't bother about her—what she wants or feels. Say, "I am a man at the end of the tether, therefore I become a man blind to everything but my own need." But keep a heart for the long run.

Look. We pay 60 lire a month for this house: 25 lire for the servant; and food is *very* cheap. You could live on 185 lire a month in plenty—and be greeted as "Signoria" when you went out together—it is the same as "Guten Tag, Herrschaften"; that would be luxury enough for Katherine.

Get up, lad, and be a man for yourself. It's the man who dares to take, who is independent, not he who gives.

I think Oxford did you harm.

It is beautiful, wonderful, here.

A ten-pound note is 253 lire. We could get you, I believe, a jolly nice apartment in a big garden, in a house alone, for 80 lire a month. Don't waste yourself—don't be silly and floppy. You know what you *could* do—you *could* write—then prepare yourself: and first make Katherine at rest in her love for you. Say, "This I will certainly do"—it would be a relief for her to hear you. Don't be a child—don't keep that rather childish charm. Throw everything away, and say, "Now I act for my own good, at last."

We are getting gradually nearer again, Frieda and I. It is very beautiful here.

We are awfully sorry Katherine is so seedy. She ought to write to us. Our love to her and you.

D. H. LAWRENCE.

If you've got an odd book or so you don't want to read, would you send it us? There is nothing for Frieda to read—and we like everything and anything.

To LADY CYNTHIA ASQUITH
Lerici, per Fiascherino, Golfo della Spezia, Italy.
Tuesday, Nov. —, 1913.[1]

Dear Mrs. Asquith,

Because I feel frightfully disagreeable, and not fit to conse-crate myself to novels or to short stories, I'll write a letter. I like to write when I feel spiteful; it's like having a good sneeze. Don't mind, will you?

You say we're happy—per Bacchino! If you but knew the thunderstorms of tragedy that have played over my wretched head, as if I was set up on God's earth for a lightning conductor, you'd say, "Thank God I'm not as that poor man." If you knew the slough of misery we've struggled and suffocated through, you'd stroke your counterpane with a purring motion, like an old maid having muffins for tea in the lamplight and reading *Stanley in Africa*. If ever you hear of me in a mad-house, and Frieda buried under a nameless sod, you'll say, "Poor things, no wonder, with all they've gone through." You talk about tears drowning the wind—my God. We are the most unfor-tunate, agonised, fate-harassed mortals since Orestes and that

[1] Mr. Moore dates this letter November 25, 1913.

gang. Don't you forget it. Put away all illusions concerning us, and see the truth.

When I had an English feel come over me, I took it frightfully badly, that we had appeared before you as if we were a perfectly respectable couple. I thought of the contamination—etc., etc.—and I really was upset. I'm glad you didn't mind; you might with justice have taken it amiss—and then, Lord, what a state I should have been in when the English feel came over me again. Heaven be blessed, England is only a spot of grease on the soup just now.

I'm sorry you've got a cold. But what do you expect, after purpling in Venice—Frieda's been in bed for four days also—like Robinson Crusoe: "First day I vomited——." I wandered under the falling vines murmuring: "What rhubarb, senna and what purgative drug——." It was sheer misery. We *have* had a time, between us: oh dear o' me! She is a bit better to-day.

I've been to Spezia. Frieda *will* hire a piano, not a hurdy-gurdy. Well, it has to come first on the workmen's steamer to Lerici, then be got down into a rowing boat, and rowed along the coast, past jutting rocks where the sea goes up and down to bring your heart in your mouth, finally landed into the shingle of this little bay, and somehow got up the steeps to the house. Well, the man found out what a journey it was, and he clings to his piano as if it were his only child, nor could I snatch it from him to-day. So we fell out—and in the midst of it a man in sailor's uniform with "White Star" on his breast came and said he was English and did we want to buy contraband English cloth. And he wasn't English—nor French, nor German, nor Italian—but spoke twenty words of each. Now I might have wrested this pianoforte out of the fervent arms of Rugi Gulielmo, but for the interruption of the sailor with a sack. As it was, I returned, boat and all, empty save of curses.

"Ecco—un pianoforte—it's not like a piece of furniture—if it was a piece of furniture—he! va bene—but—a pianoforte—he!——"

I loathe and detest the Italians. They never argue, they just get hold of a parrot phrase, shove up their shoulders and put their heads on one side, and flap their hands. And what is an honest man to do with 'em? (Forget my past when I say "Honest man.") Now I shall have to go to-morrow, and pay a regiment of facchini to transport that cursed pianoforte.

> "Take it up tenderly,
> Lift it with care,
> Fashioned so slenderly,
> Young and so fair."

And it's a tin-pot thing not fit for a cat to walk up and down. And if it *does* go to the bottom of the sea—well, God bless it and peace be with it, a gay blonde head.

> "Il pleut doucement sur la ville
> Comme il pleut dans mon coeur."[2]

As a matter of fact, it's a perfectly glittery and starry night, with a glow-worm outside the door, and on the sea a lighthouse beating time to the stars.

Well, adieu, fair lady, don't be cross and sad. Think that we have simply worn holes in our hankeys, with weeping.

Why should the cat sleep all night on my knee, and give me fleas to bear? Why?

There's a peasant wedding down below, next Saturday. The bride in white silk and orange blossom must clamber fearful roads, three hours there and back, to go to the Syndaco of l'Ameglia, to be married. Mass at 7.30 at Tellaro—*piccola colazione* at the bride's house at 8.30—*un boccone*—marriage at 10.0 at l'Ameglia—*pranzo* down here at mid-day. We are

[2] Lawrence misquotes Verlaine. These lines should read:
> "Il pleure dans mon coeur
> Comme il pleut sur la ville."
The Verlaine poem is based on a line from Rimbaud:
> "Il pleut doucement sur la ville"

invited. But it's rather sad, he doesn't want her very badly. One gets married—*si*—*come si fa!* They say it so often—*ma*—*come si fa!*

> Il pleut doucement dans la ville,
> I think I am missing a meal.

> *A rivederla, signoria,*
> D. H. LAWRENCE.

They call us "Signoria." How's that for grandeur! Shades of my poor father!

To EDWARD MARSH

Lerici, per Fiascherino, Golfo della Spezia, Italy.
24 Gennaio, 1914.

Dear Eddie,

That *Georgian Poetry* book is a veritable Aladdin's lamp. I little thought my *Snapdragon* would go on blooming and seeding in this prolific fashion. So many thanks for the cheque for four pounds, and long life to G. P.

We are still trying to get over the excitement of your rush through Fiascherino. I still think with anguish of your carrying your bag up that salita from Lerici—don't remember it against me. I have received one or two more apologies from Severino, for his having taken us for the three *saltimbanchi*: the latter, by the way, gave a great performance in Tellaro, at the bottom there by the sea, on Sunday. They performed in the open air. Elide assisted at the spectacle, but confessed to disappearing into the church when the hat came round: along with three parts of the crowd. The poor *saltimbanchi* were reduced to begging for a little bread, so stingy was Tellaro.

The night you went, was a great fall of snow. We woke in the morning wondering what the queer pallor was. And the snow lay nearly six inches deep, and was still drifting finely, shadowily, out to the sombre-looking sea.

Of course, no Elide appeared. I got up and made a roaring fire and proceeded to wash the pots, in a queer, silent, muffled Fiascherino; even the sea was dead and still.

It looked very queer. The olives on the hills bowed low, low under the snow, so the whole slopes seemed peopled with despairing shades descending to the Styx. I never saw anything so like a host of bowed, pathetic despairers, all down the hill-side. And every moment came the long creak—cre-eak of a tree giving way, and the crash as it fell.

The pines on the little peninsula were very dark and snowy, above a lead-grey sea. It was queer and Japanesy: no distance, no perspective, everything near and sharp on a dull grey ground. The water cut out a very perfect, sweeping curve from the snow on the beach.

The Mino—the cat—had been out at night as usual. He appeared shoulder-deep in snow, mewing, terrified—and he wouldn't come near me. He knows me perfectly. But that sudden fall of deep snow had frightened him out of his wits, and it was a long time before we could get him to come into the house.

At midday appeared Elide with her elder brother, Alessandro. *And* there was an outcry. Alessandro stood in the doorway, listening to the trees cracking, and crying, *"Ma dio, dio—senti signore, senti—Christo del mondo—è una rovina."* All Tellaro was praying to the Vergine in the church: they had rung a special appeal at 9.30, and the old women had flocked in. Elide looked once more at the driving snow-flakes, stamped her foot like a little horse, and cried defiantly, *"Ma se il Dio vuol' mandare il fine del mondo—che lo manda."* She was ready. Meanwhile Alessandro moaned, *"Una rovina, un danno!"*

It really was a ruin. Quite half the trees were smashed. One could not get out of our garden gate, for great trees fallen there. No post came to Tellaro—nothing happened but moaning. And the third day, in lamentation, they brought a commission to see the damage and to ask to have the taxes remitted. Now they are quite happily chopping up the ruin, crying, *"Ora si puo scaldarsi."*

Another excitement! Luigi, down at the house on the bay here, the evening of your departure came home pale with excitement, found our Felice, and said hoarsely, *"Ma zia, io ho una brutta notizia da portare. Quelli due Inglesi del signore erano arrestati stasera, al pontino di Lerici."* Loud, loud lamentations from Felice, Elide maintaining stoutly, *"Forse mancava qualche carta—di certo è una cosa di niente."* *Think* how you let us in for it—between strolling players and arrests.

There was also a great argument between Felice and Elide, as to which of you was the more beautiful. Elide said Jim Barnes,* Felice said you—and they got quite cross.

> *Addio,*
>
> D. H. LAWRENCE.

To EDWARD GARNETT

> *Lerici, per Fiascherino, Golfo della Spezia, Italy.*
> *29 Gennaio, 1914.*

Dear Garnett,

I am not very much surprised, nor even very much hurt by your letter—and I agree with you. I agree with you about the Templeman episode.[1] In the scheme of the novel, however, I *must* have Ella get some experience before she meets her Mr. Birkin. I also felt that the character was inclined to fall into two halves—and gradations between them. It came of trying to graft on to the character of ———[2] the character, more or less, of ———.[3] That I ought not to have done. To your two

---

* James Strachey Barnes, friend of Edward Marsh, later an admirer of Mussolini and author of several books on fascism. (H. T. M.)

[1] In *The Sisters,* later published as *Women in Love.*

[2] Louie. (H. T. M.)

[3] Frieda. (H. T. M.)

main criticisms, that the Templeman episode is wrong, and that the character of Ella is incoherent, I agree. Then about the artistic side being in the background. It is that which troubles me most. I have no longer the joy in creating vivid scenes, that I had in *Sons and Lovers*. I don't care much more about accumulating objects in the powerful light of emotion, and making a scene of them. I have to write differently. I am most anxious about your criticism of this, the second half of the novel, a hundred and fifty pages of which I send you to-morrow. Tell me *very* frankly what you think of it: and if it pleases you, tell me whether you think Ella would be possible, as she now stands, unless she had some experience of love and of men. I think, impossible. Then she must have a love episode, a significant one. But it must not be a Templeman episode.

I shall go on now to the end of the book. It will not take me long. Then I will go over it all again, and I shall be very glad to hear *all* you have to say. But if this, the second half, also disappoints you, I will, when I come to the end, leave this book altogether. Then I should propose to write a story with a plot, and to abandon the exhaustive method entirely—write pure object and story.

I am going through a transition stage myself. I am a slow writer, really—I only have great outbursts of work. So that I do not much mind if I put all this novel in the fire, because it is the vaguer result of transition. I write with everything vague—plenty of fire underneath, but, like bulbs in the ground, only shadowy flowers that must be beaten and sustained, for another spring. I feel that this second half of *The Sisters* is very beautiful, but it may not be sufficiently incorporated to please you. I do not try to incorporate it very much—I prefer the permeating beauty. It is my transition stage—but I must write to live, and it must produce its flowers, and if they be frail or shadowy, they will be all right if they are true to their hour. It is not so easy for one to be married. In marriage one must become something else. And I am changing, one way or the other. Thank you for the trouble you take for me. I shall be all the better in the end. Remember I am a slow producer, really.

Yours,
D. H. LAWRENCE.

To EDWARD GARNETT
Lerici, per Fiascherino, Golfo della Spezia, Italy.
22 April, 1914.

Dear Garnett,

I send you by this post as much of the *Wedding Ring*[4] as the consul[5] has as yet typed. I have only some 80 pages more to write. In a fortnight it should be done. You will perhaps get it in three weeks' time, the whole.

From this part that I have sent you, follows on the original *Sisters*—the School Inspector, and so on.

I am sure of this now, this novel. It is a big and beautiful work. Before, I could not get my soul into it. That was because of the struggle and the resistance between Frieda and me. Now you will find her and me in the novel, I think, and the work is of both of us.

I am glad you sent back the first draft of the *Wedding Ring*, because I had not been able to do in it what I wanted to do. But I was upset by the *second* letter you wrote against it, because I felt it insulted rather the thing I *wanted* to say: not me, nor what I had said, but that which I was trying to say, and had failed in.

In the work as it stands now, there will, if anything, be only small prolixities to cut down.

I hope you will like it. It is a big book now that I have got it down. I hope it will have a good sale. Both Pinker and

---

4 Later published as *The Rainbow*.
5 Thomas Dacre Dunlop, English consul at Spezia.

Curtis Brown[6] write to me making offers authorised, they insist, by leading publishers in England and America—definite offers. It was horrid to receive the accounts of *Sons and Lovers,* and to see that Duckworth has lost a number of pounds on the book—fifteen or so, was it? That is very unpleasant. Because I only had a hundred pounds even then—and I have had £35 from Kennerley.[7] If a publisher is to lose by me, I would rather it were a rich commercial man such as Heinemann. You told me in your last letter that I was at liberty to go to any other firm with this novel. Do you mean you would perhaps be relieved if I went to another firm? Because if you did not mean that, wasn't it an unnecessary thing to say? You know how willing I am to hear what you have to say, and to take your advice and to act on it when I have taken it. But it is no good unless you will have patience and understand what I *want* to do. I am not after all a child working erratically. All the time, underneath, there is something deep evolving itself out in me. And it is *hard* to express a new thing, in sincerity. And you should understand, and help me to the new thing, not get angry and say it is *common,* and send me back to the tone of the old *Sisters.* In the *Sisters* was the germ of this novel: woman becoming individual, self-responsible, taking her own initiative. But the first *Sisters* was flippant and often vulgar and jeering. I had to get out of that attitude, and make my subject really worthy. You see—you tell me I am half a Frenchman and one-eighth a Cockney. But that isn't it. I have very often the vulgarity and disagreeableness of the common people, as you say Cockney, and I may be a Frenchman. But primarily I am a passionately religious man, and my novels must be written from the depth of my religious experience. That I must keep to, because I can only work like that. And my Cockneyism and commonness are only when the deep feeling doesn't find its way out, and a sort of jeer comes instead, and sentimentality,

6 Literary agent.
7 Mitchell Kennerley, American publisher.

and purplism. But you should see the religious, earnest, suffering man in me first, and then the flippant or common things after. Mrs. Garnett says I have no true nobility—with all my cleverness and charm. But that is not true. It is there, in spite of all the littlenesses and commonnesses.

And that is why I didn't like the second letter you wrote me about the failed novel, where you rubbed it in: because you seemed to insult my real *being*. You had a right to go for my work, but in doing that, you must not make *me* cheap in your own eyes. You can be angry with a person without holding him cheap, and making him feel cheap. You believe too much in the Frenchman and the Cockney. Those are the things to criticise in me, not to rest your belief on.

Soon I shall want some money. Perhaps you might send me the little I left in Mrs. Garnett's bank—is it seven pounds or so? Don't bother if it is any trouble. I have a little still in the bank here. So I can use cheques.

If Duckworth is not really *keen* on this novel, we will give it to Pinker without its coming back here. I don't think I want to sign an agreement with Duckworth for another novel after this. I did not like to see he had lost on *Sons and Lovers*. And I *must* have money for my novels, to live. And if the other publishers definitely offer, they who are only commercial people, whereas you are my friend—well, they may lose as much as they like. For I don't want to feel under an obligation. You see I can't separate you from Duckworth and Co., in this question of novels. And *nobody* can do any good with my novels, commercially, unless they believe in them commercially—which you don't very much.

Will you also tell me who makes the agreement with Kennerley for U.S.A. publication, and what is the agreement made.

I see that *Mrs. Holroyd*[8] is coming out. Do you give me any copies? Tell me about it, will you?

8 *The Widowing of Mrs. Holroyd*, a play.

We think of staying here till the end of June, perhaps. I don't know whether we shall come straight to England, or go to Germany first. We want to be married this summer, if the decree absolute is declared all right. Then we think of coming back here for the winter. We have an invitation to the Abruzzi, to the Baronessa di Rescis, in September, and I want to go to the Abruzzi.

I am always grateful to you, and if Duckworth could have my novels and all of us be satisfied, I should be glad. But I am sure we are none of us very well satisfied with the result of *Sons and Lovers*.

I shall be glad if you like the novel now—but you will tell me. Frieda sends her regards.

Yours,

D. H. LAWRENCE.

To EDWARD GARNETT

Lerici, per Fiascherino, Golfo della Spezia, Italia.
5 Junio, 1914.

Dear Garnett,

First let me remember to thank you for letting the two books be sent to the Consul in Spezia.

About Pinker, I will do as you say, and tell him that the matter of the novel is not yet settled, and I will call on him in some fifteen or twenty days.

I don't agree with you about the *Wedding Ring*. You will find that in a while you will like the book as a whole. I don't think the psychology is wrong: it is only that I have a different attitude to my characters, and that necessitates a different attitude in you, which you are not prepared to give. As for its being my *cleverness* which would pull the thing through—that sounds odd to me, for I don't think I am so very clever, in that way. I think the book is a bit futuristic—quite unconsciously so. But when I read Marinetti[9]—"the profound intuitions of life added one to the other, word by word, according to their illogical conception, will give us the general outlines of an intuitive physiology of matter"—I see something of what I am after. I translate him clumsily, and his Italian is obfuscated—and I don't care about physiology of matter—but somehow—that which is physic—non-human, in humanity, is more interesting to me than the old-fashioned human element—which causes one to conceive a character in a certain moral scheme and make him consistent. The certain moral scheme is what I object to. In Turgenev, and in Tolstoi, and in Dostoievsky, the moral scheme into which all the characters fit—and it is nearly the same scheme—is, whatever the extraordinariness of the characters themselves, dull, old, dead. When Marinetti writes: "It is the solidity of a blade of steel that is interesting by itself, that is, the incomprehending and inhuman alliance of its molecules in resistance to, let us say, a bullet. The heat of a piece of wood or iron is in fact more passionate, for us, than the laughter or tears of a woman"—then I know what he means. He is stupid, as an artist, for contrasting the heat of the iron and the laugh of the woman. Because what is interesting in the laugh of the woman is the same as the binding of the molecules of steel or their action in heat: it is the inhuman will, call it physiology, or like Marinetti—physiology of matter, that fascinates me. I don't so much care about what the woman *feels*—in the ordinary usage of the word. That presumes an *ego* to feel with. I only care about what the woman *is*—what she IS—inhumanly, physiologically, materially—according to the use of the word: but for me, what she *is* as a phenomenon (or as representing some greater, inhuman will), instead of what she feels according to the human conception. That is where the futurists are stupid. Instead of looking for the new human phenomenon, they will only look for the phenomena of the science of physics to be

9 F. T. Marinetti, Italian futurist.

found in human beings. They are crassly stupid. But if anyone would give them eyes, they would pull the right apples off the tree, for their stomachs are true in appetite. You mustn't look in my novel for the old stable *ego* of the character. There is another *ego,* according to whose action the individual is unrecognisable, and passes through, as it were, allotropic states which it needs a deeper sense than any we've been used to exercise, to discover are states of the same single radically unchanged element. (Like as diamond and coal are the same pure single element of carbon. The ordinary novel would trace the history of the diamond—but I say, 'Diamond, what! This is carbon.' And my diamond might be coal or soot, and my theme is carbon.) You must not say my novel is shaky—it is not perfect, because I am not expert in what I want to do. But it is the real thing, say what you like. And I shall get my reception, if not now, then before long. Again I say, don't look for the development of the novel to follow the lines of certain characters: the characters fall into the form of some other rhythmic form, as when one draws a fiddle-bow across a fine tray delicately sanded, the sand takes lines unknown.

I hope this won't bore you. We leave here on Monday, the 8th. Frieda will stay in Baden Baden some 10–14 days. I am not going by sea, because of the filthy weather. I am walking across Switzerland into France with Lewis, one of the skilled engineers of Vickers-Maxim works here. I shall let you know my whereabouts.

Don't get chilly and disagreeable to me.

Au revoir,

D. H. LAWRENCE.

I shall be awfully glad to see Bunny again—and Mrs. Garnett and you.

Please keep this letter, because I want to write on futurism and it will help me. I will come and see Duckworth. Give *Bunny* my novel—I want *him* to understand it.

To CATHERINE CARSWELL
9, Selwood Terrace, South Kensington, S.W.
Monday, July 1914.

Dear Mrs. Jackson,

I must tell you I am in the middle of reading your novel. You have very often a simply *beastly* style, indirect and round-about and stiff-kneed and stupid. And your stuff is abominably muddled—you'll simply have to write it all again. But it is fascinatingly interesting. Nearly all of it is *marvellously* good. It is only so incoherent. But you can *easily* pull it together. It *must* be a long novel—it is of the quality of a long novel. My stars, just you work at it, and you'll have a piece of work you never need feel ashamed of. All you need is to get the whole thing under your control. You see, it takes one so long to know what one is really about. Your Juley is a fascinating character—not quite understood sufficiently—not quite. Ruth is good. Leave the other children sketchy.

When I've finished it—to-morrow or Wednesday—we must have a great discussion about it. My good heart, there's some honest work here, real.

I must go to Croydon to-morrow afternoon. But I'll ring you up when I've finished.

Yours,
D. H. LAWRENCE.

You must be willing to put much real work, hard work, into this, and you'll have a genuine creative piece of work. It's like Jane Austen at a deeper level.

To T. D. D.

The Cearne, Near Edenbridge, Kent.
7 July, 1914.

Dear D.,

I was glad to get your still sad letter, and sorry you are so down yet. I can't help thinking that you wouldn't be quite so

down if you and Mrs. D. didn't let yourselves be separated
rather by this trouble. Why do you do this? I think the trouble
ought to draw you together, and you seem to let it put you
apart. Of course I may be wrong. But it seems a shame that her
one cry, when she is in distress, should be for her mother. You
ought to be the mother and father to her. Perhaps if you go
away to your unhealthy post, it may be good for you. But perhaps you may be separating your inner life from hers—I don't
mean anything actual and external—but you may be taking
yourself inwardly apart from her, and leaving her inwardly
separate from you: which is no true marriage, and is a form of
failure. I am awfully sorry; because I think that no amount of
outward trouble and stress of circumstance could really touch
you both, if you were together. But if you are not together, of
course, the strain becomes too great, and you want to be alone,
and she wants her mother. And it seems to me an awful pity if,
after you have tried, you have to fail and go separate ways. I am
not speaking of vulgar outward separation: I know you would
always be a good reliable husband: but there is more than that:
there is the real sharing of one life. I can't help thinking your
love for Mrs. D. hasn't quite been vital enough to give you
yourself peace. One must learn to love, and go through a good
deal of suffering to get to it, like any knight of the grail, and the
journey is always *towards* the other soul, not away from it. Do
you think love is an accomplished thing, the day it is recognised? It isn't. To love, you have to learn to understand the
other, more than she understands herself, and to submit to her
understanding of you. It is damnably difficult and painful, but
it is the only thing which endures. You mustn't think that your
desire or your fundamental need is to make a good career, or to
fill your life with activity, or even to provide for your family
materially. It isn't. Your most vital necessity in this life is that
you shall love your wife completely and implicitly and in entire
nakedness of body and spirit. Then you will have peace and inner security, no matter how many things go wrong. And this

peace and security will leave you free to act and to produce your own work, a real independent workman.

You asked me once what my message was. I haven't got any general message, because I believe a general message is a general means of side-tracking one's own personal difficulties: like Christ's—thou shalt love thy neighbour as thyself—has given room for all the modern filthy system of society. But this that I tell you is my message as far as I've got any.

Please don't mind what I say—you know I don't really want to be impertinent or interfering.

Mrs. Huntingdon* is coming over to England this month. Probably she would bring Mrs. D. But perhaps Noémi[1] would be better. I am sorry Paddy[2] is still so seedy. He is a strange boy. I think he will need a lot of love. He has a curious heavy consciousness, a curious awareness of what people feel for him. I think he will need a lot of understanding and a lot of loving. He may, I think, have quite an unusual form of intelligence. When you said he might be a musician, it struck me. He has got that curious difference from other people, which may mean he is going to have a distinct creative personality. But he will suffer a great deal, and he will want a lot of love to make up for it.

I think our marriage comes off at the Kensington registrar's office on Saturday. I will try to remember to send you the *Times* you asked for. When I get paid for my novel, I want to send you a small cheque for doing the novel.[3] You will not mind if it is not very much that I send you.

We are very tired of London already, and very glad to be down here in the country. Probably we are going to stay in Derbyshire—and then for August going to the west of Ireland. But I shall write and tell you. Don't be miserable—I have you

* A friend from the Anglo colony at Lerici. (H. T. M.)
[1] Unidentified.
[2] Son of T. D. D.
[3] T. D. D. and his wife had typed Lawrence's manuscript of *The Rainbow*.

and Mrs. D. rather on my conscience just now—I feel as if you were taking things badly. But don't do that.

                    Auf wiedersehen,
                              D. H. LAWRENCE.

Remember me to Mrs. D.

To HARRIET MONROE

                    Bellingdon Lane, Chesham, Bucks.
                    17 Nov., 1914.

Dear Harriet Monroe,

Yesterday came your cheque for £8. Thank you very much.

To-day came the War Number of *Poetry,* for which also I thank you. It put me into such a rage—how dare Amy[4] talk about bohemian glass and stalks of flame?—that in a real fury I had to write my war poem,[5] because it breaks my heart, this war.

I hate, and hate, and hate the glib irreverence of some of your contributors—Aldington[6] with his "Do you know what it's all about, brother Jonathan? We don't." It is obvious he doesn't. And your nasty, obscene, vulgar in the last degree—"Hero" ————[7] may God tread him out—why did you put him in? You shouldn't.

At least I like the woman who wrote *Metal Checks*[8]—her idea, her attitude—but her poetry is pretty bad. I rather like the suggestion of Marian Ramie's *Face I shall never see—man I shall never see.* And *Unser Gott*[9] isn't bad—but unbeautifully ugly. Your people have such little pressure: their safety valve goes off at the high scream when the pressure is still so low.

4 Amy Lowell, American poet whom Lawrence had met in London in the summer of 1914.

5 Probably "Eloi, Eloi, Lama Sabachthani" which appeared in the May 1, 1915 issue of *The Egoist.* (H. T. M.)

6 Richard Aldington, poet, author of a Lawrence memoir, *Portrait of a Genius But* . . .

7 John Russell McCarthy. (H. T. M.)

8 Louise Driscoll. (H. T. M.)

9 By Earle Wilson Baker. (H. T. M.)

Have you no people with any force in them? Aldington almost shows most—if he weren't so lamentably imitating Hueffer.

I don't care what you do with my war poem. I don't particularly care if I don't hear of it any more. The war is dreadful. It is the business of the artist to follow it home to the heart of the individual fighters—not to talk in armies and nations and numbers—but to track it home—home—their war—and it's at the bottom of almost every Englishman's heart—the war—the desire of war—the *will* to war—and at the bottom of every German's.

Don't put common things in like the *Campfollower*[1]—why do you? They are only ugly, ugly—"putrid lips"—it is something for the nasty people of this world to batten on.

I typed my poem on a typewriter Amy Lowell gave me.[2] I think I did it quite well—and it was thrilling. I like it when you send me *Poetry,* even if it makes me rage.

> *Vale!*
> D. H. LAWRENCE.

Take care how you regard my war poem—it is good.

To MISS AMY LOWELL[3]

18 Nov., 1914.

Dear Amy Lowell,

The type-writer has come, and is splendid. Why did you give it away? I am sure you must have wanted to keep it. But it goes like a bubbling pot, frightfully jolly. My wife sits at it fascinated, patiently spelling out, at this moment, my war poem.

Oh—the War Number of 'Poetry' came—I thought it pretty bad. The war-atmosphere has blackened here—it is soaking in,

---

[1] By Maxwell Bodenheim. (H. T. M.)
[2] Miss Lowell had wanted to make Lawrence some kind of useful gift when she learned he was very poor.
[3] From *Amy Lowell.*

and getting more like part of our daily life, and therefore much grimmer. So I was quite cross with you for writing about bohemian glass and stalks of flame, when the thing is so ugly and bitter to the soul.

I like *you* in your poetry. I don't believe in affecting France. I like you when you are straight out. I really liked very much the Precinct, Rochester. There you had a sunny, vivid, intensely still atmosphere that was very true. I don't like your first long poem a bit. I think 'A Taxi' is very clever and futuristic—and good. I like the one about the dog looking [in] the window—good.

Why don't you always be yourself. Why go to France or anywhere else for your inspiration. If it doesn't come out of your own heart, real Amy Lowell, it is no good, however many colours it may have. I wish one saw more of your genuine strong, sound self in this book, full of common sense & kindness and the restrained, almost bitter, Puritan passion. Why do you deny the bitterness in your nature, when you write poetry? Why do you take a pose? It causes you always to shirk your issues, and find a banal resolution at the end. So your romances are spoiled. When you are full of your own strong gusto of things, real old English strong gusto it is, like those tulips, then I like you very much. But you shouldn't compare the sun to the yolk of an egg, except playfully. And you shouldn't spoil your story-poems with a sort of vulgar, artificial 'flourish of ink.' If you had followed the real tragedy of your man, or woman, it had been something.

I suppose you think me damned impertinent. But I hate to see you posturing, when there is thereby a real person betrayed in you.

Please don't be angry with what I say. Perhaps it really is impertinence.

At any rate, thank you very much for your book of poems, which I like because after all they have a lot of you in them —but how much nicer, finer, bigger you are, intrinsically, than your poetry is. Thank you also very much for the beautiful typewriter, with which both myself and my wife are for the present bewitched.

We are still staying on here—scarcely find it possible to move. It is cold, as you predict, but I think quite healthy. I am well, and Frieda is well. I am just finishing a book, supposed to be on Thomas Hardy, but in reality a sort of Confessions of my Heart. I wonder if ever it will come out—& what you'd say to it.

I wonder if you saw Mitchell Kennerley. Pinker, the agent, is always worrying me about what he is to do with the American publishing of the novel Kennerley holds at present, in MS. Tell me if you saw him, will you.

We are not so sad any more: it was perhaps a mood, brought on by the War, and the English autumn. Now the days are brief but very beautiful: a big red sun rising and setting upon a pale, bluish, hoar-frost world. It is very beautiful. The robin comes on to the door-step now, watches me as I write. Soon he will come indoors. Then it will be mid-winter.

I wish the War were over and gone. I will not give in to it. We who shall live after it are more important than those who fall.

Give our very warm regards to Mrs. Russell.[4]

Saluti di cuore,
D. H. LAWRENCE.

Tante belle cose from my wife to you and to Mrs. Russell.

To AMY LOWELL[5]

The Triangle, Chesham, Bucks., Dec. 18, 1914.

The day before yesterday came your letter. You sound so sad in it. What had depressed you?—Your book of poems, that they perhaps are stupid about in the papers? But there, they are always like that, the little critics. If the critics are not less than the

---

4 Mrs. Ada Russell, former actress and Miss Lowell's devoted companion.
5 From *The Intelligent Heart.*

authors they criticise, they will at once burst into equal author-
ship. And being less than the authors they criticise, they must
diminish these authors. For no critic can admit anything bigger
than himself. And we are all, therefore, no bigger than our little
critics. So don't be sad. The work one has done with all one's
might is as hard as a rock, no matter how much one suffers the
silly slings and arrows in one's silly soft flesh.

Thank you very much for going to Mitchell Kennerley for
me. I hope you were not serious when you say that in so doing
you have spoiled the "Forum" for yourself as a publishing field.
Is Kennerley indeed such a swine? As for what he owes me—he
does not send it, even if it is only ten pounds. I haven't kept
proper accounts with him, because Duckworth made the agreement and all that. I will write to them. I also will write to
Pinker, to see what he can do. I *must* get the novel out of Kennerley's hands that he has in MS.

I am re-writing it. It will be called The Rainbow. When it is
done, I think really it will be a fine piece of work.

My book of short stories is out. I am sending you a copy. I
don't think it is doing very well. The critics really hate me. So
they ought.

My wife and I we type away at my book on Thomas Hardy,
which has turned out as a sort of Story of My Heart, or a Con-
fessio Fidei: which I must write again, still another time: and
for which the critics will plainly beat me, as a Russian friend
says.

It is Christmas in a week today. I'm afraid you may not get
this letter in time: which is a pity. We shall be in this cottage.
We shall have a little party at Christmas Eve. I at once begin to
prick my ears when I think of it. We shall have a great time,
boiling ham and roasting chicken, and drinking Chianti in
memory of Italy. There will be eight of us, all nice people. We
shall enjoy ourselves afterwards up in the attico—you wait. I
shall spend 25/—on the spree, and do it quite rarely.

England is getting real thrills out of the war, at last. Yesterday and today there is the news of the shelling of Scarboro. I tell you the whole country is thrilled to the marrow, and enjoys it like hot punch.—I shall make punch at our Christmas Eve party, up in the attico with a Primus stove.

We have been in the Midlands seeing my people, and Frieda seeing her husband. He did it in the thorough music-hall fashion. It was a surprise visit. When we were children, and used to play at being grand, we put an old discarded hearthrug in the wheel-barrow, and my sister, perched there in state "at home," used to be "Mrs. Lawson" and I, visiting with a walking stick, was "Mr. Marchbanks." We'd been laughing about it, my sister and I. So Frieda, in a burst of inspiration, announced herself to the landlady as "Mrs. Lawson."

"You—" said the quondam husband, backing away—"I hoped never to see you again."

Frieda: "Yes—I know."

Quondam Husband: "And what are you doing in *this* town [?"]

Frieda: I came to see you about the children.

Quondam Husband: Aren't you ashamed to show your face where you are known! Isn't the commonest prostitute better than you?

Frieda: Oh no.

Quon. Husb.: Do you want to drive me off the face of the earth, Woman? Is there no place where I can have peace?

Frieda: You see I must speak to you about the children.

Quon. Husb.: You shall *not* have them—they don't want to see you.

Then the conversation developed into a deeper tinge of slanging—part of which was:

Q. H.: *If* you had to go away, why didn't you go away with a *gentleman?*

Frieda: He is a *great* man.

Further slanging.

Q. Husb.: Don't you know you are the vilest creature on earth?

Frieda: Oh no.

A little more of such, and a departure of Frieda. She is no further to seeing her children.

Q. Husb.: Don't you know, my solicitors have instructions to arrest you, if you attempt to interfere with the children[?]

Frieda: I don't care.

If this weren't too painful, dragging out for three years, as it does, it would be very funny I think. The Quondam Husband is a Professor of French Literature, great admirer of Maupassant, has lived in Germany and Paris, and thinks he is the tip of cosmopolitan culture. But poor Frieda can't see her children.— I really give you the conversation verbatim.

It is very rainy and very dark. I shall try to get back to Italy at the end of January.

Give my sincere sympathy to Mrs. Russell. I hope things aren't going very badly with her. All Christmas greetings to you.

D. H. LAWRENCE.

I do wish we might have a Christmas party together. I feel like kicking everything to the devil and enjoying myself willy-nilly— a wild drunk and a great and rowdy spree.

To GORDON CAMPBELL[6]

Chesham, Bucks., Dec. 19 [*20?*], *1914.*

Dear Campbell,

I was awfully glad to hear from the Murrys of the novel. They are wildly enthusiastic about it. I am very anxious for it to come. I shall be very glad when you've really got expression.

But do, for God's sake, mistrust and beware of these states of exaltation and ecstasy. They send you, anyone, swaying so far beyond the centre of gravity in one direction, there is the inevitable swing back with greater velocity to the other direction, and in the end you exceed the limits of your own soul's elasticity, and go smash, like a tower that has swung too far.

---

6 From *The Intelligent Heart.*

Besides, there is no real truth in ecstasy. All vital truth contains the memory of all that for which it is not true. Ecstasy achieves itself by virtue of exclusion; and in making any passionate exclusion, one has already put one's right hand in the hand of the lie.

I am sorry your man commits suicide in a pool. It is futile. If the Bishop—I haven't got it very clearly—but if the bishop, and the young doctor, know that the great sin, or weakness—sin, I think you said—is Egotism, then is the conclusion to be that the doctor commits the final act of egotism and vanity, and commits suicide? Or is that not the end? If you are making a great book on Egotism—and I believe you may—for God's sake give us the death of Egotism, not the death of the sinner. Russia, and Germany, and Sweden, and Italy, have done nothing but glory in the suicide of the Egoist. But the Egoist as a divine figure on the Cross, held up to tears and love and veneration, is to me a bit nauseating now, after Artzibasheff and D'Annunzio, and the Strindberg set, and the Manns in Germany.

I think the greatest book I know on the subject is the book of Job. Job was a great, splendid Egoist. But whereas Hardy and the moderns end with "Let the day perish—" or more beautifully—"the waters wear the stones; thou washest away the things which grow out of the dust of the earth; thou destroyest the hope of man:

Thou prevailest for ever against him, and he passeth: thou changest his countenance, and sendest him away."—the real book of Job ends—"Then Job answered the Lord and said:

I know that thou canst do everything, and that no thought can be withholden from thee[.]

Who is he that hideth counsel without knowledge? Therefore have I uttered that I understood not: things too wonderful for me, which I knew not.

Hear, I beseech thee, and I will speak: I will demand of thee, and declare thou unto me.

I have heard of thee by the hearing of the ear; but now mine eye seeth thee[.]

Wherefore I abhor myself, and repent in dust and ashes." If you want a story of your own soul, it is perfectly done in the book of Job—much better than in Letters from the Underworld.

But the moderns today prefer to end insisting on the sad plight. It is characteristic of us that we have preserved, of a trilogy which was really Prometheus Unbound, only the Prometheus Bound and terribly suffering on the rock of his own egotism.

But the great souls in all time did not end there. In the mediaeval period, Christianity did *not* insist on the Cross: but on the Resurrection: churches were built to the glorious hope of resurrection. Now we think we are very great, whilst we enumerate the smarts of the crucifixion. We are too mean to get any further.

I think there is the dual way of looking at things: our way, which is to say "*I* am all. All other things are but radiation out from me."—The other way is to try to conceive the whole, to build up a whole by means of symbolism, because symbolism avoids the I and puts aside the egotist; and, in the whole, to take our decent place. That was how man built the cathedrals. He didn't say "out of my breast springs this cathedral!" But "in this vast whole I am a small part, I move and live and have my being."

I understand now your passion to face the west. It is the passion for the extinction of yourself and the knowledge of the triumph of *your own will* in your body's extinction. But in the great periods, when man was great, he has faced the *East:* Christian, Mohammedan, Hindu, all.

You should try to grasp, I think—don't be angry at my tone—the *complete whole* which the Celtic symbolism made in its great time. We are such egoistic fools. We see only the *symbol* as a *subjective expression:* as an expression of ourselves. That makes us so sickly when we deal with the old symbols: like Yeats.

The old symbols were each a word in a great attempt at formulating the whole history of the soul of Man. They *are unintelligible* except in their whole context. So your Ireland of you Irishmen of today is a filthy mucking about with a part of the symbolism of a great Statement or Vision: just as the Crucifixion of Christ is a great mucking about with part of the symbolism of a great religious Vision.

The Crucifix, and Christ, are only symbols. They do not mean a man who suffered his life out as I suffer mine. They mean a moment in the history of my soul, if I must be personal. But it is a moment fixed in context and having its being only according to context. Unless I have the Father, and the hiera[r]chies of Angels, I have no Christ, no Crucifixion.

It is necessary to grasp the whole. At last I have got it, grasping something of what the mediaeval church tried to express. To me, the Latin form of expression comes very natural. To you, the Celtic I should think. I think the whole of the Celtic symbolism and great Utterance of its Conception has never been fathomed. But it must have been in accord with the Latin.

There is the Eternal God, not to be seen or known, so bright in his fire that all things pass away, evanescent at its touch. He is surrounded by the Hierarchy of the Cherubim and Seraphim, the Great Ones who partake of his being and transmit his glory: and they are *absorbed in praise eternally*. Beyond the Cherubim are the Dominions and Powers: and beyond these great ones, the Principalities, Archangels, and Angels, which come as messengers and guardians and carriers of blessing at last to mankind.

So, there are the central symbols, from the oldest vision[.]

Then God, in meditating upon himself, begot the Son. The Son receives the Divine Nature by Generation within the human flesh. In the Son, the human flesh is again crucified, to liberate the eternal Soul, the Divine Nature of God.

For the Divine Nature of God, the Spirit of the Father

procreating the human flesh forms the *ego*. And the Ego would fain absorb the position of the Eternal God. Therefore it must suffer crucifixion, so that it may rise again praising God, knowing with the Angels, and the Thrones, and the Cherubim.

And, from the mutual love of the Father and the Son, proceeds the Holy Spirit, the Holy Ghost, the Reconciler, the Comforter, the Annunciation.

It is very beautiful, and a very great conception which, when one feels it, satisfies one, and one is at rest.

But Christianity should teach us now, that after our Crucifixion, and the darkness of the tomb, we shall rise again in the flesh, you, I, as we are today, resurrected in the bodies, and acknowledging the Father, and glorying in his power, like Job.

It is very dangerous to use these old terms lest they sound like cant. But if only one can grasp and know again as a new truth, true for ones own history, the great vision, the great, satisfying conceptions of the worlds greatest periods, it is enough. Because so it is made new.

All religions I think have the same inner conception, with different expressions. Why don't you seek out the whole of the Celtic Vision, instead of messing about talking of Ireland. Beatrice[7] was somewhere on the track: but she didn't know what she was after: so she over-humanised, that is, she made subjective the symbols she used, so spoiled them: by putting them as emanations of her own Ego, instead of using them as words to convey the great whole of which her own Ego was only the Issue, as the Son is issue of the Father.

Probably this will seem all stupid to you, and you will feel you are grasping a finer, more difficult, elusive truth. But I don't believe your truths of egoistic ecstasy. Get the greatest truth into your novel, for God's sake. We need it so badly. Give us the Resurrection after the Crucifixion.

We have been reading a book on Christian Symbolism, which

7 Mrs. Campbell.

I liked *very* much, because it puts me more into order. It is a little half-crown vol. in the "Little Books on Art" series by Methuen[.] This is written by Mrs. Henry Jenner. If you don't know it, get it for Beatrice and you read it too. This copy isn't mine. And you understand the Celtic Symbolism in its entirety.

This is a Christmas greeting. For God's sake follow your novel to its *biggest* close—further than death, to the gladness. I cannot forget that the Cherubim who are nearest God and palpitate with his brightness are *absorbed in praise*. I don't know why, but the thought of the Great Bright Circle of Cherubim, godly beyond measure, are [*sic*] absorbed forever in fiery praise.

I will send you a copy of my stories for Beatrice. I think she also, like you, but she without knowing it perhaps, magnifies the great Principle of the Ego. She must also die and be born again. But I think she is tenacious, tenacious, and will have no crucifixion, let alone resurrection. But how do I know about her, after all.

Many good wishes for Christmas.

Yrs.,
D. H. LAWRENCE.

To LADY CYNTHIA ASQUITH

Greatham, Pulborough, Sussex.
Sunday, 30th January, 1915.[7a]

Dear Lady Cynthia,

We were very glad to hear from you. I wanted to send you a copy of my stories at Christmas, then I didn't know how the war had affected you—I knew Herbert Asquith was joined and I thought you'd rather be left alone, perhaps.

We have no history, since we saw you last. I feel as if I had less than no history—as if I had spent those five months in the tomb. And now, I feel very sick and corpse-cold, too newly risen

---

[7a] The correct date of this letter is probably January 31, 1915. (H. T. M.)

to share yet with anybody, having the smell of the grave in my nostrils, and a feel of grave clothes about me.

The War finished me: it was the spear through the side of all sorrows and hopes. I had been walking in Westmorland, rather happy, with water-lilies twisted round my hat—big, heavy, white and gold water-lilies that we found in a pool high up— and girls who had come out on a spree and who were having tea in the upper room of an inn, shrieked with laughter. And I remember also we crouched under the loose wall on the moors and the rain flew by in streams, and the wind came rushing through the chinks in the wall behind one's head, and we shouted songs, and I imitated music-hall turns, whilst the other men crouched under the wall and I pranked in the rain on the turf in the gorse, and Koteliansky[8] groaned Hebrew music— Ranani Sadekim Badanoi.

It seems like another life—we *were* happy—four men. Then we came down to Barrow-in-Furness, and saw that war was declared. And we all went mad. I can remember soldiers kissing on Barrow station, and a woman shouting defiantly to her sweetheart—"When you get at 'em, Clem, let 'em have it," as the train drew off—and in all the tramcars, "War." Messrs. Vickers-Maxim call in their workmen—and the great notices on Vickers' gateway—and the thousands of men streaming over the bridge. Then I went down the coast a few miles. And I think of the amazing sunsets over flat sands and the smoky sea—then of sailing in a fisherman's boat, running in the wind against a heavy sea—and a French onion boat coming in with her sails set splendidly, in the morning sunshine—and the electric suspense everywhere—and the amazing, vivid, visionary beauty of everything, heightened by the immense pain everywhere. And since then, since I came back, things have not existed for me. I have spoken to no one, I have touched no one, I have seen no one. All the while, I swear, my soul lay in the tomb—not dead,

8 S. S. Koteliansky ("Kot"), economist, Russian exile in England.

but with a flat stone over it, a corpse, become corpse-cold. And nobody existed, because I did not exist myself. Yet I was not dead—only passed over—trespassed—and all the time I knew I should have to rise again.

Now I am feeble and half alive. On the Downs on Friday I opened my eyes again, and saw it was daytime. And I saw the sea lifted up and shining like a blade with the sun on it. And high up, in the icy wind, an aeroplane flew towards us from the land—and the men ploughing and the boys in the fields on the table-lands, and the shepherds, stood back from their work and lifted their faces. And the aeroplane was small and high, in the thin, ice-cold wind. And the birds became silent and dashed to cover, afraid of the noise. And the aeroplane floated high out of sight. And below, on the level earth away down—were floods and stretches of snow, and I knew I was awake. But as yet my soul is cold and shaky and earthy.

I don't feel so hopeless now I am risen. My heart has been as cold as a lump of dead earth, all this time, because of the War. But now I don't feel so dead. I feel hopeful. I couldn't tell you how fragile and tender this hope is—the new shoot of life. But I feel hopeful now about the War. We should all rise again from this grave—though the killed soldiers will have to wait for the last trump.

There is my autobiography—written because you ask me, and because, being risen from the dead, I know we shall all come through, rise again and walk healed and whole and new in a big inheritance, here on earth.

It sounds preachy, but I don't quite know how to say it.

Viola Meynell[9] has lent us this rather beautiful cottage. We

[9] Daughter of Alice and Wilfrid Meynell. The Meynell family had a group of houses at Greatham in Sussex, one of which was lent the Lawrences. Viola Meynell, herself a poet and member of what Lawrence referred to as "the whole formidable and poetic Meynell family," was an early admirer of Lawrence's work. In the story "England, My England," Lawrence later portrayed Percy Lucas, husband of Madeline and brother-in-law of Viola, so cruelly that he estranged the whole family.

are quite alone. It is at the foot of the Downs. I wish you would come and see us, and stay a day or two. It is quite comfortable—there is hot water and a bathroom, and two spare bedrooms. I don't know when we shall be able to come to London. We are too poor for excursions. But we *should* like to see you, and it *is* nice here.

D. H. LAWRENCE.

To LADY OTTOLINE MORRELL
Greatham, Pulborough, Sussex.
Monday, 1 Feb., 1915.

Dear Lady Ottoline,

I must write you a line when you have gone, to tell you how my heart feels quite big with hope for the future. Almost with the remainder of tears and the last gnashing of teeth, I could sing the *Magnificat* for the child in my heart.

I want you to form the nucleus of a new community which shall start a new life amongst us—a life in which the only riches is integrity of character. So that each one may fulfil his own nature and deep desires to the utmost, but wherein tho', the ultimate satisfaction and joy is in the completeness of us all as one. Let us be good all together, instead of just in the privacy of our chambers, let us know that the intrinsic part of all of us is the best part, the believing part, the passionate, generous part. We can all come croppers, but what does it matter? We can laugh at each other, and dislike each other, but the good remains and we know it. And the new community shall be established upon the known, eternal good part in us. This present community consists, as far as it is a framed thing, in a myriad contrivances for preventing us from being let down by the meanness in ourselves or in our neighbours. But it is like a motor car that is so encumbered with non-skid, non-puncture, non-burst, non-this and non-that contrivances, that it simply can't go any more. I hold this the most sacred duty—the gathering together of a number of people who shall so agree to live by the *best* they know, that they shall be *free* to live by the best they know. The ideal, the religion, must now be *lived, practised.* We will have no more *churches.* We will bring church and house and shop together. I do believe that there are enough decent people to make a start with. Let us get the people. Curse the Strachey who asks for a new religion—the greedy dog. He wants another juicy bone for his soul, does he? Let him start to fulfil what religion we have.

After the War, the soul of the people will be so maimed and so injured that it is horrible to think of. And this shall be the new hope: that there shall be a life wherein the struggle shall not be for money or for power, but for individual freedom and common effort towards good. That is surely the richest thing to have now—the feeling that one is working, that one is part of a great, good effort or of a great effort towards goodness. It is no good plastering and tinkering with this community. Every strong soul must put off its connection with this society, its vanity and chiefly its fear, and go naked with its fellows, weaponless, armourless, without shield or spear, but only with naked hands and open eyes. Not self-sacrifice, but fulfilment, the flesh and the spirit in league together not in arms against one another. And each man shall know that he is part of the greater body, each man shall submit that his own soul is not supreme even to himself. "To be or not to be" is no longer the question. The question now is, how shall we fulfil our declaration, "God is"? For all our life is now based on the assumption that God is not —or except on rare occasions.

. . . We must go very, very carefully at first. The great serpent to destroy, is the will to Power: the desire for one man to have some dominion over his fellow-men. Let us have *no* personal influence, if possible—nor personal magnetism, as they used to call it, nor persuasion—no "Follow me"—but only "Behold." And a man shall not come to save his own soul. Let his soul go to hell. He shall come because he knows that his own soul is not the be-all and the end-all, but that all souls of all things do but compose the body of God, and that God indeed shall *Be*.

I do hope that we shall all of us be able to agree, that we have a common way, a common interest, not a private way and a private interest only.

It is communism based, not on poverty but on riches, not on humility but on pride, not on sacrifice but upon complete fulfilment in the flesh of all strong desire, not in Heaven but on earth. We will be Sons of God who walk here on earth, not bent on getting and having, because we know we inherit all things. We will be aristocrats, and as wise as the serpent in dealing with the mob. For the mob shall not crush us nor starve us nor cry us to death. We will deal cunningly with the mob, the greedy soul, we will gradually bring it to subjection.

We will found an order, and we will all be Princes, as the angels are.

We must bring this thing about—at least set it into life, bring it forth new-born on the earth, watched over by our old cunning and guided by our ancient, mercenary-soldier habits.

My wife sends her greetings and pledge of alliance. I shall paint you a little wooden box.

Au revoir,
D. H. LAWRENCE.

To E. M. FORSTER

Greatham, Pulborough, Sussex.
Monday (date approximately April, 1915).[1]

Dear Forster,

Don't expect any sort of answer or attention from me to-day, because everything is so strange and I feel as if I'd just come out of the shell and hadn't got any feathers to protect me from the weather. It is very snowy here, and rather beautiful.

[1] The date of this letter is more likely the beginning of February, 1915.

Will you come down next week-end and stay with us? I think nobody else will be here. As for my not listening to your answers, I've got a deep impression that you never made any.

I've only read one or two stories of yours, and should like *very much* to have the *Celestial Omnibus.*

This cottage is rather fine—a bit monastic—it was a cattle shed—now it is like a monks' refectory—the whole establishment is cloistral.

I'm glad you're not really Buddhistic—everybody said you were. I want somebody to come and make a league with me, to sing the *Chanson des Chansons—das hohe Lied*—and to war against the fussy Mammon, that pretends to be a tame pet now, and so devours us in our sleep.

But do come at the week-end.

D. H. LAWRENCE.

To BERTRAND RUSSELL[2]

Greatham, Pulborough, Sussex.
12 Feb., 1915.

Dear Mr. Russell,

We have had E. M. Forster here for three days. There is more in him than ever comes out. But he is not dead yet. I hope to see him pregnant with his own soul. We were on the edge of a fierce quarrel all the time. He went to bed muttering that he was not sure we—my wife & I—weren't just playing round his knees: he seized a candle & went to bed, neither would he say good night. Which I think is rather nice. He sucks his dummy— you know, those child's comforters—long after his age. But there is something very real in him, if he will not cause it to die. He is *much* more than his dummy-sucking, clever little habits allow him to be.

---

[2] From *D. H. Lawrence's Letters to Bertrand Russell.* The text used in that volume indicates words which Lawrence crossed out in the original letters. The text employed here does not.

I write to say to you that we *must* start a solid basis of free-dom of actual living—not only of thinking. We *must* provide another standard than the pecuniary standard, to measure *all* daily life by. We must be free of the economic question. Eco-nomic life must be the means to actual life. We must make it so at once.

There must be a revolution in the state. It shall begin by the nationalising of all industries and means of communication, & of the land—in one fell blow. Then a man shall have his wages whether he is sick or well or old—if anything prevents his working, he shall have his wages just the same. So we shall not live in fear of the wolf—no man amongst us, & no woman, shall have any fear of the wolf at the door, for all wolves are dead.

Which practically solves the whole economic question for the present. All dispossessed owners shall receive a proportionate in-come—no capital recompense—for the space of, say fifty years.

Something like this must be done. It is no use saying a man's soul should be free, if his boots hurt him so much he can't walk. All our ideals are cant & hypocrisy till we have burst the fetters of this money. Titan nailed on the rock of the modern indus-trial capitalistic system, declaring in fine language that his soul is free as the Oceanids that fly away on wings of aspiration, while the bird of carrion desire gluts at his liver, is too shame-ful. I am ashamed to write any real writing of passionate love to my fellow men. Only satire is decent now. The rest is a lie. Until we act, move, rip ourselves off the rock. So there must be an actual revolution, to set free our bodies. For there never was a free soul in a chained body. That is a lie. There might be a resigned soul. But a resigned soul is not a free soul. A resigned soul has yielded its claim on temporal living. It can only do this because the temporal living is being done for it vicariously. Therefore it is dependent on the vicar, let it say what it will. So Christ, who resigned his life, only resigned it because he knew the others would keep theirs. They would do the living,

& would later adapt his method to their living. The freedom of the soul within the denied body is a sheer conceit.

Forster is not poor, but he is bound hand & foot bodily. Why? *Because he does not believe that any beauty or any divine utterance is any good any more.* Why? Because the world is suffering from bonds, and birds of foul desire which gnaw its liver. Forster knows, as every thinking man now knows, that all his thinking and his passion for humanity amounts to no more than trying to soothe with poetry a man raging with pain which can be cured. Cure the pain, don't give the poetry. Will all the poetry in the world satisfy the manhood of Forster, when Forster knows that his implicit manhood is to be satisfied by nothing but immediate physical action. He tries to dodge himself—the sight is pitiful.

But why can't he act? Why can't he take a woman and fight clear to his own basic, primal being? Because he knows that self-realisation is not his ultimate desire. His ultimate desire is for the continued action which has been called the social passion— the love for humanity—the desire to work for humanity. That is every man's ultimate desire & need. Now you see the vicious circle. Shall I go to my Prometheus and tell him beautiful tales of the free, whilst the vulture gnaws his liver? I am ashamed. I turn my face aside from my Prometheus, ashamed of my vain, irrelevant, impudent words. I cannot help Prometheus. And this knowledge rots the love of activity.

If I cannot help Prometheus—and I am also Prometheus— how shall I be able to take a woman? For I go to a woman to know myself, and to know her. And I want to know myself, that I may know how to act for humanity. But if I am aware that I cannot act for humanity—? Then I dare not go to a woman.

Because, if I go, I know I shall betray myself & her & everything. It will be a vicious circle. I go to her to know myself, & I know myself—what?—to enjoy myself. That is sensationalism —that I go to a woman to feel myself only. Love is, that I go to a woman to know myself, & knowing myself, to go further, to explore in to the unknown, which is the woman, venture in upon the coasts of the unknown, and open my discovery to all humanity. But if I know that humanity is lame & cannot move, bound and in pain and unable to come along, my offering it discoveries is only a cynicism. Which I know & Forster knows & even Gilbert Cannan[3] knows. "They can't hear you," Gilbert Cannan says of the public. "They turn you into a sensation." So he panders to the chained Prometheus, tickles him with near sensations—a beastly thing to do. He writes Young Earnest.

If I know that humanity is chained to a rock, I cannot set set[4] forth to find it new lands to enter upon. If I do pretend to set forth, I am a cheating, false merchant, seeking my *own* ends. And I am ashamed to be that. I will not.

So then, how shall I come to a woman? To know myself first. Well and good. But knowing myself is only preparing myself. What for? For the adventure into the unexplored, the woman, the whatever-it-is I am up against.—Then the actual heart says "No no—I can't explore. Because an explorer is one sent forth from a great body of people to open out new lands for their occupation. But my people cannot even move—it is chained—paralysed. I am not an explorer. I am a curious, inquisitive man with eyes that can only look for something to take back with him. And what can I take back with me? Not revelation—only curios—titillations. I am a curio hunter.["]

Again, I am ashamed.

Well then, I am neither explorer nor curio hunter. What then? For what do I come to a woman? To know myself. But what when I know myself? What do I then embrace her for, hold the unknown against me for? To repeat the experience of self discovery. But I have discovered myself—I am not infinite. Still I can repeat the experience. But it will not be discovery. Still I repeat the experience.—That is, I can get a sensation.

---

[3] Novelist, friend of the Murrys, married to the former wife of Sir James Barrie.
[4] Sic.

The repeating of a known reaction upon myself is sensational-ism. This is what nearly *all* English people now do. When a man takes a woman, he is *merely* repeating a known reaction upon himself, not seeking a new reaction, a discovery. And this is like self-abuse or masterbation.[5] The ordinary Englishman of the educated class goes to a woman now to masterbate himself. Because he is not going for discovery or new connection or pro-gression, but only to repeat upon himself a known reaction.

When this condition arrives, there is always Sodomy. The man goes to the man to repeat this reaction upon himself. It is a nearer form of masterbation. But still it has some *object*—there are still two bodies instead of one. A man of strong soul has too much honour for the other body—man or woman—to use it as a means of masterbation. So he remains neutral, inactive. That is Forster.

Sodomy only means that a man knows he is chained to the rock, so he will try to get the finest possible sensation out of himself.

This happens whenever the form of any living becomes too strong for the life within it: the clothes are more important than the man: therefore the man must get his satisfaction beneath the clothes.

Any man who takes a woman is up against the unknown. And a man prefers rather to have nothing to do with a woman than to have to slink away without answering the challenge. Or if he is a mean souled man, he will use the woman to masterbate himself.

There comes a point when the shell, the form of life, is a prison to the life. Then the life must either concentrate on breaking the shell, or it must turn round, turn in upon itself, and try infinite variations of a known reaction upon itself. Which produces a novelty. So that "The Rosary" is a new com-bination of known re-actions—so is Gilbert Cannan's "Young

5 Lawrence's spelling.

Earnest"—so is the cinematograph drama & all our drama & all our literature.

Or, the best thing such a life can do, that knows it is confined, is to set-to to arrange and assort all the facts & knowledge of the contained life. Which is what Plato did & what most of our writers are doing on a mean scale. They know that they are enclosed entirely by the shell, the form of living. There is no going beyond it. They are bound down.

Now either we have to break the shell, the form, the whole frame, or we have got to turn to this inward activity of setting the house in order & drawing up a list before we die.

But we shall smash the frame. The land, the industries, the means of communication & the public amusements shall all be nationalised. Every man shall have his wage till the day of his death, whether he work or not, so long as he works when he is fit. Every woman shall have her wage till the day of her death, whether she work or not, so long as she works when she is fit—keeps her house or rears her children.

Then, and then only, shall we be able to *begin* living. Then we shall be able to *begin* to work. Then we can examine marriage and love and all. Till then, we are fast within the hard, unliving, impervious shell.

You must have patience with me & understand me when my language is not clear.

I shall come and see you on the Sunday, March 7th, if you still invite me, because I want to meet Lowes Dickinson[6] & the good people you are going to introduce me to.

It is very nice and spring-like. The birds are beginning to sing. I laugh at them. Their voices are quite rusty & stiff with a winter of disuse. The blackbird goes at it so hard, to get his whistle clear, & the wood-pigeon is so soon disheartened.

Yours sincerely,

D. H. LAWRENCE.

[6] G. Lowes Dickinson, political philosopher, of Kings College, Cambridge.

To LADY OTTOLINE MORRELL[7]

Greatham, Pulborough, Sussex.
[*22 February, 1915.*]

Dear Lady Ottoline,

We shall be so glad to see you tomorrow.... There must be a great talk. I want to hear about your estate in Oxford, and the cottage, the cottage, the cottage.

Murry is here because Katharine[8] has gone to Paris. He is one of the men of the future—you will see. He is with me for the Revolution. He is just finishing his novel—his first—*very* good. At present he is my partner—the only man who quite simply is with me—One day he'll be ahead of me. Because he'll build up the temple if I carve out the way—the place.

How big we talk

à demain,
D. H. LAWRENCE.

To PHILIP MORRELL[9]

Greatham, Pulborough, Sussex.
Tuesday, April [*20*] *1915.*

My dear Morrell,

Of course the costs for the monastic house are impossible beyond all consideration. I thought that the whole thing would be done for about £200. The prices are monstrous. The only thing to do under these circumstances of war and exorbitancy is to employ the minimum of building or alteration. Certainly it is utterly impossible to go on for these extravagances. What a vile, thieving, swindling life! What a horrible generation! One can only want to hide oneself away from its contact.

7 From *I Will Send Address: New Letters of D. H. Lawrence.* Bracketed date has been taken from postmark.
8 Katherine Mansfield. This is Lawrence's spelling.
9 From *I Will Send Address: New Letters of D. H. Lawrence.* The bracketed date was supplied by Mr. Mark Schorer.

Lady Ottoline said we could have three rooms in the gardener's cottage. If we could really have those for a time, it would be quite enough. For heavens sake don't build a single brick on our account. The thought of your being swindled to this extent makes me feel I would rather be a rabbit in a rabbit-hole, than hire a bricklayer for even half an hour. No, the only satisfaction I get is to think that, by living in the three—or two—rooms of the gardener's cottage, all that bleeding is saved. The miserable miscreant vermin, with their prices! It is too horrible and degrading.

It will be, as you say, only possible to begin on the monastic buildings when things become normal again—if ever they do. But really, if they *are* the spare rooms in the gardener's cottage, we should like to stay there for a time. It would be very disappointing not to come to Garsington[1] at all.

Those vile greedy contractors, they set my blood boiling to such a degree, I can scarcely bear to write.

But I shall be *very* glad if you are not put to much expense on our account. You are both so generous that I could feel it only a vileness to trespass on your generosity. We shall be *very* grateful for the two or three rooms in the gardener's cottage, and always grateful for the gift of the monastic buildings. I only feel those vile sordid contractors have stolen these away from us.

Please don't think any more about *any* alterations or hired workmen on our account—a little furniture in the three rooms is more than enough.

Yours very sincerely,

D. H. LAWRENCE.

---

[1] The Morrells' place in Oxfordshire.

To LADY OTTOLINE MORRELL[2]

Greatham, Pulborough, Sussex.
23 April, 1915.

My dear Lady Ottoline,

We were shocked about M—[3]: it really is rather horrible. I'm not sure whether you aren't really more wicked than I had at first thought you. I think you can't help torturing a bit.

But I think it has shown [?] something—as if you, with a strong, old-developed *will* had enveloped the girl, in this will, so that she lived under the dominance of your will: and then you want to put her away from you, eject her from your will. So that when she says it was because she couldn't bear being left, that she took the poison, and it is a great deal true. Also she feels quite bewildered and chaotic. I think she really does know nothing about herself, in her consciousness. We English, with our old-developed public selves, and the consequent powerful will, and the accompanying rudimentary private or instinctive selves, I think we are very baffling to any other nation. We are apt to assume domination, when we are not really personally implicated. A young foreigner can't understand that—not a girl like M—.

Why must you always use your *will* so much, why can't you let things be, without always grasping and trying to know and to dominate. I'm too much like this myself.

There, now I'm scolding at you, even. But *why* will you use power instead of love, good public control instead of affection. I suppose it is breeding.

Don't mind what I say.—I send you another batch of MS. . . . if you think it good, or bad, do tell me.

Be careful not to spend money on us at Garsington *now*: just the gardener's rooms, I beg you. Perhaps later on we shall all be rich. . . . Still we must form the nucleus of a new society, as we

---

[2] From *I Will Send Address: New Letters of D. H. Lawrence.*
[3] Maria. (Maria Nys, a Belgian refugee, later Mrs. Aldous Huxley)

said at the first. But you use your will so much, always your will.

Our love to you,

D. H. LAWRENCE.

To LADY OTTOLINE MORRELL

Greatham, Pulborough, Sussex.

30 April, 1915.

My dear Lady Ottoline,

Never mind the numbering of the pages of the MS. Just tell me the last page of this secondary numbering when you write, is it 356?—and send the batch to Pinker: Talbot House, Arundel St., Strand. I'm glad you like it.

You were quite cross with me last time, because of my elaborate theory. Never mind—don't let us bother.

We went to Worthing yesterday on the motor-bus: very beautiful: even I loved Worthing: and such light, such quantities of light beating and throbbing all around. I felt like Persephone come up from hell. But to-day I would rather say, like Eurydice: *jamque vale!*

How dark my soul is! I stumble and grope about and don't get much further. I suppose it must be so. All the beauty and light of the days seems like an iridescence on a very black flood. Mostly one is underneath: sometimes one rises like the dove from the ark: but there is no olive branch.

What a sentimental simile: myself as a dove: a sparrow is nearer the mark.

If you are in London next week—Wednesday till Monday—we are there then, so let us go somewhere together, shall we?—to Kew or Hampton Court—London excursioners.

This is very beautiful weather. But it is going to rain. I can smell the soot in the chimney.

I wish I were going to Thibet—or Kamschatka—or Tahiti—to the ultima, ultima, ultima Thule. I feel sometimes I shall go mad, because there is nowhere to go, no "new world." One of these days, unless I watch myself, I shall be departing in some rash fashion, to some foolish place. . . .

I almost wish I could go to the war—not to shoot: I have vowed an eternal oath that I won't shoot in this war, not even if I am shot. I should like to be a bus conductor at the front— anything to escape this, that is.

The death of Rupert Brooke fills me more and more with the sense of the fatuity of it all. He was slain by bright Phoebus' shaft—it was in keeping with his general sunniness—it was the real climax of his pose. I first heard of him as a Greek god under a Japanese sunshade, reading poetry in his pyjamas, at Grant- chester,—at Grantchester upon the lawns where the river goes. Bright Phoebus smote him down. It is all in the saga.

O God, O God, it is all too much of a piece: it is like madness.

Yesterday, at Worthing, there were many soldiers. Can I ever tell you how ugly they were. "To insects—sensual lust." I like sensual lust—but insectwise, no—it is obscene. I like men to be beasts—but insects—one insect mounted on another— oh, God! The soldiers at Worthing are like that—they remind me of lice or bugs: "to insects—sensual lust." They will murder their officers one day. They are teeming insects. What massive creeping hell is let loose nowadays.

It isn't my disordered imagination. There is a wagtail sitting on the gate-post. I see how sweet and swift heaven is. But hell is slow and creeping and viscous and insect-teeming: as is this Europe now, this England.

Vale!

D. H. LAWRENCE.

To S. S. KOTELIANSKY[4]
> *Greatham, Pulborough, Sussex, Thursday.*

My Dear Kot,

B[5] has just gone. I like her, but she gets on my nerves with her eternal: "but *do* you think"—"but, look here, *isn't* it rather that. . . ." I want to say: "For God's sake woman, stop haggling." And she is so deprecating, and so persistent. Oh God! But— *basta!*

I must tell you, *caro mio*, that I liked you very much while you were here. You must continue to be patient with me.

But you positively *must not* be so inert. You are getting simply a monolith. You *must* rouse yourself. You *must* do something—anything. Really it is a disgrace to be as inert as you are. Really, it is unforgivable. Write for the papers, do anything, but don't continue in this negation.

I think I shall send you my philosophy to type again for me. I have begun it again. I will not tell them, the people, this time that they are angels in disguise. Curse them, I will tell them they are dogs and swine, bloodsuckers.

I will send you *The Idiot* to read.

Will you type my philosophy again?—one copy only this time, on common paper? I shall have to get it done somewhere or other. But if the burden on you, monolith, is too great, then refuse.

I have been fighting the powers of darkness lately. Still they prevail with me. But I have more or less got my head out of the inferno, my body will follow later. How one has to struggle, really, to overcome this cursed blackness. It would do me so much good if I could kill a few people.

Is Katharine[6] at home, or have you heard from her? And how

4 From *Letters to S. S. Koteliansky.* This letter is postmarked April or May, 1915. Signature not given.
5 Mr. Moore thinks this is probably Barbara, in which case it refers to Dr. Barbara Low, later a psychoanalyst. Dr. Low was the aunt of Ivy Low who became Mrs. Maxim Litvinov.
6 Katherine Mansfield. This spelling is Lawrence's.

is Murry? I will write to him. I feel all right again towards him. My spleen has worked itself off.

I am still in bed with my cold. It is a sort of cold in my inside—like a sore throat in one's stomach. Do you understand? I am going to stay in bed till it is better. Thank God B isn't here to nag me—poor thing.

My dear Kot, now that the spring has come, *do* rouse up, and *don't* be sad and inert. It is so terrible to be such a weight upon the face of the earth. But you were almost all right this time you were here. Next time you must come when nobody else is here.

Frieda sends her love, with mine. I am reading the Dostoievsky letters. What an amazing person he was—a pure introvert, a purely disintegrating will—there was not a grain of the passion of love within him—all the passion of hate, of evil. Yet a great man. It has become, I think, now, a supreme wickedness to set up a Christ worship as Dostoievsky did: it is the outcome of an evil will, disguising itself in terms of love.

But he is a great man and I have the greatest admiration for him. I even feel a sort of subterranean love for him. But he never, never wanted anybody to love him, to come close to him. He exerted repelling influence on everybody.

Write to me soon—Yrs.

To LADY OTTOLINE MORRELL

Greatham, Pulborough, Sussex.
14 May, 1915.

My dear Lady Ottoline,

I wonder if you are still in Buxton, and if you got the last batch of MS. which I sent you, enclosed with a copy of the *Imagist Anthology* which contains some of my verses. If you got them, tell me, will you?

We were in London for four days: beautiful weather, but I don't like London. My eyes can see nothing human that is good, nowadays: at any rate, nothing public. London seems to me like some hoary massive underworld, a hoary ponderous inferno. The traffic flows through the rigid grey streets like the rivers of hell through their banks of dry, rocky ash. The fashions and the women's clothes are very ugly.

Coming back here, I find the country very beautiful. The apple trees are leaning forwards, all white with blossom, towards the green grass. I watch, in the morning when I wake up, a thrush on the wall opposite the window—not a thrush, a blackbird—and he sings, opening his beak. It is a strange thing to watch his singing, opening his beak and giving out his calls and warblings, then remaining silent. He looks so remote, so buried in primeval silence, standing there on the wall, and bethinking himself, then opening his beak to make the strange, strong sounds. He seems as if his singing were a sort of talking to himself, or of thinking aloud his strongest thoughts. I wish I was a blackbird, like him. I hate men.

> "The ousel cock of sable hue
> And orange-yellow bill."

The bluebells are all out in the wood, under the new vivid leaves. But they are rather dashed aside by yesterday's rain. It would be nice if the Lord sent another flood and drowned the world. Probably I should want to be Noah. I am not sure.

I've got again into one of those horrible sleeps from which I can't wake. I can't brush it aside to wake up. You know those horrible sleeps when one is struggling to wake up, and can't. I was like it all autumn—now I am again like it. Everything has a touch of delirium, the blackbird on the wall is a delirium, even the apple-blossom. And when I see a snake winding rapidly in the marshy places, I think I am mad.

It is not a question of me, it is the world of men. The world of men is dreaming, it has gone mad in its sleep, and a snake is strangling it, but it can't wake up.

When I read of the *Lusitania,* and of the riots in London, I know it is so. I think soon we must get up and try to stop it. Let us wait a little longer. Then when we cannot bear it any longer, we must try to wake up the world of men, which has gone mad in its sleep.

I cannot bear it much longer, to let the madness get stronger and stronger possession. Soon we in England shall go fully mad, with hate. I too hate the Germans so much, I could kill every one of them. Why should they goad us to this frenzy of hatred, why should we be tortured to ———[7] madness, when we are only grieved in our souls, and heavy? They will drive our heaviness and our grief away in a fury of rage. And we don't want to be worked up into this fury, this destructive madness of rage. Yet we must, we are goaded on and on. I am mad with rage myself. I would like to kill a million Germans—two millions.

I wonder when we shall see you again, and where you are. I have promised to stay here for another month at least, to teach Mary Saleeby.[8] Her mother has a nervous breakdown, and they asked me to teach the child. I do it for the child's sake, for nothing else. So my mornings are taken up, for 3½ hours each day.

Don't take any notice of my extravagant talk—one must say something. Write soon and tell us where you are, and how you are. I feel a little bit anxious about you, when you do not write.

Vale!

D. H. LAWRENCE.

To J. B. PINKER

Greatham, Pulborough, 31 May, 1915.

Dear Pinker,

In response to the wire from E. Garnett, I send you the final batch of MS. of the *Rainbow*. One or two little things: you

---

[7] Bloody. (H. T. M.)
[8] Daughter of Monica Meynell Saleeby.

will see the pages are not numbered: we all lost count after a certain point. Will you let somebody number the pages: also see that they run on, that none of the MS. is missing: also please see that the chapters are correctly numbered.

I hope you will like the book: also that it is not very improper. It did not seem to me very improper, as I went through it. But then I feel very incompetent to judge, on that point.

My beloved book, I am sorry to give it to you to be printed. I could weep tears in my heart, when I read these pages. If I had my way, I would put off the publishing yet awhile.

One other little thing: I want on the fly-leaf, in German characters, the inscription "Zu Else"—i.e.,

𝔷𝔲 𝔈𝔩𝔰𝔢

Put that in for me, will you? It is just "To Else." But it must be in Gothic letters.

We shall have peace by the time this book is published.

Yours,
D. H. LAWRENCE.

To BERTRAND RUSSELL[9]

Greatham, Pulborough, Sussex.
Friday 15 July. [*1915*]

In your lecture on the State, you must criticise the extant *democracy*, the young idea. That is our enemy. This existing phase is now in its collapse. What we must hasten to prevent is this young democratic party from getting into power. The idea of giving power to the hands of the working class is *wrong*. The working man must elect the immediate government, of his work, of his district, not the ultimate government of the nation. There must be a body of chosen patricians. There must be woman governing equally with men, especially all the inner

---

[9] From *D. H. Lawrence's Letters to Bertrand Russell.* The bracketed date was supplied by Mr. Moore, editor of that volume.

half of life. The whole must culminate in an absolute *Dictator,* & an equivalent *Dictatrix.* There must be none of your bourgeois presidents of Republics. The women's share must be equal with the men's. You must work this out in your own way. But you must do it.

Can't you see the whole state is collapsing. Look at the Welsh strike. This war is going to develop into the last great war between labour & capital. It will be a ghastly chaos of destruction, if it is left to Labour to be constructive. The fight must immediately be given a higher aim than the triumph of Labour, or we shall have another French Revolution. The deadly Hydra now is the hydra of Equality. Liberty, Equality & Fraternity is the three-fanged serpent. You must have a government based upon good, better & best. You must get this into your lectures, at once. You are too old-fashioned. The back of your serpent is already broken.

A new constructive idea of a new state is needed *immediately.* Criticism is *unnecessary.* It is behind the times. You *must* work out the idea of a new state, not go on criticising this old one. Get anybody & everybody to help—Orage,[1] Shaw, anybody, but it must be a *new State.* And the idea is, that every man shall vote according to his understanding, & that the higher understanding must dictate for the lower understandings. And the desire is to have a perfect government perfectly related in all its parts, the highest aim of the government is the highest good of the *soul,* of the individual, the fulfilment in the Infinite, in the Absolute.

In a fortnight I shall come & take account of you.

D. H. L.

---

[1] A. E. Orage (1873-1934), editor of *The New Age* which published Mansfield, Pound, Aldington and other important young writers before the first war; later, editor the *New English Weekly.* (H. T. M.)

To J. B. PINKER

Greatham, Pulborough, 26 July, 1915.

Dear Pinker,

I send you back the slips and pages. I have cut out, as I said I would, all the *phrases* objected to. The passages and paragraphs marked I cannot alter. There is nothing offensive in them, beyond the very substance they contain. And that is no more offensive than that of all the rest of the novel. The libraries won't object to the book any less, or approve of it any more, if these passages are cut out. And I can't cut them out, because they are living parts of an organic whole. Those who object, will object to the book altogether. These bits won't affect them particularly.

Tell Methuen, he need not be afraid. If the novel doesn't pay him back this year, it will before very long. Does he expect me to be popular? I shan't be that. But I am a safe speculation for a publisher.

These slips and pages I return to you are *not revised proofs.* I am now at page 192 of the revised proofs, the final form, and I must go on from there.

Yours sincerely,
D. H. LAWRENCE.

To LADY CYNTHIA ASQUITH

1, Byron Villas, Vale of Health, Hampstead, N.W.
16 August, 1915.

My dear Lady Cynthia,

We also waited at Appenrodt's till 5.30: you must have gone to the wrong one. Bad luck.

I am sorry that gloom tumbles on top of gloom with you. But the dead are the only people one need not fret about nowadays.

The Lectures you ask about. I don't know if they will ever

begin. I don't see how I am to start. Russell and I were to do something together. He was to give a *real* course on political reconstruction ideas. But it is no good. He sent me a synopsis of the lectures, and I can only think them pernicious. And now his vanity is piqued, because I said they *must* be different. He cannot stand the *must,* and yet they *must* be different, if they are to be even decent.

I am so sick of people: they preserve an evil, bad, separating spirit under the warm cloak of good words. That is intolerable in them. The Conservative talks about the old and glorious national ideal, the Liberal talks about this great struggle for right in which the nation is engaged, the peaceful women talk about disarmament and international peace. Bertie Russell talks about democratic control and the educating of the artisan, and all this, all this goodness, is just a warm and cosy cloak for a bad spirit. They all want the same thing: a continuing in this state of disintegration wherein each separate little ego is an independent little principality by itself. What does Russell really want? He wants to keep his own established ego, his finite and ready-defined self intact, free from contact and connection. He wants to be ultimately a free agent. That is what they all want, ultimately—that is what is at the back of all international peace-for-ever and democratic control talks [—] they want an outward system of nullity, which they call peace and goodwill, so that in their own souls they can be independent little gods, referred nowhere and to nothing, little mortal Absolutes, secure from question. That is at the back of all Liberalism, Fabianism and democracy. It stinks. It is the will of the louse. And the Conservative either wants to bully or to be bullied. And the young authoritarian, the young man who turns Roman Catholic in order to put himself under the authority of the Church, in order to enjoy the aesthetic quality of obedience, he is such a swine with cringing hind-quarters, that I am delighted, I dance with joy when I see him rushing down the Gadarene slope of the war.

I feel like knocking my head against the wall: or of running off to some unformed South American place where there is no thought of civilised effort. I suppose I could learn to ride a horse and live just by myself for myself.

But it is too bad, it is too mean, that they are all so pettily selfish, these good people who sacrifice themselves. I want them—just Russell, or Murry—anybody—to say: "This is wrong, we are acting in a wrong spirit. We have created a great, almost overwhelming incubus of falsity and ugliness on top of us, so that we are almost crushed to death. Now let us move it. Let us have done with this foolish form of government, and this idea of democratic control. Let us submit to the knowledge that there are aristocrats and plebeians born, not made. Some amongst us are born fit to govern, and some are born only fit to be governed. Some are born to be artisans and labourers, some to be lords and governors. But it is not a question of tradition or heritage. It is a question of the incontrovertible soul. If we have right spirit, even the most stupid of us will know how to choose our governors, and in that way we shall give the nucleus of our classes. There are such falsities of distinction now. Let us get rid of them.

It is a question of the spirit. *Why* are we a nation? We are a nation which must be built up according to a living idea, a great architecture of living people, which shall express the greatest truth of which we are capable. There must be King and Queen, and Lords and Ladies, and Burghers and Burgesses, and Servants: but not ——— ——— and ——— ———, not Lord ——— or Earl ——— (or ———) or ——— ———.¹ It is a question of spirit even more than of intelligence. A bad spirit in a nation chooses a bad spirit in a governor. We must begin to choose all afresh, for the pure, great truth. We must have a new King, who stands for the truth, and a new Queen,

¹ The names which belong in these blank spaces have not yet been made available for publication.

a House of Lords and a House of Ladies, but lords of the spirit and the knowledge, and ladies the same. If we have a right spirit, then our Lords and our Ladies will appear, as the flowers come forth from nowhere in the spring. If we continue in our bad spirit, we shall have Horatio Bottomley for our Prime Minister before a year is out.

We must rid ourselves of this ponderous incubus of falsehood, this massive London, with its streets and streets of nullity: we must, with one accord and in purity of spirit, pull it down and build up a beautiful thing. We must rid ourselves of the idea of money. A rich man with a beautiful house is like a jewel on a leper's body. You know that. Your Stanway is a jewel on a leper's body: so near to Burslem, Hanley and Stoke and Wolverhampton. Our business is not in jewellery, but in the body politic. You know that. What good is it to a sick, unclean man, if he wears jewels.

I hope you are with me in this. Russell says I cherish illusions, that there *is* no such spirit as I like to imagine, the spirit of unanimity in truth, among mankind. He says that is fiction. Murry says that the spirit matters, but that an idea is bad. He says he believes in what I say, because he believes in me, he might help in the work I set out to do because he would be believing in me. But he would not believe in the work. He would deplore it. He says the whole thing is personal: that between him and me it is a case of Lawrence and Murry, not of any union in an *idea*. He thinks the introduction of any idea, particularly of any political idea, highly dangerous and deplorable. The thing should be left personal, each man just expressing himself. Frieda says things are not so bad as I pretend, that people are good, that life is also good, that London is also good, and that this civilisation is great and wonderful. She thinks if the war were over, things would be pretty well all right.

But they are all wrong.

I've got a real bitterness in my soul, just now, as if ———
and ———² were traitors—they are traitors. They betray the
real truth. They come to me, and they make me talk, and they
enjoy it, it gives them a profoundly gratifying sensation. And
that is all. As if what I say were meant only to give them gratification, because of the flavour of personality, as if I were a cake
or a wine or a pudding. Then they say I, D. H. L., am wonderful, I am an exceedingly valuable personality, and that the
things I say are extravaganzas, illusions. They say I cannot
think.

All that is dynamic in the world, they convert to a sensation,
to the gratification of what is static. They are static, static,
static, they come, they say to me, "You are wonderful, you are
dynamic," then they filch my life for a sensation unto themselves, all my effort, which is my life, they betray, they are like
Judas: they turn it all to their own static selves, convert it into
the static nullity. The result is for them a gratifying sensation,
a tickling, and for me a real bleeding.

But I know them now, which is enough.

I don't know how to begin to lecture or write, publicly, these
things of the real truth and the living spirit. Everything is so
awful and static, so large and ponderous, like the physical mass
of London lying on the plain of south England. And one must
shift that mass: it is the mountain that faith must move. I do
believe there are people who wait for the spirit of truth. But
I think one can't find them personally. I had hoped and tried
to get a little nucleus of living people together. But I think it is
no good. One must start direct with the open public, without
associates. But how to begin, and when, I don't know yet.

I hope you don't mind having all this fired off at you. I half
feel I ought not to send it. But I intend to send it.

Only, I don't want any friends, except the friends who are
going to *act,* put everything—or at any rate, put *something* into

2 See previous footnote.

the effort by bringing about a new unanimity among us, a new movement for the pure truth, an immediate destruction—and reconstructive revolution in actual life, England, now.

Yours,

D. H. LAWRENCE.

To BERTRAND RUSSELL[3]

1, Byron Villas, Vale of Health, Hampstead N. W.

14 Sept., 1915.

Dear Russell,

I'm going to quarrel with you again. You simply don't speak the truth, you simply are not sincere. The article you send me is a plausible lie, and I hate it. If it says some true things, that is not the point. The fact is that you, in the Essay, are all the time a lie.

Your basic desire is the maximum of desire of war, you are really the super-war-spirit. What you want is to jab and strike, like the soldier with the bayonet, only you are sublimated into words. And you are like a soldier who might jab man after man with his bayonet, saying "this is for ultimate peace." The soldier would be a liar. And it isn't in the least true that you, your basic self, want ultimate peace. You are satisfying in an indirect, false way your lust to jab and strike. Either satisfy it in a direct and honorable way, saying "I hate you all, liars and swine, and am out to set upon you," or stick to mathematics, where you can be true—But to come as the angel of peace—no, I prefer Tirpitz a thousand times in that rôle.

You are simply *full* of repressed desires, which have become savage and anti-social. And they come out in this sheep's clothing of peace propaganda. As a woman said to me, who had been to one of your meetings: "It seemed so strange, with his face looking so evil, to be talking about peace and love. He can't have *meant* what he said."

I believe in your inherent power for realising the truth. But

3 From *D. H. Lawrence's Letters to Bertrand Russell.*

I don't believe in your will, not for a second. Your will is false and cruel. You are too full of devilish repressions to be anything but lustful and cruel. I would rather have the German soldiers with rapine and cruelty, than you with your words of goodness. It is the falsity I can't bear. I wouldn't care if you were six times a murderer, so long as you said to yourself, "I am this." The enemy of all mankind, you are, full of the lust of enmity. It is *not* the hatred of falsehood which inspires you. It is the hatred of people, of flesh and blood. It is a perverted, mental blood-lust. Why don't you own it.

Let us become strangers again, I think it is better.

D. H. Lawrence.

To EDWARD MARSH

1, Byron Villas, Vale of Health, Hampstead.
6 Nov., 1915.

My dear Eddie,

You jeered rather at *The Rainbow,* but notwithstanding, it is a big book, and one of the important novels in the language. I tell you, who know. Now the magistrates have suppressed the sale of the book, and ordered Methuen to deliver up all copies in existence.

And I am so sick, in body and soul, that if I don't go away I shall die. A man said we could live on his little estate in Florida. I want you, if you can, to give me a little money to go with: if you can, easily, that is. God knows I don't want to mulct you. I'll give it you back if ever I have any money: I owe you £10 already. And I will give you full and final possession of some poems, when I have any you like. And I will ask you not to send me any part in the proceeds of *Georgian Poetry.* Because if I can get a little money now, so that my wife and I can go away, I will work at anything over there. But I feel so sick, I shall never be able to get through a winter here.

Yours,
D. H. Lawrence.

To KATHERINE MANSFIELD
1, Byron Villas, Vale of Health, Hampstead, N.W.
Sunday, 12 Dec., 1915.

My dear Katherine,

Murry turned up on Friday, to my moderate surprise. He doesn't look well, tells us of his dreadful experience in France, and is *very* chirpy. At the present I am not very much in sympathy with him, so I won't say any more about it. He came yesterday with Goodyear,[4] whom I like, but who is on the same Oxford introspective line, who has an "inner life" to concern himself with—which bores me. I'm sick to death of people who are wrapped up in their own inner lives, inner selves.

We are on the point of departure, where to I don't know. We leave this flat on the 20th; the furniture is sold, the lease transferred altogether. So after the 20th we are free. We spend Christmas with my sister: c/o Mrs. Clarke, Grosvenor Rd., Ripley, Derbyshire. After that I don't know what happens. I am afraid they will not let me leave the country, unless I get an exemption from service, which I haven't yet got. We may go somewhere in Somerset or Devon, I don't know. We *may* even get off to Florida. It is on the knees of the gods, and I am not troubling. At any rate we leave London permanently. I cannot live here.

No doubt you hear of Murry's scheme for publishing books, the authors to be publishers. But what I wonder is, are there either books or authors, at the present moment. There are Gilbert Cannans and Beresfords,[5] but I have nothing to do with them. I intend to lie fallow for a bit. I know one or two very young people—20, 21, 22—who seem to have something real in them, for a new phase. But it is necessary that these unite together; a perfectly new *body* of purpose, that is the only thing that will avail anything. Perhaps it will come—but nobody can

4 Frederick Goodyear, friend of the Murrys, later killed in the war.
5 J. D. Beresford, popular novelist, in whose house in Cornwall the Lawrences were to stay in the early months of 1916.

force it into being. So for the time being, everything is unre-
solved, and must remain so until it resolves of itself. Mental
decisions are of no use. It is a matter of underground development, development of new being in the roots of life, not in the
head.

One thing I know, I am tired of this insistence on the
personal element; personal truth, personal reality. It is very
stale and profitless. I want some new non-personal activity,
which is at the same time a genuine vital activity. And I want
relations which are not purely personal, based on purely
personal qualities; but relations based upon some unanimous
accord in truth or belief, and a harmony of *purpose,* rather than
of personality. I am weary of personality. It remains now
whether Murry is still based upon the personal hypothesis:
because if he is, then our ways are different. I don't want a
purely personal relation with him; he is a man, therefore our
relation should be based on *purpose*; not upon that which we
are, but upon that which we wish to bring to pass. I am sick
and tired of personality in every way. Let us be easy and impersonal, not for ever fingering over our own souls, and the souls
of our acquaintances, but trying to create a new life, a new
common life, a new complete tree of life from the roots that are
within us. I am weary to death of these dead, dry leaves of
personalities which flap in every wind.

My dear Katherine, you know that in this we are your sincere
friends, and what we want is to create a new, good, common
life, the germ of a new social life altogether. That is what we
want. But we must grow from our deepest underground roots,
out of the *unconsciousness,* not from the conscious concepts
which we falsely call ourselves. Murry irritates me and falsifies
me, and I must tell him so. He makes *me* false. If that must
always be so, then there is no relation between us. But we must
try that there *is* a living relation between us, all of us, because
then we shall be happy. Frieda sends her love, I mine.

D. H. LAWRENCE.

To LADY OTTOLINE MORRELL
1, Byron Villas, Vale of Health, Hampstead, N.W.
12 Dec., 1915.

My dear Ottoline,

Thank you for the letter and the pound. The last I *did not want.*

I hear Heseltine[6] and Kouyoumdjian[7] are coming to you to-morrow. Heseltine is a bit backboneless and needs stiffening up. But I like him very much; Kouyoumdjian seems a bit blatant and pushing: you may be put off by him. But that is because he is *very foreign,* even though he doesn't know it himself. In English life he is in a strange, alien medium, and he can't adjust himself. But I find the core of him *very good.* One must be patient with his jarring manner, and listen to the sound decency that is in him. He is not a bit rotten, which most young cultivated Englishmen are.

Murry is back, and I am rather out of sympathy with him. Bertie[8] came. He is growing *much better:* he is going to become young and new. I have more hopes.

We leave here on the 20th, go to my sister's in Derbyshire for Christmas, and then I don't know where. I must say I feel again a certain amount of slow, subterranean hope. It won't put forth any leaves, nor show any activity yet, I believe: but it seems to be full and nascent somewhere in the underearth of my soul. Probably we shall go to the West—Devon, Somerset— for a while after Christmas, I don't know. I must let things work themselves into being. One can do nothing now, forcing is disastrous. I shall not go to America until a stronger force from there pulls me across the sea. It is not a case of my will.

I went to a recruiting station yesterday to be attested and to get a military exemption. But I hated it so much, after waiting nearly two hours, that I came away. And yet, waiting there in

6 Philip Heseltine, later the composer Peter Warlock.
7 Dikran Kouyoumdjian, later the novelist Michael Arlen.
8 Bertrand Russell.

the queue, I felt the *men* were very decent, and that the slumbering lion was going to wake up in them: not against the Germans either, but against the great lie of this life. I felt all the men were decent, even the police and the officials. It was at Battersea Town Hall. A strange, patient spirit possessed everybody, as under a doom, a bad fate superimposed. But I felt the patience rested upon slumbering strength, not exhaustion, and the strength would begin before long to stretch itself like a waking lion. I felt, though I *hated* the situation almost to *madness,* so vile and false and degrading, such an utter travesty of action on my part, waiting even to be attested that I might be rejected, still I felt, when suddenly I broke out of the queue, in face of the table where one's name was to be written, and went across the hall away from all the underworld of this spectral submission, and climbed a bus, and after a while saw the fugitive sunshine across the river on the spectral sunlit towers at Westminster, that I had triumphed, like Satan flying over the world and knowing he had won at last, though he had not come into even a fragment of his own. I feel somewhere that the triumph is mine, remote, oh very remote and buried underground, but the triumph is mine. It is only the immediate present which frightens me and bullies me. In the long run I have the victory; for all those men in the queue, for those spectral, hazy, sunny towers hovering beyond the river, for the world that is to be. Endless patient strength and courage, that is all that is necessary—and the avoiding of disaster.

Let me only be still, and know we can force nothing, and compel nothing, can only nourish in the darkness the unuttered buds of the new life that shall be. That is our life now: this nourishing of the germs, the unknown quicks when the new life is coming into being in us and in others—I have hope of Bertie too—only patience, only patience, and endless courage to reject false dead things and false, killing processes.

With love from Frieda and me,

D. H. LAWRENCE.

To EDWARD MARSH
Porthcothan, St Merryn, North Cornwall.
12 Feb., 1916.

My Dear Eddie,

Cynthia Asquith writes me that somebody says I "abuse you."
If ever I have abused you to anybody, I am very sorry and
ashamed. But I don't think I ever have: though Heaven knows
what one says. Yet I don't feel as if I had. We have *often*
laughed at you, because you are one of those special figures one
can laugh at; just as I am, only I'm ten times more ridiculous.
But I'm sure we've laughed kindly and affectionately: I know
the Murrys and us, we've always laughed affectionately. I did
feel rather bitter the way you took the war: "What splendid
times we live in": because the war makes me feel very badly,
always. And I may have been furious about that: I must be more
restrained. But I don't think I've abused you, apart from the
war, which is something special: and even for that I don't think
I have.

But whatever I have said, may have said, for I can't remember, I always feel a real gratitude to you, and a kindness, and
an esteem of the genuine man. And I'm sorry if ever I've gone
against those true feelings for you. I have thought that it was
best for us to keep no constant connection, because of your
position in the Government, and of my feelings about the war.
But that I do out of respect for your position.

However, if ever I have abused you, though I can't remember,
then forgive me: for indeed I am not ungrateful, and I never
want to abuse you. If the war makes us strangers, it does not,
I hope, make us in the least enemies.

I have been seedy down here, and felt like dying. I must not
get into such states. Next month will appear a vol. of my
Italian Sketches, which I will send you. Only don't say, as you
said of *The Rainbow:* toujours perdrix. Because you know one
suffers what one writes.

And a little later will come a book of poems. I know you don't care much for my verses: but I'll send them along when they appear.

It's been a bad time, this last year. I wish it were ended.

Frieda sends her regards, I mine.

D. H. LAWRENCE.

To LADY OTTOLINE MORRELL
Porthcothan, St. Merryn, North Cornwall.
15 Feb., 1916.

My dear Ottoline,

We love the counterpane. It is the kind of thing that really rejoices my heart. I am very fond of woollen things too—even more than silk, I think. I don't think the pale blue and black are bad: they make me laugh. I don't know why, but the whole shawl gives me a sudden feeling of laughter. I really like it very much: and so does Frieda. We had puzzled over a word in one of your letters—countrypair, you wrote, I think—and wondered what it *was* you thought of sending us. How jolly it is to have this coloured countrypair. I want to wear it like a Red Indian.

I shall read the *History of Egypt* and tell you how I like it. I now send you back one or two of your books. The Dostoievsky lay in the window-seat and in the night the rain beat in and spoiled it. I am sorry. Perhaps I ought to buy you another. But you don't like it very much. I *love* the book about St. Francis and Dante—or whatever it is—the *Salimbene's Biography*. I love to see these people as they were when the Christian idea was still only a graft upon their lives, had not entered in their blood. But what times to live in. I should think not two men in a hundred died a natural death then. It is always so interesting to see the original self in man being modified by a big universal idea. One has to recover the original self now.

[125]

I have nearly done the first, the destructive, half of my philosophy. At last it can stand. It is the last word. I am sure it marks the end of a great epoch: at least for me. When this chapter is typed I shall send you as much as is done, for you to read. I feel that probably you won't like it, for a time. But do read it.

To-day we have a letter from Bertie: very miserable. He doesn't know why he lives at all: mere obstinacy and pride, he says, keep him alive. His lectures are all right in themselves, but their *effect* is negligible. They are a financial success. But all the people who matter are too busy doing other things to come to listen. He lives only for fussy trivialities, and for nothing else.

That is the whole gist of his letter. I am sorry for him, but my heart doesn't soften to him just yet: I don't know why. I feel he is obstinate in going his own way, and until he ceases to be obstinate, all is useless.

I had a similar despairing letter from the Murrys. Something must have happened to the French mail—the mail to France— I had written them, and so had Frieda. I forgot to tell you, she has £130 a year from her father; he has what he makes. He can make quite a lot by his journalism. It is rather surprising that newspaper editors hold him in such esteem.

About ——— and M——[9] I tell him he ought to tell her. I suppose he will. It is queer. He declares he does not like this one, P—— but he does really. He declares he wants her to go. But he is really attached to her in the senses, in the unconsciousness, in the blood. He is always fighting away from this. But in so doing he is a fool. She is very nice and very real and simple, we like her. His affection for M—— is a desire for the light because he is in the dark. If he were in the light he would want

---

[9] Although this paragraph very likely refers to the triangular relation of Heseltine, his wife Minnie and an artist's model who was called "Puma" (the "Pussum" of *Women in Love*), Catherine Carswell believed it referred to Gilbert and Mary Cannan, in which case P—— is not identified. (H. T. M.)

the dark. He wants M—— for *companionship,* not for the blood connection, the dark, sensuous relation. With P—— he has this second, dark relation, but not the first. She is quite intelligent, in her way, but no mental consciousness; no white consciousness, if you understand, all intuition, in the dark, the consciousness of the senses. But she is quite fine and subtle in that way, quite, and I esteem her there *quite* as much as I esteem him.

Perhaps he is very split, and would always have the two things separate, the real blood connection and the real conscious or spiritual connection, always separate. For these people I really believe in two wives. I don't see why there should be monogamy for people who can't have full satisfaction in one person, because they themselves are too split, because they act in themselves separately. Monogamy is for those who are whole and clear, all in one stroke. But for those whose stroke is broken into two different directions, then there should be two fulfilments.

For myself, thank God, I feel myself becoming more and more unified, more and more a oneness. And Frieda and I become more and more truly married—for which I thank Heaven. It has been such a fight. But it is coming right. And then we can all three be real friends. Then we shall be really happy, all of us, in our relation.

I am better. I got a cold and my chest was a bit raw, but that is going again. Here the winds are so black and terrible. They rush with such force that the house shudders, though the old walls are very solid and thick. Only occasionally the gulls rise very slowly into the air. And all the while the wind rushes and thuds and booms, and all the while the sea is hoarse and heavy. It is strange, one forgets the rest of life. It shuts one in within its massive violent world. Sometimes a wave bursts with a great explosion against one of the outlying rocks, and there is a tremendous ghost standing high on the sea, a great tall whiteness. I hope it will be more restful by and by, and you will come down here.

I shall send you most of the books back, because we are so wandering.

We have got daffodils and little yellow narcissi, and blue-and-white violets, on the table, that the children bring us from the gardens. It is really spring. The willow catkins are already silver, very gleaming. We are going soon to look for another house. I wonder where we shall find it? Quite near, I think.

Heseltine is very keen about the publishing scheme. He has sent off a circular to be printed at his expense. Do you know, I believe he is one of those people who are born to be conveyors of art: they are next to artists, and they convey art to the world. I shouldn't wonder if he made the publishing scheme a real success in the long run.

I feel quite anti-social, against this social whole as it exists. I wish one could be a pirate or a highwayman in these days. But my way of shooting them with noiseless bullets that explode in their souls, these social people of to-day, perhaps it is more satisfying. But I feel like an outlaw. All my work is a shot at their very innermost strength, these banded people of to-day. Let them cease to be. Let them make way for another, fewer, stronger, less cowardly people.

Frieda sends her love—my love to you.

D. H. LAWRENCE.

To BERTRAND RUSSELL[1]

> [*Porthcothan, St. Merryn, Cornwall.*]
> *Saturday* [*February 19, 1916*].

My dear Russell,

I didn't like your letter. What's the good of living as you do, anyway. I don't believe your lectures *are* good. They are nearly over, aren't they?

What's the good of sticking in the damned ship and har-

---

[1] From *D. H. Lawrence's Letters to Bertrand Russell*. Address and date, in brackets, supplied by Mr. Moore, editor of that volume.

anguing the merchant-pilgrims in their own language. Why don't you drop overboard? Why don't you clear out of the whole show?

One must be an outlaw these days, not a teacher or preacher. One must retire out of the herd & then fire bombs into it. You said in your lecture on education that you didn't set much count by the unconscious. That is sheer perversity. The whole of the consciousness and the conscious content is old hat—the millstone round your neck.

Do cut it—cut your will and leave your old self behind. Even your mathematics are only *dead* truth: and no matter how fine you grind the dead meat, you'll not bring it to life again.

Do stop working & writing altogether and become a creature instead of a mechanical instrument. Do clear out of the whole social ship. Do for your very pride's sake become a mere nothing, a mole, a creature that feels its way & doesn't think. Do for heavens sake be a baby, & not a savant any more. Don't *do* anything any more—but for heavens sake begin to *be*—start at the very beginning and be a perfect baby: in the name of courage.

Oh, and I want to ask you, when you make your will, do leave me enough to live on. I want you to live for ever. But I want you to make me in some part your heir.

We have got to clear out of this house in a week's time. We are looking for another house. You had better come & live near us: but not if you are going to be a thinker and a worker, only if you are going to be a creature, an infant. The Murrys are coming to live with us in April, they say.

Heseltine is starting the publishing scheme. I shouldn't wonder if he would make something of it, if he isn't conscripted. I feel as if we were all living on the edge of a precipice. Soon I shall be penniless, & they'll shove me into munitions, & I shall tell 'em what I think of 'em, & end my days in prison or a madhouse. But I don't care. One can still write bombs. But I don't want to be penniless and at their mercy. Life is very good of itself, and I am terrified lest they should get me into their power. They seem to me like an innumerable host of rats, & once they get the scent, one is lost.

My love to you. Stop working and being an ego, & have the courage to be a creature.

Yours,

D. H. LAWRENCE.

To LADY OTTOLINE MORRELL

Higher Tregerthen, Zennor, St. Ives, Cornwall.

7 April, 1916.

My dear Ottoline,

The Murrys have come and we are very busy getting their cottage ready: colouring the walls and painting and working furiously. I like it, and we all enjoy ourselves. The Murrys are happy with each other now. But they neither of them seem very well in health. That will come, however.

Our cottage is practically done. At last I am in my own home and feel content. I feel I have a place here. The cottage looks *very nice*. I made a dresser, with cupboard below, and shelves for plates above, also book-shelves. These are painted royal blue, and the walls are pale pink, and the ceiling with its beams is white. This is downstairs, a rather low, square room with thick walls. Upstairs looks really beautiful: a good-sized room with a large deep window looking at the sea, and another window opposite looking at the hill-slope of gorse and granite. Your embroidery hangs on the slanting wall of the big window, and the countrypair on the bed is brilliant and gay: it is very nice.

We have only these two rooms, and a long scullery-kitchen with sloping roof at the back. But it is quite enough, there is all the world outside, the sea and moor-hills quite open. The Murrys like it also.

Frieda wrote to you. I am glad she said what she feels. That is always best. Then if anything remains, it can begin to grow, free from the weeds. I do feel that the only thing to try for is a free, natural, unstrained relationship, without exclusions or enclosures. But it's very difficult.

I did not thank you for Thucydides. He is a very splendid and noble writer, with the simplicity and the directness of the most complete culture and the widest consciousness. I salute him. More and more I admire the true classic dignity and self-responsibility.

I have just finished reading Romain Rolland's *Life of Michael Angelo*. Do you know it? If not, I will give it to you. In its way, I think it is good. Having reached the same point of overripeness in humble Christianity, as Michael Angelo had reached in proud Christianity, Romain Rolland is understanding. It is *amazing* how plainly one sees, in Michael Angelo, the transference from the great mediaeval and classic epoch of Power and Might and Glory to the great modern epoch of Service and Equality and Humility. Michael Angelo reverted back into the old Catholic form, like Vittoria Colonna. But he was the new thing as well. Only, it is quite true, he was more concerned with the End than the Beginning, with the Last Judgment. What he felt most was the downfall of the old God of Power and Might, the death of the God, the descent from the Cross, the body in torture. But he turned his eyes to the Great God of Power and Might, whose sons we are.

And now Romain Rolland, at the end of the very epoch which Michael Angelo initiated, looks back and sees only the sorrow and the charity and the Gethsemane ecstasy. Now it is time for us to leave our Christian-democratic epoch, as it was time for Europe in Michael Angelo's day to leave the Christian-aristocratic epoch. But we cannot leap away, we slip back. That is the horror. We slip back and go mad. The world is going mad, as the Italian and Spanish Renaissance went mad. But where is our Reformation, where is our new light? Where is even our anathema? They had Savonarola and Luther, but we only slip wallowing back into our old mire of "Love thy Neighbour." It is very frightening. In Michael Angelo's day, Vittoria Colonna had a choice between Lutheranism, or even "Free Catholicism," and the "Reactionary Catholicism." Now there is no choice. There is no choice between new and old, only between old and old. It is so serious that one is hardly moved, one only wonders, and feels outside everything. What is the choice between Oxford and Cambridge, Philip Snowden[2] and F. E. Smith?[3] It is only one old hat or another.

Thank you very much for offering to help us with money. For the present we can manage. I wish I could always be sure of earning enough to keep us, but I can't. At the Renaissance, Art was holy, "A work of art is an act of faith." People came from France and Holland and Germany to be present when Michael Angelo's "Last Judgment" was inaugurated. Now art is degraded beneath mention, really trampled under the choice of a free democracy, a public opinion. When I think of art, and then of the British public—or the French public, or the Russian—then a sort of madness comes over me, really as if one were fastened within a mob, and in danger of being trampled to death. I hate the 'public,' the 'people,' 'society,' so much that a madness possesses me when I think of them. I hate democracy so much. It almost kills me. But then, I think that 'aristocracy' is just as pernicious, only it is much more dead. They are both evil. But there is nothing else, because everybody is either "the people" or "the capitalist."

One must forget, only forget, turn one's eyes from the world: that is all. One must live quite apart, forgetting, having another world, a world as yet uncreated. Everything lies in *being,* although the whole world is one colossal madness, falsity, a stupendous assertion of not-being.

Murry will read Tylor's *Primitive Culture* before I return it.

2 Viscount Snowden, Chancellor of the Exchequer in Ramsey McDonald's cabinets of 1924 and 1929-31. (H. T. M.)
3 Conservative M. P., later Earl of Birkenhead.

It is a very good sound substantial book, I had far rather read it than the *Golden Bough* or Gilbert Murray.

With affection.

Yours,

D. H. LAWRENCE.

To LADY CYNTHIA ASQUITH

Higher Tregerthen, Zennor, St. Ives, Cornwall.
Wednesday, April 26th, 1916.

My dear Lady Cynthia,

It seems as if we were all going to be dragged into the *danse macabre.* One can only grin, and be fatalistic. My dear nation is bitten by the tarantula, and the venom has gone home at last. Now it is dance, *mes amis,* to the sound of the knuckle-bones.

It is very sad, but one isn't sad any more. It is done now, and no use crying over spilt milk. "Addio" to everything. The poor dear old ship of Christian democracy is scuttled at last, the breach is made, the veil of the temple is torn, our epoch is over. *Soit!* I don't care, it's not my doing, and I can't help it. It isn't a question of "dancing while Rome burns," as you said to me on the omnibus that Sunday evening—do you remember? It is a question of bobbing about gaily in chaos. "Carpe diem" is the motto now: pure gay fatalism. It makes me laugh. My good old moral soul is *crevé.*

Will you tell me, if you can, what it would be wisest for me to do, at this juncture? Ought one to attest, and if so, what sort of job can I do? I don't *want* to do anything; but what will be, will be, and I haven't any conscience in the matter. If I have to serve, all right: only I should like a job that was at least sufferable. Do think a little, and advise me: or ask Herbert Asquith to tell me what I could do. I think it is all rather ridiculous— even when it is a question of life and death; such a scurry and a scuffle and a meaningless confusion that it is only a farce.

It is very lovely down here, the slopes of desert dead grass and heather shearing down to a sea that is so big and blue. I don't want a bit to have to go away. But it will keep. And the cottage is *very nice,* so small and neat and lovely. There is one next door, the same as this, that you must have when the pot bubbles too hard out there in the world. Will you be coming this way, when you are making your round of visits?

I am still waiting for my book of *Italian Sketches* to appear. Now there is a strike among the printers in Edinburgh. But it won't be long. It is quite a nice book. I will send you a copy.

I am doing another novel—that really occupies me. The world crackles and busts, but that is another matter, external, in chaos. One has a certain order inviolable in one's soul. There one sits, as in a crow's nest, out of it all. And even if one is conscripted, still I can sit in my crow's nest of a soul and grin. Life mustn't be taken seriously any more, at least, the outer, social life. The social being I am has become a spectator at a knockabout dangerous farce. The individual particular me remains self-contained and grins. But I should be mortally indignant if I lost my life or even too much of my liberty, by being dragged into the knockabout farce of this social life.

I hope we shall see you soon. We might have some good times together—real good times, not a bit macabre, but jolly and full. The macabre touch bores me excessively.

Frieda is boiling the washing in a saucepan. I am, for the moment, making a portrait of Taimur-i-lang—Tamerlane, the Tartar: copying it from a 15th-century Indian picture. I like it very much.

Mila salute di cuore.

D. H. LAWRENCE.

To LADY CYNTHIA ASQUITH
                    Higher Tregerthen, Nr. St. Ives, Cornwall.
.... Did you not answer my letter because I asked you what to do about military service? Never mind, I don't

want to listen. I take the question back. We'll take what comes, and leave what doesn't come. As for the rest, I hope I haven't offended you any further—there seems to be a little adder of offence under every bush.

But adders are slim and princess-like things, in reality—there are many here.

I feel that things are going to get better soon—in the world.

D. H. LAWRENCE.

To CATHERINE CARSWELL

Higher Tregerthen, Zennor, St. Ives, Cornwall.
9th July, 1916.

My dear Catherine,

I never wrote to tell you that they gave me a complete exemption from all military service, thanks be to God. That was a week ago last Thursday. I had to join the Colours in Penzance, be conveyed to Bodmin (60 miles), spend a night in barracks with all the other men, and then be examined. It was experience enough for me, of soldiering. I am sure I should die in a week, if they kept me. It is the annulling of all one stands for, this militarism, the nipping of the very germ of one's being. I was very much upset. The sense of spiritual disaster everywhere was quite terrifying. One was not sure whether one survived or not. Things are very bad.

Yet I liked the men. They all seemed so *decent*. And yet they all seemed as if they had *chosen wrong*. It was the underlying sense of disaster that overwhelmed me. They are all so brave, to suffer, but none of them brave enough, to reject suffering. They are all so noble, to accept sorrow and hurt, but they can none of them demand happiness. Their manliness all lies in accepting calmly this death, this loss of their integrity. They must stand by their fellow man: that is the motto.

This is what Christ's weeping over Jerusalem has brought us to, a whole Jerusalem offering itself to the Cross. To me, this is infinitely more terrifying than Pharisees and Publicans and Sinners, taking *their* way to death. This is what the love of our neighbour has brought us to, that, because one man dies, we all die.

This is the most terrible madness. And the worst of it all, is, that it is a madness of righteousness. These Cornish are most, most unwarlike, soft, peaceable, ancient. No men could suffer more than they, at being conscripted—at any rate, those that were with me. Yet they accepted it all: they accepted it, as one of them said to me, with wonderful purity of spirit—I could howl my eyes out over him—because "they believed first of all in their duty to their fellow man." There is no falsity about it: they believe in their duty to their fellow man. And what duty is this, which makes us forfeit everything, because Germany invaded Belgium? Is there nothing beyond my fellow man? If not, then there is nothing beyond myself, beyond my own throat, which may be cut, and my own purse, which may be slit: because *I* am the fellow-man of all the world, my neighbour is but myself in a mirror. So we toil in a circle of pure egoism.

That is what "love thy neighbour as thyself" comes to. It needs only a little convulsion, to break the mirror, to turn over the coin, and there I have myself, my own purse, I, I, I, we, we, we—like the newspapers to-day: "Capture the trade—unite the Empire—*à bas les autres.*"

There needs something else besides the love of the neighbour. If all my neighbours chose to go down the slope to Hell, that is no reason why I should go with them. I know in my own soul a truth, a right, and no amount of neighbours can weight it out of the balance. I know that, for me, the war is wrong. I know that if the Germans wanted my little house, I would rather give it them than fight for it: because my little house is not important enough to me. If another man must fight for his house, the more's the pity. But it is his affair. To fight for possessions, goods, is what my soul *will not* do. Therefore it will not fight for the neighbour who fights for his own goods.

All this war, this talk of nationality, to me is false. I *feel* no nationality, not fundamentally. I feel no passion for my own land, nor my own house, nor my own furniture, nor my own money. Therefore I won't pretend any. Neither will I take part in the scrimmage, to help my neighbour. It is his affair to go in or to stay out, as he wishes.

If they had compelled me to go in, I should have died, I am sure. One is too raw, one fights too hard already, for the real integrity of one's being. That last straw of compulsion would have been too much, I think.

Christianity is based on the love of self, the love of property, one degree removed. Why should I care for my neighbour's property, or my neighbour's life, if I do not care for my own? If the truth of my spirit is all that matters to me, in the last issue, then on behalf of my neighbour, all I care for is the truth of *his* spirit. And if his truth is his love of property, I refuse to stand by him, whether he be a poor man robbed of his cottage, his wife and children, or a rich man robbed of his merchandise. I have nothing to do with him, in that wise, and I don't care whether he keep or lose his throat, on behalf of his property. Property, and power—which is the same—is *not* the criterion. The criterion is the truth of my own intrinsic desire, clear of ulterior contamination.

I hope you aren't bored. Something makes me state my position, when I write to you.

It is summer, but not very summery, such heavy rain. I told you the Murrys had gone away, to south Cornwall. Now she doesn't like that. I believe she is in London at present. She is very dissatisfied with him.

We are keeping on their house for the rest of their year. It is *so* near, that if strangers came, it would be intolerable. So I am buying a very little furniture—it is so cheap and *so* nice here, second-hand—to furnish a sitting-room and a bedroom, for the visitors. I think Dollie Radford[4] is coming in about a week's

4 Wife of Ernest Radford, poet.

[137]

time, then Barbara Low. We get such pleasure, looking at old tables and old chairs: a big round rose-wood table, very large, 4 ft. 4 ins. diameter and solid, 10/–: three very nice birch-wood chairs, 7/6.: an armchair, 5/–: the sitting-room is furnished: it is an upper room, with big windows, and shelves.

It is such a pleasure, buying this furniture—I remember my sermon. But one doesn't really care. This cottage, that I like so much—and the new table, and the chairs—I could leave them all to-morrow, blithely. Meanwhile, they are very nice.

I have finished my novel, and am going to try to type it. It will be a labour—but we have got no money. But I am asking Pinker for some. And if it bores me to type the novel, I shan't do it. There is a last chapter to write, some time, when one's heart is not so contracted.

I think you are not very wise to go to the Hebrides with Carswell's people—you would be so much happier with him alone—or with friends.

Greiffenhagen[6] seems to be slipping back and back. I suppose it has to be. Let the dead bury their dead. Let the past smoulder out. One shouldn't look back, like Lot's wife: though why *salt*, that I could never understand.

Have you got a copy of *Twilight in Italy?* If not, I have got one to give you. So just send me word, a p.c.

Frieda sends many greetings.

Yours,

D. H. LAWRENCE.

I am amused to hear of Carswell's *divorce* case.

[6] Painter whose pictures Lawrence had enjoyed copying.

To MISS AMY LOWELL[7]

> *Higher Tregerthen, Zennor, St. Ives, Cornwall.*
> *23 August, 1916.*

My dear Amy,

Thank you so much for the cheque for £8[8], which came today. Those Imagiste books seem to blossom into gold like a monthly rose. I am very glad, too, to hear of the good things the papers are deigning to say. You should see my English critics walking round me in every sort of trepidation, like dogs round a mongoose.

I will ask Duckworths to send you the poems & the Italian Sketches. You know we may only send books abroad, through the publisher or a bookseller. Otherwise, of course, I should gladly autograph them for you.

Thank God they did not make me a soldier. I had to join up, & spend a night in barracks, and then they gave me a total exemption. If they hadn't, I should have been a stretched corpse in a fortnight: that I knew, at four o'clock in the morning, on that fatal night in barracks at Bodmin. There is something in military life that would kill me off, as if I were in an asphyxiating chamber. The whole thing is abhorrent to me—even the camaraderie, that is so glamorous—the Achilles & Patroclus business. The spirit, the pure spirit of militarism is sheer death to a nature that is at all constructive or social-creative. And it is not that I am afraid or shy: I can get on with the men like a house on fire. It is simply that the spirit of militarism is essentially destructive, destroying the individual and the constructive social being. It is *bad*. How Aldington[9] will stand it I don't know. But I can tell that the glamour is getting hold of him: the 'now we're all men together' business, the kind of love that was between Achilles & Patroclus. And if once that lays hold of

---

[7] From *Amy Lowell.*

[8] Lawrence's share in the royalties from the second anthology of Imagist Poets edited by Amy Lowell.

[9] Richard Aldington, English poet, novelist and biographer.

a man, then farewell to that man forever, as an independent or constructive soul.

I am glad you think the war is virtually over. Official London seems to be saying, with much confidence, two more years of it. But nobody knows. God help us if this is going on for two years more. These last two years have made one at least two centuries older. In two years more, we shall have ceased to be human beings at all. Certainly England has spit on her hands and taken hold at last. The whole nation is hanging on tense and taut, throwing all her weight on the rope at last, in the tug of war. It is our tradition—to get our blood up at the eleventh hour. Well, the English blood is up now, the bull-dog is hanging on—alas that it ever need have come to pass. What will be the end, when the war *is* at last over, the mind refuses to consider: but it will be nothing good.

So one's soul knows misfortune and terror. But there is a limit to grief for one's fellow man: one becomes callous, since nothing can be done.

Here we live very quietly indeed, being far from the world. Here we live as if on one of the blessed Isles, the moors are so still behind us, the sea so big in front. I am very much better, much stronger, now. All the winter I was so ill. I hope it won't be so again this year. But I think not. I am busy typing out a new novel, to be called 'Women in Love.' Every day I bless you for the gift of the typewriter. It runs so glibly, & has at last become a true confrère. I take so unkindly to any sort of machinery. But now I & the typewriter have sworn a Blut-bruderschaft.

We go down & bathe among the rocks—not the typewriter, but Frieda & I. Today there were great rollers coming from the west. It is so frightening, when one is naked among the rocks, to see the high water rising to a threatening wall, the pale green fire shooting along, then bursting into a furious wild incandescence of foam. But it is great fun. It is so lovely to recognise the non-human elements: to hear the rain like a song, to feel the wind going by one, to be thrown against the rocks by the wonderful water. I cannot bear to see or to know humanity any more.

Your remoter America must be splendid. One day, I hope to come to see it, when there is peace and I am not poor. We are living on credit as usual. But what does it matter, in a world like this. Hilda Aldington[1] says to me, why don't I write hymns to fire, why am I not in love with a tree. But my fire is a pyre, & the tree is the tree of Knowledge.

I wonder if I have said anything censurous in my letter—I think not. The honeysuckle smells so sweet tonight—what are the flowers in New Hampshire? Often I have longed to go to a country which has new, quite unknown flowers & birds. It would be such a joy to make their acquaintance. Have you still got humming birds, as in Crèvecoeur? I like Crèvecoeur's 'Letters of an American Farmer,' *so* much. And how splendid Hermann Melville's 'Moby Dick' is, & Dana's 'Two Years before the Mast.' But your classic American literature, I find to my surprise, is *older* than our English. The tree did not become new, which was transplanted. It only ran more swiftly into age, impersonal, nonhuman almost. But how good these books are! Is the *English* tree in America almost dead? By the literature, I think it is.

Remember me warmly to Mrs. Russell. Many greetings to you from my wife & me. You will never come back to the England you knew before. But at any rate, when you do come, you must come here.

D. H. LAWRENCE.

Doran is to publish both the books of mine in America.

---

[1] H. D., poet, wife of Richard Aldington.

To MISS AMY LOWELL²

Do write a book called Fire Rockets.

Higher Tregerthen, Zennor, St. Ives, Cornwall.
14 Novem., 1916.

My dear Amy,

I was infinitely touched when there came this morning a cheque for £60, sent by you through the bankers. One is so moved by the kindness: the money, after all, is necessity, but the kindness is given. This I shall always treasure up, the kindness, even if I can pay you back the money. Because, after all, there is not much real generosity in the world.

I was rather sorry Frieda wrote and asked you for money: how do we know what you have to do with your money. But it is wearying, to be so much unwell, and penniless. I shall begin at once to move towards Italy: though heaven knows when we shall really get away. And I hope, from Italy, to come on to America, next year, when I am better and the winter has gone.

Why don't you come to Rome for a while? Think how jolly that would be, if we were all in Rome at the same time. Perhaps you would like it better, in these times, than London.

You[r] book, Men, Women and Ghosts, came two days ago. We have both read all the poems. I like this book better than 'Sword Blades.' I think The Cremona Violin is both a lovely story and lovely verse: an exquisite picture into the bargain. Then I like The Fruit Shop, the sense of youngness and all the gorgeous fruitfulness in store, then the sudden destructiveness of Bonaparte, a smash of irony. I like that. Some of the movements of the Hammers really startle one's heart—one listens, and hears, and lives, it is almost frightening. Only I don't care for the Ship. 'Reaping' seems to me one of the very best—a real straight jet of a story—but of course there isn't the newness of sensation one gets in Hoops—it belongs to the old knowledge

2 From *Amy Lowell.*

—but it is *very* good. I always liked 'Spring Day'—sometimes
the prose is best of all, better than any verse-form.—And then,
after all, I like Towns in Colour more than anything in the
book: and of these Opera and Aquarium most.

It is very surprising to me, now I have come to understand
you Americans a little, to realise how much older you are than
us, how much further you and your art are really developed,
outstripping us by far in decadence and non-emotional aestheti-
cism, how much beyond us you are in the last stages of human
apprehension of the physico-sensational world, apprehension of
things non-human, not conceptual. We still see with concepts.
But you, in the last stages of return, have gone beyond tragedy
and emotion, even beyond irony, and have come to the pure
mechanical stage of physical apprehension, the *human* unit
almost lost, the primary elemental forces, kinetic, dynamic—
prismatic, tonic, the great, massive, active, *inorganic* world,
elemental, never softened by life, that hard universe of Matter
and Force where life is not yet known, come to pass again. It is
strange and wonderful. I find it only in you and H. D.,[3] in
English: in your 'Bath,' and the fire of the lacquer music-stand,
& Acquarium, [*sic*] & some Stravinsky, and here & there in
Roxbury Garden—which, to my mind, is not quite chemical
and crystallographical *enough*. Of course, it seems to me this is
a real *cul de sac* of art. You can't get any further than

> 'Streaks of green & yellow iridescence
> Silver shiftings
> Rings veering out of rings
> Silver—gold—
> Grey-green opaqueness sliding down'

You see it is uttering pure sensation *without concepts,* which
is what this futuristic art tries to do. One step further and it
passes into *mere noises,* as the Italian futurismo poems have

3 Hilda Aldington, wife of Richard Aldington.

done, or mere jags and zig-zags, as the futuristic paintings. There it ceases to be art, and is pure accident, mindless.—But there is this to fulfil, this last and most primary state of our being, where we are shocked into form like crystals that take place from the fluid chaos. And it is this primary state of being which you carry into art, in

> 'Gold clusters
> Flash in soft explosions
> On the blue darkness
> Suck back to a point

And disappear . . .'—for example. You might have called your book 'Rockets and Sighs.' It would have been better than Men, Women & Ghosts.

If ever I come to America I will write about these things. But won't you try to come to Rome. Think of the Naples aquarium, and the Naples museum—and Rome itself. We might enjoy it so much.

Thank you once more, dear Amy. Remember me to Mrs. Russell. My wife is writing to you.—I have just finished a novel, of which I am proud.—Did you get my 'Amores' and 'Twilight in Italy'? Do let us have a letter.

Yours ever,

D. H. LAWRENCE.

These things are your best, by far, I think: Spring Day, Towns in Colour, Hammers, p. 344, some p. 346, & p. 347 of the Stravinsky. The shock and clipping of the physicomechanical world are your finest expression.

To CATHERINE CARSWELL[4]

Zennor, Cornwall, Nov. 27, 1916.

My dear Catherine,

I heard from Ottoline Morrell this morning, saying she hears she is the villainess of the new book.[5] It is very strange, how rumours go round.—So I have offered to send her the MS.—So don't send it to Pinker till I let you know.

I got Sportsman's Sketches and have read them. No, I don't like Turgenev very much; he seems so very critical, like Katherine Mansfield and also a sort of male old maid. It amazes me that we have bowed down and worshipped these foreigners as we have. Their art is so clumsy, really, and clayey, compared with our own. I read "Deerslayer" just before the Turgenev. And I can tell you what a come-down it was, from the pure and the exquisite art of Fennimore [*sic*] Cooper—whom we count nobody—to the journalistic bludgeonings of Turgenev. They are all—Turgenev, Tolstoi, Dostoevsky, Maupassant, Flaubert —so very *obvious* and coarse, beside the lovely, mature and sensitive art of Fennimore Cooper or Hardy. It seems to me that our English art, at its best, is by far the subtlest and loveliest and most perfect in the world. But it is characteristic of a highly-developed nation to bow down to that which is more gross and raw and affected. Take even D'Annunzio and my Trespasser—how much cruder [and] stupider D'Annunzio is, really. No, enough of this silly worship of foreigners. The most exquisite literature in the world is written in the English language.

Don't talk much about my novel, will you? And above all don't give it to anybody to read, but Don. I feel it won't be published yet, so I would rather nobody read it. I hope Ottoline Morrell won't want the MS. And if you can prevent Aunt Barbara[6] from knowing you have the book by you, *do*—because,

---

4 From *The Intelligent Heart.*
5 Lady Ottoline recognized herself as Hermione in *Women in Love.*
6 Barbara Low.

having read the beginning, she is sure to claim the right to read the rest.

How are you feeling?—better, I hope. And how is your work going now? Let it go as slowly as it likes.

It is a sunny cold morning—I shall go out now.

D. H. LAWRENCE.

To LADY CYNTHIA ASQUITH

Zennor, St. Ives, Cornwall.
19th December, 1916.

. . . I wonder if you could help me in another little matter? I have finished and sent in the novel, *Women in Love,* which is more or less a sequel to *The Rainbow.* It is a very fine piece of work, and I will stand by it for ever. But there is the same danger ahead as ever: it is, perhaps, almost as likely to be suppressed as was *The Rainbow:* which seems to me monstrous, a serious and profound piece of work like that. I wondered if I could dedicate it to some patron, in the old-fashioned way, and so secure it some patronage which would save it from the barkings of the little newspaper curs. Do you know anybody of any weight or importance, who would take it under his, or her, protection, so far as to accept a serious dedication? It is a much finer book than *The Rainbow,* and I would rather it were never published at all than insulted by petty dogs as that was. However, in your mad scurry of train-catching, you might think it over for me. . . .

To LADY CYNTHIA ASQUITH

Zennor, St. Ives, Cornwall.
8th January, 1917.

I didn't answer your letter about *Women in Love* because it seems the book will not find a publisher in England at all. Indeed, nobody will print me nowadays, the public taste is averse from me. It is a nasty quandary. The books I have don't sell, so it's a bad look-out.

I wrote to Eddie[7] asking him if he thought we could get passports to U.S.A. Of course we have the passports of November, 1915—but they won't do, I believe. We have some friends going over to New York in March, and I should like to go with them. I am pretty sure of selling my stuff if I am in America. I don't want to write or talk about the war at all—only stories and literary stuff: because I think the war will end this year, and even if it doesn't I can't help it any more. I feel there is disaster impending for England. Not that I want to run away—only I feel useless, it is quite useless my trying to live and write here. I shall only starve in ignominy: should be starving now if an American hadn't given me £60.

After the Cornwallis-West affair[8]—and how disgusting that is, how loathsome the attitude of the papers, how indecent the whole publicity—I know one ought not to ask for anything from you. But I believe it is quite legal for us to go to America: I am medically exempt, we are not spies, and I will neither write nor talk about the war to the Americans—they have nothing to do with it, it is our affair, alas! So just confer a little with Eddie about it, will you? I shall have just enough money to take us to New York if we can go on the first of March with our friends. And I *can't* go on living here on a miserable pittance which Pinker, my literary agent, will allow me. I can't take a pittance from Pinker: it is too insulting and it is worse than useless my living in England any more.

I don't think America is a paradise. But I know I can sell my stories there, and get a connection with publishers. And what I want is for us to have sufficient to go far west, to California or

7 Edward Marsh.

8 Mr. Moore believes this refers to the break-up of the marriage of George Cornwallis-West and Mrs. Patrick Campbell, and the attendant scandal. (Before marrying Mrs. Campbell, Cornwallis-West had been married to the mother of Winston Churchill.) Lady Cynthia was secretary to Sir James Barrie, a close friend of Mrs. Campbell.

the South Seas, and live apart, away from the world. It is really my old Florida idea—but one must go further west. I hope in the end other people will come, and we can be a little community, a monastery, a school—a little Hesperides of the soul and body. That is what I will do finally. . . .

But in the end I will go far away and make a little new world, like a seed which drops in a fertile soil, and germinates with a new earth and a new heaven. I don't believe in practical life, nor this materialism, nor in submitting to falsity because there is nothing else to do.

D. H. LAWRENCE.

I hope we shall always be friends.

To J. B. PINKER

Zennor, St. Ives, Cornwall, 3 August, 1917.

Dear Pinker,

Your letter and the poems came to-day. Truly the ways and the taste of publishers is mysterious and beyond finding out.

The only thing I feel strongly about is the *Song of a Man who is Loved.* CAN you or anybody tell me why they want it omitted? I'm sure Alice Meynell might print it without reproach. I don't want to omit it. I send a copy of it. Please convince them they are absurd on this point.

I will omit *Meeting Among the Mountains,* if they want it. But *do* ask them why they wish it. It has already been printed in the *English Review,* and in *Georgian Poetry.* The *Georgian Poetry* public is a very big one, according to sales, and they are sure to be glad to come upon something they know already. The lines I will alter, though for some of them it is a great pity, spoiling the clarity and precision of the expression. I will look after my bad taste in *Eve's Mass* and *Candlemass.* Strange are the ways of man, strangest of all, the publishers.

Do convince them that the *Song of a Man who is Loved* is beautiful, necessary, and innocuous as a sprig of mignonette. If they still persist, make them say *what* they object to. For I cannot believe that this poem shall be omitted.

Yrs.,

D. H. LAWRENCE.

P.S.—Do you think anybody would care to publish as a little book or pamphlet, the *Reality of Peace,* four numbers of which (out of seven) came in the *English Review?*

If Chatto's leave out the *Meeting Among the Mountains,* I must leave out all reference to *Georgian Poetry,* which is a name which I am sure gives a good deal of sanction among a certain class.

P.P.S.—I have already changed all the lines and the two titles. There remain only the two poems to be decided on. *Meeting* I don't feel strongly about—but the other I do.

To MISS AMY LOWELL[9]

Higher Tregerthen, Zennor, St. Ives, Cornwall.

30 Aug., 1917.

My dear Amy,

How are you, and what are you doing? It is ages since I have heard of or from you. How is your health, and what are you writing?

I am all right in health. Frieda has been laid low with neuritis in her leg: very bad for a month, but righting now. I think she'll soon be sound.

Here the community seriously thinks of building an ark, for the cataclysmic deluge has certainly set in. It rains and rains, and it blows the sea up on the land, in volleys and masses of wind. We are all being finely and subtly sea-pickled, sea-changed, sure enough, 'into something new and strange.' I shouldn't be a bit surprised to find one morning that fine webs had grown between my toes, and that my legs were slippery

9 From *Amy Lowell.*

with sea-weedy scales. I feel quite spray-blind, like any fish, and my brain is turning nacreous. I verily believe I am metamorphosed—feel as if I daren't look to see.

The corn is cut, and being washed back again to the bowels of the earth. I made a wonderful garden: but the pea-rows are already beaten and smashed and dissolved to nauseous glue, and the leaves are blown to bits from off the marrow vines, leaving the voluptuous smooth-skinned marrows naked like virgins in the hands of the heathen. All's wrong with the world, in contradiction to Browning. But I don't care—why should I!

Nobody will publish my novel 'Women in Love'—my best bit of work. The publishers say 'it is too strong for an English public.' Poor darling English public, when will it go in for a little spiritual athletics. Are these Tommies, so tough and brown on the outside, are they really so pappy and unbaked inside, that they would faint and fall under a mere dose of 'Women in Love'?—Let me mix my metaphors thoroughly, let me put gravy-salt into the pudding, and pour vanilla essence over the beef, for the world is mad, yet won't cry 'Willow, Willow,' and drown itself like Ophelia.

Chatto & Windus are this autumn bringing out a new book of verse of mine 'Look, We Have Come Through.' They are actually going to give me 20 guineas in advance of royalties.—I will send you a copy as soon as I can. (not of the guineas)—This is one bright beam in my publishing sky.—But I shall have to go and look for daylight with a lantern.

That is to say, with an eye to material things as well as spiritual: at last I am learning to squint:—I am doing a set of essays on 'The Transcendental Element in American (Classic) Literature.' It sounds very fine and large, but in reality is rather a thrilling blood-and-thunder, your-money-or-your-life kind of thing: hands up, America!—No, but they are very keen essays in criticism—cut your fingers if you don't handle them carefully.—Are you going to help me to hold up the 'Yale Review' or the 'New Republic' or some such fat old coach, with this ten-barrelled pistol of essays of mine, held right in the eye of America? Answer me that, Donna Americana. Will you try to suborn for me the conductor of one of these coaches?—Never say nay.—Tis a chef-d'oeuvre of soul-searching criticism. Shall I inscribe it to you? Say the word!

To
Amy Lowell
Who buttered my bread
these few fair words
For she can butter her own parsnips.
Being well-to-do
She gave to the thankless
Because she thought it was worth it.

Frieda says you will be offended. Jamais de la Vie! cry I.— But please yourself.

Ah me—it's a long way to Tipperary, if Tipperary means a place of peacefulness.—I shall come to America directly the war is over. No doubt you don't want me—but it will be one of the moments of my life when I can say 'Farewell and Adieu' to Europe; the 'It is finished' of my Golgotha. As for Uncle Sam, I put my fingers to my nose, at him.

D. H. LAWRENCE.

To LADY CYNTHIA ASQUITH

Zennor, St. Ives, Cornwall, 12th October, 1917.

My dear Lady Cynthia,

Now comes another nasty blow. The police have suddenly descended on the house, searched it, and delivered us a notice to leave the area of Cornwall, by Monday next. So on Monday we shall be in London, staying, if possible c/o Mrs. Radford 32, Well Walk, Hampstead, N.W.

This bolt from the blue has fallen this morning: why, I know not, any more than you do. I cannot even conceive how I have incurred suspicion—have not the faintest notion. We are as innocent even of pacifist activities, let alone spying of any sort as the rabbits in the field outside. And we must leave Cornwall, and live in an unprohibited area, and report to the police. It is *very* vile. We have practically no money at all—I don't know what we shall do.

At any rate we shall be in London Monday evening. You can see us if you feel like it during the week.

This order comes from W. Western, Major-General i/c Administration, Southern Command, Salisbury. They have taken away some of my papers—I don't know what. It is all very sickening, and makes me very weary.

I hope things are all right with you.

D. H. LAWRENCE.

To CECIL GRAY

44, Mecklenburgh Square, W.C.1, Wednesday.

You are only half right about the disciples and the alabaster box. If Jesus had paid more attention to Magdalene, and less to his disciples, it would have been better. It was not the ointment-pouring which was so devastating, but the discipleship of the twelve.

As for me and my "women," I know what they are and aren't, and though there is a certain messiness, there is further reality. Take away the subservience and feet-washing, and the pure understanding between the Magdalene and Jesus went deeper than the understanding between the disciples and Jesus, or Jesus and the Bethany women. But Jesus himself was frightened of the knowledge which subsisted between the Magdalene and him, a knowledge deeper than the knowledge of Christianity and "good," deeper than love, anyhow.

And both you and Frieda need to go one world deeper in knowledge. As for spikenard, if I chance to luxuriate in it, it is by the way: not so very Philippically[1] filthy either. Not that it matters.

I don't mind a bit being told where I am wrong—not by you or anybody I respect. Only you don't seem to be going for me in anything where I am really wrong: a bit Pharisaic, both you and Frieda: external.

It seems to me there is a whole world of knowledge to forsake, a new, deeper, lower one to *entamer*. And your hatred of me, like Frieda's hatred of me, is your cleavage to a world of knowledge and being which you ought to forsake, which, by organic law, you must depart from or die. And my "women" represent, in an impure and unproud, subservient, cringing, bad fashion, I admit—but represent none the less the threshold of a new world, or underworld, of knowledge and being. And the Hebridean songs, which represent you and Frieda in this, are songs of the damned: that is, songs of those who inhabit an underworld which is forever an underworld, never to be made open and whole. And you would like us all to inhabit a suggestive underworld which is never revealed or opened, only intimated, only *felt* between the initiated.—I won't have it. The old world must burst, the underworld must be open and whole, new world. You want an emotional sensuous underworld, like Frieda and the Hebrideans: my "women" want an ecstatic subtly-intellectual underworld, like the Greeks—Orphicism—like Magdalene at her feet-washing—and there you are.

D. H. LAWRENCE.

To LADY CYNTHIA ASQUITH
13b, Earl's Court Square, S.W., Tuesday (1917).[1a]
It is a pity you wouldn't come this evening—and you didn't write and say why, after all.

1 Refers to Philip Heseltine.
1a The date of this letter is December 18, 1917. (H. T. M.)

We are leaving here on Friday—going, I think, to Dollie Radford's cottage in the country near Newbury.

But it seems we are never going to have any peace. To-day there has been a man from the Criminal Investigation Department inquiring about us—from Gray.[2] It is quite evident that somebody from Cornwall—somebody we don't know, probably —is writing letters to these various departments—and we are followed everywhere by the persecution. It is just like the Cornish to do such a thing. But it is *very* maddening. The detective pretended to Gray that I was a foreigner—but what has the Criminal Investigation Department to do with that? Altogether it is too sickening.

Ask your man at Scotland Yard if he can tell you how I can put a stop to it—if there is any way of putting a stop to it. I hate bothering you—but really, this is getting a bit too thick. I shall soon have every department in the country on my heels for no reason whatever. Surely I can find out from the Criminal Dept. what the persecution is about?

Just write a letter to your man at Scotland Yard, will you? At least this last vileness against me I ought to be able to quash. Address me at:

44, Mecklenburgh Square, W.C.1.

will you, unless you hear from me. That address will always find me.

I hate worrying you—but perhaps you will forgive me.

Frieda sends her love.

D. H. LAWRENCE.

To LADY CYNTHIA ASQUITH

Chapel Farm Cottage, Hermitage,
Nr. Newbury, Berks, Sunday.[2a]

Got your letter to-day—glad you like the poems—I myself think they are highly amusing and interesting—they might

---

2 Cecil Gray, composer.
2a The date of this letter is March, 1918. (H. T. M.)

have quite a run—so why should I sell them out for £9? Why, America gives me £9 for three or four poems—Beaumont must make a different sort of agreement with me. I shall tell him. Would you have preferred to be inscribed with your title, not only your bare name? It is as you like.

I don't know if I've had anything from the Literary Fund. The only thing I've ever had from any fund or body was £50, which I had two months after the war began and which came from the Authors' Society, I believe, though whether they drew it out of the Literary Fund I don't know. I believe Alfred Sutro got it for me. I am very willing to have £100 from any fund whatsoever—as for obligation, I shall certainly go on writing and I am not married to the censor. I have begun a novel now[2b] —done 150 pages, which is as blameless as Cranford. It shall not have one garment disarranged, but shall be buttoned up like a Member of Parliament. Still, I wouldn't vouch that it is like *Sons and Lovers:* it is funny. It amuses me terribly.

Tell my well-wisher to get me the £100, which will be a great boon to me, as being a mere necessity, and not to mind about any obligation, which is surely *infra dig.* on the part of gentlemen. Why has the world become so ambidextrous that the left hand must always be implicated in what the right hand does! Pah—people—pfui!

D. H. LAWRENCE.

To KATHERINE MANSFIELD

Middleton, Thursday [? *early Dec., 1918*].

My dear Katherine,

I received your letter this morning. I want to write a few little things I have on my mind.

First, I send you the Jung book, borrowed from Kot[3] in the midst of his reading it. Ask Jack not to keep it long, will you,

---

[2b] Probably *Aaron's Rod.*
[3] S. S. Koteliansky, Russian economist, exiled in England.

as I feel I ought to send it back. Beware of it—this mother-incest idea can become an obsession. But it seems to me there is this much truth in it: that at certain periods the man has a desire and a tendency to return unto the woman, make her his goal and end, find his justification in her. In this way he casts himself as it were into her womb, and she, the Magna Mater, receives him with gratification. This is a kind of incest. It seems to me it is what Jack does to you, and what repels and fascinates you. I have done it, and now struggle all my might to get out. In a way, Frieda is the devouring mother. It is awfully hard, once the sex relation has gone this way, to recover. If we don't recover, we die. But Frieda says I am antediluvian in my positive attitude. I do think a woman must yield some sort of precedence to a man, and he must take this precedence. I do think men must go ahead absolutely in front of their women, without turning round to ask for permission or approval from their women. Consequently the women must follow as it were unquestioningly. I can't help it, I believe this. Frieda doesn't. Hence our fight.

Secondly, I do believe in friendship. I believe tremendously in friendship between man and man, a pledging of men to each other inviolably. But I have not ever met or formed such friendship. Also I believe the same way in friendship between men and women, and between women and women, sworn, pledged, eternal, as eternal as the marriage bond, and as deep. But I have not met or formed such friendship.

Excuse this sudden burst into dogma. Please give the letter to Jack. I say it to him particularly.

The weather continues dark, warm, muggy and nasty. I find the Midlands full of the fear of death—truly. They are all queer and unnerved. This flu. is very bad. There has only been one flicker of sunshine on the valley. It is very grim always. Last evening at dusk I sat by the rapid brook which runs by the highroad in the valley bed. The spell of hastening, secret water goes over one's mind. When I got to the top—a very hard climb —I felt as if I had climbed out of a womb.

The week-end I was at Ripley. Going, on Sat. night, the train runs just above the surface of Butterley reservoir, and the iron-works on the bank were flaming, a massive roar of flame and burnt smoke in the black sky, flaming and waving again on the black water round the train. On Butterley platform—when I got out—everything was lit up red—there was a man with dark brows, odd, not a human being. I could write a story about him. He made me think of Ashurbanipal. It seems to me, if one is to do fiction now, one must cross the threshold of the human people. I've not done *The Fox* yet—but I've done *The Blind Man*—the end queer and ironical. I realise *how* many people are just rotten at the quick.

I've written three little essays, "Education of the People." I told you Freeman, on *The Times,* asked me to do something for his *Educational Supplement.* Will you ask Jack please to send me, by return if possible, Freeman's initials, and *The Times* address, that will find him, so that I can send him the essays and see if he will print them. It will be nice if I can earn a little weekly money.

I begin to despair altogether about human relationships— feel one may just as well turn into a sort of lone wolf, and have done with it. Really, I need a little reassuring of some sort.

D. H. L.

Do you know the poem—Heine, I think:

> *Aus alten Märchen winkt es*
> *Hervor mit weisser Hand,*
> *Da singt es und da klingt es*
> *Von einem Zauberland,*
> *Wo grossen Blumen schmachten*
> *In goldnen Abendlicht*
> *Und traurig sich betrachten*
> *Mit bräutlichem Gesicht.*

I only object to *"traurig"*—it fascinates me—if I remember it right.

Don't you think you and Jack might come here for Christmas? Would you be well enough? I've been getting wood in the well-fields—it's rather beautiful, these dark, gleamy afternoons.

To KATHERINE MANSFIELD

Middleton-by-Wirksworth.
Tuesday [December, 1918].

My dear Katherine,

No, it's damn well no good bothering about people. I had an S.O.S. from ———— ————[4] to-day, and she wants her Jung. Let her have it by the week-end, will you—post it to her direct —and *print* the address, dear Katherine, so that the Jewish Magpie shall not settle chattering on my roof. You will understand I can't be chattered at.

I went to Ripley—found my poor sister rather sick and wretched. We must get her husband home, to do the work. I am writing to ————,[5] though he's no good—I mean, he will never lift a finger. Does Jack know anybody at the Ministry of Labour, who might tell us the best way to go about to get my brother-in-law out of the Marines? There is a special clause for one-man businesses, you know.

I also saw the Eastwood friends: one just on the point of dying. Katherine—*on ne meurt pas:* I almost want to let it be reflexive—*on ne se meurt pas: Point!* Be damned and be blasted everything, and let the ————[6] world come to its end. But one does not die. *Jamais.*—I bolted home to Matlock in the train. The Derwent (the river at Matlock) rushes very fast. This for some reason gives me extreme pleasure. I believe it would you.

4 Barbara Low. (H. T. M.)
5 Unidentified.
6 Bloody.

We must find some way, next year, of getting *out* of the world: and if Jack doesn't want to go, let him stay and write for *The Nation*. IF we are self-sufficient, a few of us, WHAT do we want with the world?

When do you think you will be strong enough to come up here? Don't be long.

I'm sending you *The Times* essays, in despair of ever getting the address. You will be cursing me, probably, for bothering you. But do read them and post them on at once if you can, for the sake of the publication.

I wrote the fox story—rather odd and amusing. What is your story? Perhaps I'll send both the "Fox" and the "Education" essays to Frieda, and she'll bring them on to you. Let me see your story. Somehow I hate doing that *European History* for the Oxford Press.[7] Curse it—why shouldn't one do as one likes.

We'll stand free and swear allegiance, anyhow, shall we?

D. H. L.

To KATHERINE MANSFIELD
c/o Mrs. Clarke, Grosvenor Rd., Ripley, Nr. Derby.
Friday, 27 Dec., 1918.

My dear Katherine,

We got your parcel on Christmas morning. We had started off, and were on the brow of the hill, when the postman loomed round the corner, over the snow. It was all white and snowy and sunny, with a wind like an axe. I floated out my hanky for a flag over the snow, and Frieda dropped the tangerines in her anxiety to get the wheatsheaf unwrapped, and it was terribly cold and windy just on that edge. Frieda's wheatsheaf looked so strange, such a queer indescribable darkish colour, somehow elephant, over the snow which is so candid in comparison. It was queer and like Africa, and a bit like a meteor.

---

[7] *Movements in European History,* to which Lawrence signed the name Lawrence H. Davison.

She has worn it on her yellow slip, with the red silk shirt and red coat, at our two parties here—but I can't get used to it now, it seems like a little torch or brand of elephant-grey, tropical, lush twilight. Funny how things disturb one. But my hanky fluttered very nice and lively. I wish you could have been there on the hill summit—the valley all white and hairy with trees below us, and grey with rocks—and just round us on our side the grey stone fences drawn in a network over the snow, all very clear in the sun. We ate the sweets, and slithered downhill, very steep and tottering. The children had the tangerines and the fan.

We read your letter in the wind, dropping down to Cromford. It made me feel weary, that we couldn't be all there, with rucksacks—I'd got mine on—setting off for somewhere good, over the snow. It *is* disappointing. And unless one decorates one's house for oneself alone, best leave it bare, for other people are all wall-eyed. I do so want to GET OUT—out of England—really, out of Europe. And I *will* get out. We must do it.

There was hardly any snow in the valley—all green, with the yew-berries still sprinkling the causeway. At Ambergate my sister had sent a motor-car for us—so we were at Ripley in time for turkey and Christmas pudding. My God, what masses of food here, turkey, large tongues, long wall of roast loin of pork, pork-pies, sausages, mince-pies, dark cakes covered with almonds, cheese-cakes, lemon-tarts, jellies, endless masses of food, with whisky, gin, port wine, burgundy, muscatel. It seems incredible. We played charades—the old people of 67 playing away harder than the young ones—and lit the Christmas tree, and drank healths, and sang, and roared—Lord above. If only one hadn't all the while a sense that next week would be the same dreariness as before. What a good party we might have had, had we felt really free of the world.

We had a second turn-to yesterday—and at half past eleven went roaring off in the dark wind to Dr. Feroze's—he is a Parsee—and drank two more bottles of muscatel, and danced in his big empty room till we were staggered, and quite dazed.

To-night we are going back to Middleton—and I feel infuriated to think of the months ahead, when one waits paralysed for some sort of release. I feel caged, somehow— and I *cannot* find out how to earn enough to keep us—and it maddens me.

Still, it might be very much worse. One might be tied tight to a job, or to a sickness. I do wish you were better. But you *sound* stronger. I long to make *plans*—new plans. But not Europe: oh, God!

I pledge you "the days to come."

D. H. L.

To MRS. NANCY HENRY

Middleton-by-Wirksworth, Derby.
Monday, 3 Feb., 1919.

Dear Mrs. Henry,

I am so sorry you have been laid-up, do hope you'll get sound again soon. The weather is vicious, I think. I've been in bed a day or two also. Here the snow lies: it is rather lovely, but very cold.

I don't know whether I ought to step in with advice. But I DO think it would be unwise to give up your job, unless you have some other provision. Never has it been so difficult to make money by any form of art: never has the artist had such a bad chance: and never has the world been so coldly indifferent, never has it clutched its shillings more tightly. Everybody feels we are just marking time before a debacle, and nobody is going to waste one *serious* moment on art at all, or on charity. Your husband doesn't know what the world is like now. It is not as it was five years ago. If you are going to put yourself in a position to starve, starve you actually will: have no illusion about it. The day has gone by when fairy godmothers stepped in. The tension of the struggle for the possession of money grows so strong, that you must actually be on one side or the other, either earning or producing money, or you are less than nothing. And he, if he is going to produce music, let him produce it out of the courage of his own soul. That other business is a form of prostitution.

One should not prostitute oneself, even to art. The art can't be vital, anyway—must be spurious. If you are wise you will keep your job: there are days coming when art will not save us: neither you nor me nor anybody.

I am glad you like the history. I send you here the last four chapters. I thought of calling it *Movements in European History*. Do you think that is all right? I suppose it will be anonymous—Ely won't want my name—and I don't want it on the book, either. If a pseudonym is useful to the publishers, we can apply one. Let me know about maps, will you? I hate bothering you when you are knocked up.

Kindest regards from us both.

D. H. LAWRENCE.

To KATHERINE MANSFIELD

Thursday.[7a]

Frieda said you were cross with me, that I *repulsed* you. I'm sure I didn't. The complication of getting Jack and you and F. and me into a square seems great—especially Jack. But you I am sure of—I was ever since Cornwall, save for Jack—and if you must go his way, and if he will *never* really come our way—well! But things will resolve themselves.

I dreamed such a vivid little dream of you last night. I dreamed you came to Cromford, and stayed there. You were not coming on here because you weren't well enough. You were quite clear from the consumption—quite, you told me. But there was still something that made you that you couldn't come up the hill here.

So you went out with me as I was going. It was night, and very starry. We looked at the stars, and they were different. All the constellations were different, and I, who was looking for

7a The date of this letter is probably April 10, 1919. (H. T. M.)

Orion, to show you, because he is rising now, was very puzzled by these thick, close, brilliant new constellations. Then suddenly we saw one planet, so beautiful, a large, fearful, strong star, that we were both pierced by it, possessed, for a second. Then I said, "That's Jupiter"—but I felt that it wasn't Jupiter —at least not the everyday Jupiter.

Ask Jung or Freud about it? Never! It was a star that blazed for a second on one's soul.

I wish it was spring for us all.

D. H. L.

To LADY CYNTHIA ASQUITH

Chapel Farm Cottage, Hermitage,
Nr. Newbury, Berks, 16th Sept., 1919.

Will Simon[8] be called Peter, and *super hanc Petram* shall you found your fortress? I suppose we shall have to see you Madonnaing in the penny pictorials for a while. But beware, you know what comes to over-pictorialised ladies. Didn't one fall through a sky-light? Don't Madonna for the Sunday press.

So I expect you are on your legs again, cast forth from the hallucinary Patmos of your bed. Simon! Simon! It has a Judaic sound. Better make a dart for the foam again, Aphrodite is better than any Judith, or than any Mary. *Plus fière.* Loathsome Judaea.

What other news, save Simon? Are you richer? Are you glad to go back to Sussex Place? What is your husband doing? When I say richer, I merely mean "Bradburys." Are you preparing to sally forth into the *monde* as a sort of young matron? Pfui!! Ah, bad! What is the new line? You'll have to have a new line. *Mère de trois.* It's a bit of a quandary. Capitoline Juno? Ox-eyed Hera? *Ficherie! Mais toujours mère de trois. Super hanc Petram.* That's how it always is, nowadays. *Fate attenzione al sasso.* Mind the stone. *Cave Petram.*

---

8 Lady Cynthia's new baby.

No, I'm not angry with the world. I've got tired of being angry. I also want a new line. It's time the world began to amuse me. I insist on being amused.

I believe in a little while I shall be having a sort of success: in America. Better spend it in England. Time one had a bit of fun.

Frieda, who still insists on "feeling" her trials, gets very cross, or weeps, when the letters come from Germany. She has set her mind on going: and she can't go. Another quandary. Patience is justified of all her children......................
Frieda will get her passport: *quand nous avons changé tout cela.* But really I don't care a jot about changing it.

Beaumont*..........slowly filters through the poems. He must be nearing the end. Perhaps by Christmas he will actually spawn his production.

Martin Secker will bring out *Women in Love* in the spring. Probably it will come out this autumn in America.

When I lunched with ——————[1] he says, "Isn't it remarkable, how the poets are returning to Beauty!"—he was afraid to walk with me up the Mall afterwards, and ran away like a respectable rabbit. What I want to know is, was it my appearance, or my reputation, or his? *Bel Dio!*

Pleasant mild autumn, many mushrooms, smoke from cottage gardens, chilly evenings, etc.—*toujours perdrix*—no, not even that—*toujours lapin en casserole.*

When I am in town again—before long—I will call at Sussex Place, if I am duly invited. Frieda sends her love: emotional goods not rationed.

D. H. L.

---

* Cyril Beaumont, at present an authority on the ballet, then a bookseller and small publisher who issued Lawrence's *Bay* in November 1919. (H. T. M.)
[1] Unidentified.

To J. B. PINKER
                    Palazzo Ferraro, Capri, Italy, 27 Dec., 1919.
Dear Pinker,

We are here for a time—moving out of Europe before long, I hope.

I think there is not much point in our remaining bound to one another. You told me when we made our agreement that we might break it when either of us wished. I wish it should be broken now. What bit of work I have to place, I like to place myself. I am sure it isn't much worth to you.

Let me know, will you?

                                                    D. H. LAWRENCE.

To CATHERINE CARSWELL
                    Palazzo Ferraro, Capri, Naples, 4 Jan., 1920.
My dear Catherine,

I had your letter to-day—we have moved and moved in such a state of restlessness. I could not write letters. Picinisco was beautiful beyond words, but *so* primitive, and *so* cold, that I thought we should die. The mountains stood round in a ring, glittering white like devils. On the Saturday before Christmas it snowed all day long: so on Monday we did extricate ourselves: got up at 5.30, walked 5 miles to Atina, caught the post omnibus 10 miles drive to the only station, Cassino. We got to Naples, caught the Capri boat at 3.0 p.m. The sea rose as we left the bay—by 7.30 we came in to the shallow port of Capri, but the seas were running so high, the boats couldn't come out to take us off. Back we had to go, to be all night rolling on board, in the semi-shelter of Sorrento. The Italians *were* sick: oh, dear: luckily we managed to keep all right.

We have got an apartment—two beautiful rooms and a kitchen we share—160 francs a month—at the top of this old palazzo, which has a staircase like a prison, not a palace. It is

[165]

extremely beautiful—just on the very neck of the little town, on the very neck of the island: we can touch the queer bubbly *duomo,* almost, from our balcony: all the island life goes beneath us: and then away on the right, the sea, Ischia in the distance, and the Bay of Naples: on the left the wide open Mediterranean. In each case it is a short mile down to the sea—but steep down. The narcissus flowers still are many in the rocks, but passing: sweet they are, Greece. A few pink cistus-flowers too. It is warm, but rather stormy. We have had one fire one evening—for the rest, we aren't cold. Your plaid, however, is a valuable thing: and your little jersey a treasure for Frieda. They are just the things for Italy: to wrap oneself up indoors a bit. Naples—nice. There is a young and amusing Roumanian who fans his *fornello* so hard and seizes me to pour Socialism into me. It is pleasant and Bohemian. I wish you were both here: this is the life we could enjoy together.

We lunch or dine sometimes with —————— ——————,[2] and he is nice. But one feels the generations of actors behind him and can't be quite serious. What a queer thing the theatre is, in its influence. He seems quite rich, and does himself well, and walks a sort of æsthetic figure—"head of the realistic school of England, isn't he?" asks my Roumanian—walking in a pale blue suit to match his eyes, and a woman's large brown velour hat to match his hair. It was a sight on New Year's Eve, when we were down in Morgano's café—the centre of Capri, downstairs. F. and I sat with an old, old Dutchman and a nice man called Brooks, drinking a modest punch, and listening to the amazing bands which come in, with the Tree, on New Year's Eve: a weird, barbaric affair. The Anacapri lot intoned a ballad, utterly unintelligible, of about 38 verses, with the most amazing accompaniments. At about 11.0 came in —————— with *rich* Americans—rather drunk. The Tiberio band came — —————— —————— took the tree and bobbed it in the faces of the Ameri-

2 Throughout this passage Lawrence is referring to Compton Mackenzie. (H. T. M.)

cans, and looked like Christ before Pilate in the act. The
Tiberio boys, two of them, danced the Tarantella to the same
grunting music—a funny indecent pederastic sight it was (Don
will chase my spelling—I mean paederastic). At midnight the
——— crowd ordered champagne and tried to look wine and
womenish. But my God, it was an excruciating selfconscious
effort, a veritable Via Dolorosa for ———, who felt his stomach
going. Oh God, the wild rakishness of these young heroes! How
conscious they are of the Italian crowd in the background. They
never see the faint smile of the same crowd—such a smile.—A
glass of champagne is sent out to the old road-sweeper—*de
rigeuer* (can't spell). Meanwhile we sip our last drop of punch,
and are the Poor Relations at the other end of the table—
ignored—to our amusement. ——— is going to begin to-
morrow, at 10.30 precisely, "Rich Relatives." He thinks *Relatives,* as an offset to *Relations, so* good.

Well, I find I am nearly as spiteful as the rest of Capri. This
island is covered with a small brand of cosmopolitans—English,
American, Russian, German—everything. The English-speaking
crowd are the uttermost, uttermost limit for spiteful scandal.
My dear Catherine, London is a prayer-meeting in comparison.
We get it from Mary Cannan! Here we found her! And she is
one of the decentest people here on this island—brings us butter
and figs: butter costs 20 francs a kilo. But she is staying with an
arch-scandalmonger—wife of a local judge of some sort—he's
English. The stories Mary is told are *incredible.* We've got a
long way to go, such mere people as us. It would be an interesting document, to set down this scandal verbatim. Suetonius
would blush to his heels, and Tiberius would feel he's been a
flea-bite.

Now for your news: *good.* Of one thing I'm certain, and that
is, your novel is the best that Melrose or any of the rest of them
has had the chance of seeing. I wonder if I could review it anywhere? But there, I should do it no good. But it's coming out,

and that'll hearten you to another shot, especially as J. P. will be growing up. We'll carry the field yet, you see if we don't.

But about the £50—don't give it to us, you really need it more.

Though in the next breath, I must lament the dearness of Italy: butter 20 francs, wine 3 francs a litre the cheapest—sugar 8 francs a kilo, oil 7 or 8 francs a litre, carbone a franc for two kilos—a porter expects ten francs for bringing one's luggage from the sea—and so on. With the exchange at 50, it is just possible, and only just.

Still, you might come for Easter. How jolly it would be. You could have a room with us here, independent and splendid. Nourish the idea.

I liked Ellisina³ very much: glad Fanny⁴ is all right again, *hate* these shocks: hope Don is feeling happy. A million good wishes.

D. H. L.

To MARTIN SECKER
                    Palazzo Ferraro, Capri (Naples), 16 Jan., 1920.
Dear Secker,

I had your letter with the offer for *The Rainbow* and *Women in Love*—and I talked it over also with Mackenzie. I had written to Duckworth asking him if he would sell back my copyrights: he replied he could not see his way to sell them back, but was ready to make me an offer for the re-publication of *The Rainbow*. I wrote and asked him what offer he could make. There it stands.

With regard to your letter—I should never sell *The Rainbow* for £200. I'd rather go back to my old arrangement with Duckworth, of royalty and £50 advance: or even no advance. The fact that I have no money would never make me jump at a lump

3 Ellisina Santoro, cousin of Catherine Carswell. (H. T. M.)
4 Not identified.

sum. I have lived so long without money, that I know I can go
on living without money, and £200 is really nothing to a man
who has nothing. Moreover I believe in my books and in their
future, and don't really bother. *Vogue la galère*—she won't sink,
anyhow, of that I'm sure.

But apart from this: I should like to join with you: I should
like to be a part-publisher of my own work: I should like to be
one in a real guild. Mackenzie and I get on with one another:
also Brett Young.

I should like to be with you, because you really care about
books. The thought of our being partners all in Secker & Co.
pleases me, so long as we are really in sympathy, and so long as
we are all free souls.

Mackenzie suggested £200 for *The Rainbow,* £300 for
Women in Love, and £500 for the book which I am expecting—
it is in the post now—and which I will call provisionally *A
Mixed Marriage:*[4a] this total of £800 is to represent the sale of all
copyrights until your books prove a return of £1,000, after
which I am to resume my royalty of 20 per cent, the proceeds of
which are to pass into the firm of Secker & Co., until such time
as I shall have, say, £2,000 invested in the firm—after which
they are to be my own separate property. This, with minor
provisions, is Mackenzie's scheme. And this seems to me pretty
sound.

But I don't want you to imagine for an instant that I am
trying to force an issue, with Mackenzie's help. I don't want
anything that doesn't seem to you just and fair. But I want you
also to treat me justly and fairly. I hate tentative methods. I
do like plain outspokenness. I don't want to cadge anything.
Tell me exactly and flatly what you think. In an affair like this,
we have either to be a genuine *alliance,* a certain real accord
between us: or else we must keep entirely to the old, purely
commercial relationship, such as I had with Duckworth, and

4a Later *The Lost Girl.*

which I found always, with Duckworth, decent—or else we merely part.

Then, honestly, I think you are wrong about the title *Women in Love*. Everybody jumps at it, as an excellent title. *The Rainbow* and *Women in Love* are really an organic artistic whole. I cannot but think it would be well to issue them as *Women in Love,* Vol. I and Vol. II. *The Rainbow* must appear as a new book. Best give it a new title and make some few alterations. I should like to know what alterations you would suggest. As far as the legal proceedings of the suppression are concerned, Pinker could supply you with all information: so could that man—Thring, is it?—Secretary to the Authors' Society. I was given distinctly to understand that the magistrate's order destroyed only the existing edition: that any further edition would have to be proceeded against all over again, it could not be automatically suppressed. Best re-issue as a new book, with a new title, anyhow.—The magistrates proceeded on the reviews by James Douglas, in the *Star,* and one by Clement Shorter, I think in *Pall Mall.* The scene to which exception was *particularly* taken was the one where Anna dances naked, when she is with child. I don't think it's very important, anyhow sufficiently past.

The MS. which is now in the post, coming from Germany, has lain in Bavaria since early 1914. It is a novel, two-thirds finished—quite unlike my usual style—more eventual—I am very keen to see it. I thought if I finished it, it would be quite *unexceptionable,* as far as the censor is concerned, and you might publish it soon after *The Rainbow,* if you liked—or leave it till *Women in Love* is also done.

These are just suggestions. Tell me just what you think. Let us either agree sincerely, or remain merely commercial, or break off. I wish we could meet, pity you are so far.

Yrs.,

D. H. LAWRENCE.

Pinker replied that, if I really wished, he would let me go. I have written to say I want to go. So I am as good as free in this respect. I want to act for myself.

To AMY LOWELL[5]

Palazzo Ferraro, Capri, Feb. 13, 1920.

My dear Amy,

Today I have your letter, and cheque for thirteen hundred Lire. How very nice of you to think of us this New Year. But I wish I needn't take the money: it irks me a bit. Why can't I earn enough, I've done the work. After all, you know, it makes one angry to have to accept a sort of charity. Not from you, really, because you are an artist, and that is always a sort of partnership. But when Cannan[6] writes and tells me he has collected a few dollars—which, of course, I have not received— he wrote me to tell me he was collecting a few, but never wrote again. Cannan annoys me with his sort of penny-a-time attempt at benevolence, and the ridiculous things he says about me—and everybody else—in the American press. I am a sort of charity- boy of literature, apparently. One is denied one's just rights, and then insulted with charity. Pfui! to them all.—But I feel you and I have a sort of odd congenital understanding, so that it hardly irks me to take these Liras from you, only a little it ties me up. However, you must keep one's trust in a few people, and rest in the Lord.

I am extremely sorry you are not well, and must have an operation. Such a thought is most shattering. Hope to heaven it won't hurt much and will make you right.—Blackwell is a good publisher for getting at the young life in England. He's much more in touch with the future, than old Macmillan.

Secker has done another edition of my *New Poems,* properly

---

[5] From *The Intelligent Heart.* Salutation and subscription taken from *Amy Lowell* where this letter appears in a somewhat cut version.
[6] Gilbert Cannan, novelist.

bound now. I shall have him send you a copy. I asked Beaumont to send you a copy of a tiny book of mine "Bay," which he has hand-printed. He is not very responsible—tell me if you have received it.

No, don't go to England now, it is so depressing and uneasy and unpleasant in its temper. Even Italy isn't what it was, a cheerful insouciant land. The insouciance has gone. But still, I like the Italians deeply; and the sun shines, the rocks glimmer, the sea is unfolded like fresh petals. I am better here than in England.—Things are expensive, and not too abundant. But one lives for the same amount, about, as in England: and freer to move in the air and over the water one is, all the while. Southwards the old coast glimmers its rocks, far beyond the Siren Isles. It is very Greek—Ulysses['] ship left the last track in the waves. Impossible for Dreadnoughts to tread this unchangeable morning-delicate sea.

Frieda came down to Florence from Germany: a bit thinner and wiser for her visit. Things are wretchedly bad there. I must have food sent all the time to F's mother from England, and for the children—there absolutely isn't enough to eat.

We have got two beautiful rooms here on the top of this old palace, in the very centre of Capri, with the sea on both hands. Compton Mackenzie is here—a man one can trust and like, which—as far as the first goes—is more than one can say of Cannan.—But Capri is a bit small, to live on. Perhaps I shall go to the mainland—perhaps not. Anyway this address will always find me. I have just begun a new novel.

I feel we shall see you in Italy. I do hope you will be better. Is Mrs. Russell with you always? A thousand greetings from both.

D. H. LAWRENCE.

Fontana Vecchia, Taormina, Sicilia.

To CURTIS BROWN

4th April, 1921.

Dear Curtis Brown,

Will you undertake to place my stuff? And will you let me know your terms? If so, make it for not more than five years, so that we needn't be tied to one another.

There are three pieces of MS. in hand.

1. *Birds, Beasts and Flowers.* Of these two went to Squire of *The Mercury;* viz., *Hibiscus and Salvia Flowers* and *Purple Anemones.* These two poems and *The Ass,* are in handwriting. If Barbara Low has not done so, please send copies (typed) of these three poems to Robert Mountsier. No one has seen any of these poems, save Squire's two.

2. *Mr. Noon (Part I).* Try and serialise this, and for serial purposes cut as much as you like. Secker's agreement claims the book. I enclose the said agreement: it is for five books, but *Rainbow* makes one of the five, and *Lost Girl* another: leaves three, of which here two.

3. *Diary of a Trip to Sardinia* (provisional title). Am sending photographs of first part—hope to send other photographs shortly of Sardinia itself. Try and sell this book to periodicals— or part of it. And I don't care how much the editors cut it.

But before you do anything definite *at all* please communicate with

Robert Mountsier,
417, West 118 Street,
New York City.

He has all my stuff in hand over there, trying to unravel a beautiful tangle of publishers and agreements and Pinker. Please work absolutely in unison with Mountsier.

I wish I'd come to you ten years back; you wrote me just too late. But now, don't tie me too tight—I get restive.

Am leaving Taormina on Saturday—wandering. But write

c/o Thomas Cook, Piazza delle Terme, Rome.

I enclose the Oxford Press agreement. I have received six presentation copies of the book, but have no idea what they are doing, especially as regards America. American rights are mine.

Shall I turn over to you all the back agreements? Very little remains to Pinker. Or shall we only go on with what lies ahead? Let us consider.

Luck to us.

D. H. LAWRENCE.

To EARL BREWSTER[7]

Ludwig-Wilhelmstift, Baden-Baden, Germany.

Dear Brewster,

Your letter to-day—Sunday—and I'll answer smack off because I prefer to do things on the spur.

I Damn the Norwegian chap.

II We must meet before you go East.

III *Sons and Lovers* is supposed, technically, to have no construction. The world is full of technical fools.

IV You probably do know me better than I know you, because I don't know you—hardly at all. You Buddhistic people are dark birds, and hardly know yourselves what you build your nests of, I believe.

V What I mean by the eternal quality—and what you mean—I believe we should never make the two fit. But I agree quite about the not grasping; first because of thorns, then because it's so horrid (not sorrowful but enraging) to be grasped.

VI I here and now, finally and forever, give up knowing anything about love, or wanting to know. I believe it doesn't exist, save as a word: a sort of wailing phoenix

[7] From *D. H. Lawrence: Reminiscences and Correspondence.* The date of this letter is May 1921.

that is really the wind in the trees. In fact I here and now, finally and forever, leave off loving anything or everything or anybody. Basta la mossa!

VII   All right, let white include all colours, if you like. Only, white does *not* include all colours. It is only pure colourless light which includes all colours. And of even that I am doubtful. I doubt the exact sciences more than anything else—I don't know *anything* about Nirvana, and I never shall.

VIII   Does the admission of difference presuppose the possibility of superseding? When any life-creature has reached a certain—I don't mean that—I mean any vivid *being* can no more be superseded than life itself can be superseded. I consider the tiger is a *being,* a created being. If you kill all tigers still the tiger-soul continues. The mankind which kills the tiger assumes, willynilly, the tiger's nature and need of being. Just as white America assumes, inevitably and frighteningly, the Red Indian nature—little by little. But the point is I don't *want* the tiger superseded. Oh, may each she-tigress have seventy-seven whelps. And may they all grow in strength and shine in stripes like day and night, and may each one eat at least seventy miserable featherless human birds, and lick red chops of gusto after it. Leave me my tigers, leave me spangled leopards, leave me bright cobra snakes, and I wish I had poison fangs and talons as good. I *believe* in wrath and gnashing of teeth and crunching of coward's bones. I believe in fear and in pain and in oh, such a lot of sorrow. As for your white Nirvana, my boy: paint stripes on it, and see how it looks. I'll bet it has a tiger's hungry sides and buzzing, disagreeable tail. Only it's like Well's[7a] Invisible Man, it makes no show except when it's had its dinner.

7a Sic.

IX As for Mr. Hume: Ambition, avarice, self-love, vanity, friendship, generosity, public spirit: the *words* are all the same: the actuality is so different in each individual, as to make the statement feeble. You need only translate generosity into German or Russian, and you'll see that Mr. Hume knew nothing about it. As for Die liebe, Minne, l'amour, love, l'amore, Amor, and the two blessed Greek words which we pretend stand for love: look at 'em. But I believe there is a certain life concord. But life expressions are so different, it is idiocy to count them like cash. Give me differences.

X Nirvana-ing is surely a state of continuing as you are. But I know nothing about it. Rather hate it.

XI I'll go Eastward when the West pays me enough for my books to carry me there.

XII Tell Mrs. X* yes, to write to me, and please to invite us to look at the convent.** I have a mind to—or a nose to sniff out a Franciscan rat.

XIII I wish they had been tears.

D. H. LAWRENCE.

On the same paper is the following letter, fenced off with these words: "PRIVATE GROUNDS TRESPASSERS PROSECUTED by order Jas Buddh."

Dear Mrs. Brewster,

All right, write your *own* first name as if you weren't trying to hide it: succeeding in hiding it, too. Might as well be Absalom for all I make of it.[1]

Guess old Z[2] does it for stinginess. As for me this is the only sheet of paper you'll get out of me this time.

* Unidentified. In publishing their Lawrence letters, the Brewsters used irrelevant initials for most of the proper names.
** In Assisi.
[1] Mrs. Brewster's first name was Achsah.
[2] Unidentified.

Who on earth is the third lovable woman in *Sons and Lovers?*
As for Miriam, I dreamed of her two nights ago. But the word
love has for me gone pop: there isn't anything any more. Not
tragically of course: but just so: quite a new sort of feeling.

M.G.[3] is an ass who would say a pudding on a dish looked
like Buddha, if only you crossed the spoon and fork in front to
look like two cross-legs. Your St. Francis needs a good *schiaffo,*
and a pint of Chianti. Never ate enough.

I am finishing Aaron.[4] And you won't like it *at all.* Instead of
bringing him nearer to heaven, in leaps and bounds, he's mis-
behaving and putting ten fingers to his nose at everything.
Damn heaven. Damn holiness. Damn Nirvana. Damn *it all.*

What a mercy your daughter[5] doesn't shed a woeful tear at
mention of men. I suppose I buddhistically removed her beyond
sorrow: though a Punch and Judy show might have been better.

Epaphroditus is good. Wish I had my Greek lexicon. What is
Epaphros?

I don't want that tranquillity of heart which springs from
within. Too much at my own expense. I want a bit of a good
time—can't sit supping forever at these inside Baden-Baden
cure-springs.

Weather-report. My wife and I are in a little inn about 3
miles from Baden—among the hills, just on the edge of the
Black Forest—the deep, deep green meadows, with bell flowers
and big daisies, and the old black and white village scattered
amongst, and amongst trees; the reddish castle ruin sticking
above, out of green maple and beeches: the opening walnut-
trees beside the loop of the road: the great woods on the final
hills, many-pointed fir-woods, and edges of flaming beech: the
hills just steeply ceasing, and the wide Rhine-plain beyond, seen
from the window, with a loop of river: the nice little northern,

---

3 Identified by Mr. Brewster only as someone who had said that Mrs. Brewster's painting of St. Francis looked like Lawrence.
4 *Aaron's Rod.*
5 Harwood. In May 1921 she was 8 years old.

barefoot children playing, playing so childlike, not Italian adult-infant; the yellow oxen in the long wagons of grass: everybody nice but rather spent, rather life-empty: and all so different from before the war: and so different from Taormina. Cheap too—35 marks a day each—70 marks for us two: about 6/–. Good food—good German sausages and beer, *good* Rhine wine, *good* whipped cream, and the first strawberries. No sausageless Nirvana: no! no! Get a new *cook*. (Enquire of Anna DiChiara.[6])

We must contrive to meet. Is that convent habitable? Couldn't we turn it into a den of thieves, and pitch a camp there? I mean the Assisi, not the Burmese. I may have to come to Italy—Florence—in the summer, to do a book for the Medici Society. Not sure. But I need not stay long in Florence. Are you staying all summer in Capri? We'll be wandering South in September, if we don't meet anywhere else, might meet then. But you sail in October!! Send a line of sound practical plotting.

> DAVID (not Daniel) HERBERT
> (i.e. Bright Lord), LAWRENCE.

Ah, the flesh-pots! We had *asparagus* (German the best in the world), *strawberries* and *Rhine wine* and *Roast Pork* for dinner. WHAT did you have?

To NELLY MORRISON

32, Via dei Bardi, Firenze, 1 Sept., 1921.

Dear Nelly Morrison,

I had your letter yesterday. Everything goes well with us: we like your flat more every day: have all our meals on the terrace, when the wind isn't too strong. I find it lovely and cool, and am writing a story about Venice. Later I want to write one about Florence and this house: modern, of course.

---

[6] The di Chiaras were friends in Capri. Mrs. di Chiara was an American.

Is Venice very lovely just now? Writing about it makes me realise how beautiful it is.

Peggy[7] is pretty well, I think. She's not going to die of a broken heart, whatever else she dies of. So don't flatter yourself. Yesterday Tina[8] gave her a bath on the terrace here, in the red trough. She trembled and looked pathetic, but loved all the notice taken of her.

Poor Tina has trouble with her teeth, bad inflammation of the lower gums: looks a wretch and feels it, but is rather better now, after certain lotions, etc., from the dentist.

I tried Casanova, but he smells. One can be immoral if one likes, but one must not be a creeping, itching, fingering, inferior being, led on chiefly by a dirty sniffing kind of curiosity, without pride or clearness of soul. For me, a man must have pride, good natural inward pride. Without that, cleverness only stinks. But I will treat the battered volumes as gingerly as such *crotte* deserves.

Two days ago, Mrs. Gilbert Cannan arrived from France. She is an old friend. She was here when Tina was bathing Peggy, and drying the same Peggy in the shut-up bedroom— next the salotta here: Mrs. Cannan immediately began pining to come and stay in it for a week or two. She made me promise to write and ask you if you would let it to her for three weeks or a month, and she would engage to vacate it at once if you should need it or want it. She would have her meals with us, but I am not sure if I want a permanent guest. But do as you wish.

The plants are watered very regularly, and seem quite well. Juta[9] is due to arrive to-morrow in Florence.

Greet Gino,[10] and be greeted yourself by us both.

Yrs.,

D. H. LAWRENCE.

7 Probably Mrs. Morrison's dog, left in her flat.
8 Probably Mrs. Morrison's maid.
9 Jan Juta, painter, later illustrated Lawrence's *Sea and Sardinia*.
10 Unidentified.

To EARL BREWSTER[2]

Fontana Vecchia, Taormina, Sicilia.
Sabato 8 Ottobre 1921.

Dear Brewster,

I thought to have heard from you—but nothing. I wrote you the next morning after we were back. I forgot to send the Liras 100—and here it is. I believe it should be a few Liras more, but leave it at the hundred.

My post has brought me nothing nice: no, not one single nice word since I am back. But that doesn't alter things. I am determined to sail away before next March. Where to depends largely on where I can get a ship to. I will hear what you have to say of Ceylon.

My plan is, ultimately, to get a little farm somewhere by myself, in Mexico, New Mexico, Rocky Mountains, or British Columbia. The desire to be away from the body of mankind—to be a bit of a hermit—is paramount. In the old world, even of Buddha, I have no deep hope. But I would like to see it, too, and speak with it.

I would like you and Achsah Brewster and the child to settle somewhere near. I would rather dig a little, and tend a few fruit-trees with you, than meditate with you. I would rather we did a bit of quite manual work together—and spent our days in our own solitude and labour.

There I think that's the ultimate of what I want. Tell me how you finally feel.

D. H. LAWRENCE.

I would much rather approach America from the Pacific than from the Atlantic.

I sent you *Psychoanalysis and the Unconscious*. If you were near enough I would like you to read the MS. of its sequel[2a]—I have it now.

---

2 From *D. H. Lawrence: Reminiscences and Correspondence.*
2a *Fantasia of the Unconscious.*

To EARL BREWSTER[3]

Fontana Vecchia, Taormina, Sicilia.
Tuesday.

Dear Brewster,

Well, you are packed up, apparently, and on your way. I had your second letter just this minute—also Mrs. Brewster's. Santa Lucia seems quite a long stride, really, if Quattro Venti is *left* behind. Ach Gott, that first stride of clearing out of one's house genuinely *costs*.

Here we sit: the rain has begun: and I feel rather gloomy. Europe is my own continent, so I feel bad about it. I feel as if it was dying under my eyes. Maybe it isn't at all: but I get the feeling just the same, you see. It's almost precisely as if somebody were dying: one's mother for example. One's unconscious simply bristles and listens for death. That is how Taormina, Italy, all affects me since summer. So when I leave Europe, I feel I want to go for ever.

As a good omen, I was that very instant dreaming in my siesta dream that you had written from *Ceylon* and that it was lovely there—when the banging of the express boy on my door woke me. And I was just in some odd way seeing Ceylon myself. Let's hope we'll tie the broken end of the dream to reality.

I'll write to you in Ceylon. I wish you had had time to read my *Fantasia of the Unconscious* before you went. I've just finished correcting it. Write to me quickly from Ceylon, and tell me first impressions, and if one could live there cheaply enough. I am sure upper Ceylon is lovely. I am rather inclined to think, myself, that people matter more than place. But the east seems to me the world to meditate in, Europe the world to feel in. America the world to act in.

But I don't feel very sure about anything.

I will write quite often.

D. H. LAWRENCE.

[3] From *D. H. Lawrence: Reminiscences and Correspondence.* The date of this letter is probably October 1921.

To MABEL STERNE[4]

Fontana Vecchia, Taormina, Sicilia.
5th November, 1921.

Dear Mabel Dodge Sterne,

I had your letter this afternoon and read it going down Corso: and smelt the Indian scent, and nibbled the medicine: the last being like licorice root, the scent being a wistful dried herb.[5]

Truly, the q-b[6] and I would like to come to Taos—there are no little bees. I think it is quite feasible. I think I have enough dollars in America to get us there. Are you practical enough to tell me how much it would cost, per month, for the q-b and myself to keep house in Taos? We are *very* practical, do all our own work, even the washing, cooking, floor-cleaning and everything here in Taormina: because I loathe servants creeping around. They poison the atmosphere. So I prefer to wash my own shirt, etc. And I *like* doing things.—Secondly, is there a colony of rather dreadful sub-arty people?—But even if there is, it couldn't be worse than Florence.—Thirdly, are your Indians dying out, and is it rather sad?—Fourthly, what do the sound, *prosperous* Americans do in your region?—Fifthly, how does one get there? What is the nearest port? I might get a cargo boat to bring us, from Palermo.

I believe I've heard of Taos, and even seen pictures of it, photographs—at Leo Stein's[7] house in Settignano. Have I? And are you a relative of the Maurice Sterne,[8] artist, who was at Anticoli this summer? I've only heard of him.

4 From *Lorenzo in Taos.*

5 In order to draw Lawrence to Taos, Mrs. Sterne had included with her invitation several Indian herbs whose magical powers she hoped would supplement her own.

6 The q-b (queen bee) was Frieda Lawrence who was so referred to throughout *Sea and Sardinia.*

7 Artist, brother of Gertrude Stein.

8 Maurice Sterne was Mabel Sterne's third husband. Even after Mrs. Sterne married Tony Luhan, her fourth husband, the letters in this volume appear as addressed to Mabel Sterne.

I believe what you say—one must somehow bring together the two ends of humanity, our own thin end, and the last dark strand from the previous, pre-white era. I verily believe that. Is Taos the place?

I have already written the second book to Psychoanalysis and the Unconscious, and posted the MS. to Seltzer—called provisionally, *Fantasia of the Unconscious*. I am satisfied with it for what it is. But it is the third book, which I have still to write, and which I can't write yet, not till I have crossed another border, it is this that will really matter. To me, I mean. I feel hopeless about the public. Not that I care about them. I want to live my life, and say my say, and the public can die its own death in its own way, just as it likes.

I think we may leave here in January or February. I think we will come to Taos. Write me what advice or instructions you think necessary, by return. I should have your letter by the new year.

I want to leave Europe. I want to take the next step. Shall it be Taos?—I like the *word*. It's a bit like Taormina.

D. H. LAWRENCE.

We could sail from any Italian port, or even from Malta. Do you know anything about ships from New Orleans or Galveston or anywhere near? I should really like to miss New York, for the first shot. If you should find it worth while to cable I'll pay when I arrive—or send cheque.—I would prefer to sail in January—don't know why.—Are there any trees? Is there any water?—stream, river, lake?—How far are you from El Paso or from Santa Fe. I don't see Taos on the map.

D. H. L.

If possible I would not go to New York: perhaps Galveston, Texas, or Los Angeles. Please say.

D. H. L.

Please don't tell anybody that we think of coming to Taos. Shall we bring any household things?—sheets, towels, etc.? How warm must the clothing be? How cold, and how hot is Taos?

The man who does most things for me is Robert Mountsier, 417 West 118 Street, New York. He might write you.

To EDWARD GARNETT

> *Fontana Vecchia, Taormina, Sicilia.*
> *10 Nov. 1921.*

Dear Garnett,

Thank you for the MS. of the story, which came to-day. I hope it was not a nuisance to you to send it.

No, I won't read *Homer*, my atom of Greek is too infinitesimal. But if you want to read *Homer*, I'll send him you. Somebody made me a gift of him. And then, if you want to read *Homer*, why, you needn't make the mistake of reading me.

No, my dear Garnett, you are an old critic and I shall always like you, but you are also a tiresome old pontiff and I shan't listen to a word you say, but shall go my own way to the dogs and bitches, just as heretofore. So there.

I ordered *Women in Love* for you from Secker. If he doesn't send it you, go to 5, John St. and kill him at once. When you get it, if you get it, and when you read it, if you read it, don't for a moment imagine you are wrestling with the *Iliad*. Just remember that it is your young friend so-and-so, wipe away all your Homeric illusions, and bear nobly on.

It is lovely here, and the morning landscape is just like Homer. But only the landscape. Not man. I hope you *will* come one day.

If it is quite easy for you to find out, tell me what translations of the Sicilian Giovanni Verga have appeared in English. His two chief novels are *I Malavoglia* and *Mastro don Gesualdo*. Then the short sketches, the volumes, are *Cavalleria Rusticana* and *Novelle Rusticane* and *Vagabondaggio* and another. He is *extraordinarily* good—peasant—quite modern—Homeric—and it would need somebody who could absolutely handle English in the dialect, to translate him. He would be most awfully difficult to translate. That is what tempts me: though it is rather a waste of time, and probably I shall never do it. Though if I don't, I doubt if anyone else will—adequately, at least.

I am glad Bunny is set up all right with a wife. Of course you'd *say* she was Irish even if she was a nigger as black as soot with lips like life-belts. But I'm sure she's nice, Irish or not. I haven't heard from him, so I can't send him two antimacassars or a set of toilet-tidies until I do. Of course he may have turned over a new leaf and started, like *John Bull,* to disapprove of me. I hope not, it is so unoriginal.

I will send back the *Grenzen der Seele.*

Tell me if you come across any more MS.

Secker is due to have all my next three books, but he may prefer to have novels.

Greet Mrs. Garnett—and I hope everything is lovely at the Cearne. Here the roses are just rushing into bloom, in masses, now the rain has come. But to-day is suddenly cold, and it has snowed on Etna and on Calabria.

> *Saluti,*
> D. H. LAWRENCE.

To DONALD CARSWELL

> *Fontana Vecchia, Taormina, Sicilia.*
> *15 Novem., 1921.*

Dear Don,

Many thanks for your letter: also to Catherine for hers. About the trews,[9] that is all I want to know. Very good. I've done the story and can just correct it where it needs.

---

9 Trousers. Lawrence was writing "The Captain's Doll" and had inquired of Carswell about the trousers worn by the Scots regiments. (H. T. M.)

Am glad you're going to earn money. What has Speyer[1] done to forfeit his nationality?—or to make them say so?

I hear the weather is cold and awful in England. Here it has had a sharp cold touch. But now scirocco in hot billows of wet and clinging mist—and rain. Damn scirocco.

We've got no news except that a woman called Mabel Dodge Sterne writes from Taos, New Mexico, saying we can have a furnished adobe house there, for ourselves, and all we want, if we'll only go. It seems Taos is on a mountain—7,000 feet up— and 23 miles from a railway—and has a tribe of 600 free Indians who she says are interesting, sun-worshippers, rain-makers, and unspoiled. It sounds rather fun. I believe there's a little bunch of American artists there, though. But that might make it easier just to live. Fun it would be if one could get a merchant ship to New Orleans or Galveston, Texas, and miss that awful New York altogether, don't you think? Tell me if you know anything about such a place as Taos.—Of course I haven't settled anything—and we have talked so often of a move, and never made it.—But don't tell anybody else, will you?

I am expecting every day *Sea and Sardinia*—the slight Sardinian travel book, from New York. It has got Juta's coloured illustration. As soon as I get copies I'll send you and Cath one. Also Seltzer is bringing out *Tortoises,* poems, as a chap-book, this month. I'll send that too when I get it. I wanted to send Cath the *Adolf:* the Rabbit Sketch: but have lost MS. and printed copy and everything. How the devil I've managed it I don't know. Shall have to write to New York for a copy of the *Dial,* where it appeared. Ask Catherine another thing. Seltzer wanted to bring out the poem, *Apostolic Beasts,* as a chap-book too. (I know it should be Evangelic or Apocalyptic.) And he wanted, if so, to have a cover design representing the four

1 Sir Edgar Speyer, German-born banker, husband of Leonora Speyer, musician and poet. During the war, Sir Edgar's loyalty to Britain had been questioned; in December 1921 his naturalization and that of his daughters was revoked.

beasts of the Evangelists—from the Apocalypse—Man, Lion, Bull, and Eagle.—In mediaeval Missals and Books of Hours and such, sometimes one comes across fascinating diagrams of the four beasts. If ever you see one, tell me where and if it would reproduce for a cover design.

Everybody hated *Aaron's Rod*—even Frieda. But I just had a cable from Seltzer that he thinks it wonderful. Maybe it is just a publisher's pat. Anyhow it is better than a smack in the eye, such as one gets from England for everything—as Cath for her *Camomile*. If only she'd called it *Rose-hearted Camellia*, they'd have supped it up. Pah! *canaille. Canaille, canaglia, Schweinhunderei!*

The post is very bad here. One train fell in a river in Calabria, and all post and all luggage lost irretrievably: stolen, of course. Now the Fascisti and Communisti are at it in Rome. The Catholic Church is a deep one. It is trying to form a Catholic world league, *political,* and taking more the Communistic line. It is working hard in Germany and Austria and here—and in France—and also America. It may turn out a big thing. I shouldn't wonder if before very long they effected a mild sort of revolution here, and turned out the King. It would be a clergy-industrial-socialist move—industrialists and clergy to rule in name of the people. Smart dodge, I think. If the exchange falls again they'll effect it. Then they'll ally with Germany and Austria and probably France, and make a European ring excluding England. That seems to be the idea.

Hope your ship is sailing nicely, and J. P.[2] and all flourishing.

D. H. LAWRENCE.

There are clouds of all sorts of new birds in the garden, suddenly come south. And the storks are passing in the night, whewing softly and murmuring as they go overhead.

2 The Carswells' baby, John Patrick.

To EARL BREWSTER[3]

Fontana Vecchia, Taormina, Sicilia.
18 Jan. 1922.

Dear Brewster,

Your letter of 16 December just came. And suddenly, for the first time, I suddenly feel you may be right and I wrong: that I am kicking against the pricks. I have misinterpreted "Life is sorrow." That is a first truth, not a last truth. And one must accept it as one's first truth, and develop from that. I verily believe it.

The groundwork of life is sorrow. But that once established, one can start to build. And until that is established one can build nothing: no life of any sort. I begin to agree. I took it one must *finish* with the fact that *Life is sorrow*. Now again I realize that one must get there, and having arrived, then begin to live.

Good then: as a basis, *Life is sorrow*. But beyond that one can smile and go on.

Only—only—I somehow have an imperative need to fight. I suppose it depends *how* one fights.

No, I believe you are right. Probably there, east, is the *source:* and America is the extreme periphery. Oh God, must one go to the extreme limit, then to come back?

I only know it seems so much *easier,* more peaceful to come east. But then peace, peace! I am so mistrustful of it: so much afraid that it means a sort of weakness and giving in. Yet I believe you're right. The very word you say, that Ceylon is *heavy,* makes me think you are right.

And the fact that I have felt so *spiteful* against Buddha makes me feel I was unsure all the time, and kicking against the pricks.

We have made all arrangements to go to Taos, New Mexico. But we have booked no passage. Shall I come to Ceylon? Dio

3 From *D. H. Lawrence: Reminiscences and Correspondence.*

mio, I am so ridiculous, wavering between east and west.

I believe I shall not go to America.

What is the good after all of going to where everything is just *unlearnt* and confused to the utmost. Perhaps it is true, Buddhism is true realism, *things as they are.* And America is utterly *things as they are not.* But the future—where is that? Must one go through the utter unreality of America: or keep a continuity? I'd better begin to make sure.

Later: Well now, I'm writing at once about ships to Colombo. I shall cable to you if we are actually coming, when we book passages. I hope to sail next month.

So—arrivederci.

D. H. LAWRENCE.

To MABEL STERNE[4]

Fontana Vecchia, Taormina, Sicily.

27 Jan. 1922.

Dear Mabel Dodge Sterne,

Is it vile of us to put off Taos for the moment. But I have a Balaam's Ass in my belly which won't budge, when I turn my face west. I can't help it. It just stubbornly swerves away in me. I *will* come. But I detour. I am writing to book berths on the Osterley from Naples, Feby. 26th for Colombo, Ceylon. The address will be,

c/o E. H. Brewster, "Ardnaree," Lake View Estate, Kandy, Ceylon. But the telegraphic address just: Brewster, Ardnaree, Kandy. I feel it is my destiny to go east before coming west. Only to stay a short time: perhaps a year. But to get quite calm and sure and still and strong. I feel America is so *unreligious*: it's a bad word: and that it is on the brink of a change, but the change isn't quite ready yet, so I daren't come. And I feel you yourself are *harried* out there. Come and join us in Ceylon —as soon as you can—and then after, let us go together to Taos.

4 From *Lorenzo in Taos.*

I had your letter of New Year's Day. I sent you *Tortoises.* I will come to the Indians, yes. But only via the East. There is something will not let me sail west for America.

You want to send Brill[5] to hell, and all the analytic therapeutic lot. And I don't like Stein,[6] a nasty, nosy, corrupt Jew. Voilà! Time we got clear of all that stuff.

No, *never* adapt yourself. Kick Brill in the guts if he tries to come it over you. Kick all America in the guts: they need it. Foul enough, with their overriding of life. But when the hand has fallen on them a bit heavier, they will change. Only wait. But meanwhile withdraw for a little peace: a breathing space.

No, spit on every neurotic, and wipe your feet on his face if he tries to drag you down to him.... All that "arty" and "literary" crew, I know them.......................My blood turns to gall: I want to go and have it sweetened a bit: away from them all, in the old, old east. Later we'll tackle 'em.

Come to Ceylon. Come at once—via San Francisco and China—and we'll prepare ourselves for the later Onslaught on to that Land of Promise of yours,

Benedicite,

D. H. LAWRENCE.

To BARONIN VON RICHTHOFEN[7]

R.M.S. "Osterley," Tuesday, 7 March.

Arabian Sea.

Dear Mother-in-Law,

Perhaps I can post this letter at Aden this evening, but we do not stop. We have come so far and so lovely. We stopped three hours in Port Said, and it was quite like the Thousand

5 Dr. A. A. Brill, one of the pioneer psychoanalysts in America, first translator of Freud.

6 Leo Stein, brother of Gertrude Stein.

7 From *"Not I, But the Wind . . ."* as translated there from the German. The date of this letter is March 7, 1922.

and One Nights. It was 9 o'clock in the morning, and the ladies of Port Said were all abroad shopping. Little black waddling heaps of black crêpe and two houri eyes between veil and mantle. Comic is the little peg that stands above the nose and keeps veil and headcloth together. There came a charabanc with twenty black women parcels. Then one of the women threw back her veil and spat at us because we are ugly Christians. But you still see everything—beggars, water carriers, the scribe who sits with his little table, and writes letters, the old one who reads the Koran, the men who smoke their "chibouks" in the open café and on the pavement—and what people! Beautiful Turks, Negroes, Greeks, Levantines, Fellaheen, three Bedouins out of the desert like animals, Arabs, wonderful. We have taken coal on board, and then at midday off again into the Suez Canal, and that is very interesting. The Canal is eighty-eight miles long, and you can only travel five miles an hour. There you sit on this great ship and you feel really on land, slowly travelling on a still land ship. The shores are quite near, you can surely throw an orange at the Arabs that work on the shores. Then you see beautifully, wonderfully, the Sahara Wüste, or desert—which do you say? The waterway goes narrow and alone through red-yellow sands. From time to time Arabs with camels work on the shores and keep on shouting "Hallo, Hallo" when the big ship passes so slowly. In the distance little sharp sand hills so red and pink-gold and sharp and the horizon sharp like a knife edge so clear. Then a few lonely palms, lonely and lost in the strong light, small, like people that have not grown very tall.

Then again only sand, gold-pink and sharp little sand hills, so sharp and defined and clear, not like reality but a dream. Solemn evening came, and we so still, one thought we did not seem to move any more. Seagulls flew about like a sand-storm, and a great black bird of prey alone and cruel, so black between thousands of white screaming, quick-flying sea birds. Then we came to the Dead Sea, flat seas that extend very far, and slowly the sun sank behind the desert with marvellous colours, and as the sun had set, then such a sky like a sword burning green and pink. Beautiful it was, I have never seen anything so super-human. One felt near to the doors of the old Paradise, I do not know how, but something only half human, something of a heaven with grey-browed, overbearing and cruel angels. The palm trees looked so little the angels should be much bigger and every one with a sword. Yes, it is a frontier country.

Next morning we were in the Red Sea. There stands Mount Sinai, red like old dried blood, naked like a knife and so sharp, so unnaturally sharp, like a dagger that has been dipped in blood and has dried long ago and is a bit rusty and is always there like something dreadful between man and his lost Para-dise. All is Semitic and cruel, naked, sharp. No tree, no leaf, no life: the murderous will and the iron of the idea and ideal—iron will and ideal. So they stand, these dreadful shores of this Red Sea that is hot like an oven without air. It is a strange exit through this Red Sea—bitter. Behind lie finally Jerusalem, Greece, Rome and Europe, fulfilled and past—a great dreadful dream. It began with Jews and with Jews it ends. You should see Sinai, then you could know it. The ideal has been wicked against men and Jehovah is father of the ideal and Zeus and Jupiter and Christ are only sons. And God be praised Sinai and the Red Sea are past and consummated.

Yesterday morning we came through the Straits of Bab-el-Mandeb, again into the open. I am so glad that we came this way. Yesterday we always saw land—Arabia naked and desert but not so red and sharp and like dried blood. Today we see no land but later on we shall pass Cape Socotra. This ship has gained fifteen hours. We are fifteen hours before time. Perhaps we arrive in Colombo on Sunday evening instead of Monday. It is very warm, but there is always air. The sea is covered with little white sea-horses, but the ship is still and sure. We have not had one single bad moment. All here on board so friendly and so good and comfortable. I work on the translation of

"Maestro Don Gesualdo" and I let my inkpot fall on the deck. The "Osterley" shall wear my black sign for ever. At 11 o'clock in the morning we do not get Bovril any more, but ice cream. The women all wear colourful summer frocks. In the evening we dance. We see now the little flying fish. They are all silver and they fly like butterflies, so wee. There are also little black dolphins that run about like little black pigs.

Benediciti,

D. H. LAWRENCE.

To MABEL STERNE[8]

Ardnaree, Kandy, Ceylon, 10 April, 1922.

Dear Mabel Dodge Sterne,

I have your two letters, but still no sign of book or necklace. Speriamo.

No, the East doesn't get me at all. Its boneless suavity, and the thick, choky feel of tropical forest, and the metallic sense of palms and the horrid noises of the birds and creatures, who hammer and clang and rattle and cackle and explode all the livelong day, and run little machines all the livelong night; and the scents that make me feel sick, the perpetual nauseous over-tone of cocoanut and cocoanut fibre and oil, the sort of tropical sweetness which to me suggests an undertang of blood, hot blood, and thin sweat: the undertaste of blood and sweat in the nauseous tropical fruits; the nasty faces and yellow robes of the Buddhist monks, the little vulgar dens of the temples: all this makes up Ceylon to me, and all this I cannot bear. Je m'en vais. Me ne vo'. I am going away. Moving on.

I have cabled for money from New York, and anxiously await the return cable so that I can book berths on the Orsova. on the 24th of this month, for West Australia: about 10 days from Colombo to Fremantle. The address there will be *c/o*

8 From *Lorenzo in Taos.*

Mrs. Jenkins,[9] Strawberry Hill, Perth, W. Australia. I don't know how long we shall stay there: but I shall take my steamer-ticket right to Sydney. I want to look at Australia, and try what it's like. If I don't care for it, then I can very easily come on. There are steamers every fortnight from Sydney to San Francisco; and San Francisco is not very far from Taos. And I shall be fulfilling my real desire to approach America from the West, over the Pacific. I hope I shall arrive in Taos with ten cents left in my pocket—ten cents left to me in the world, even. Knees of the Gods.

I still of course mistrust Taos very much, chiefly on account of the artists. I feel I never want to see an artist again while I live. The Indians, yes: if one is sure that they are not jeering at one. I find all dark people have a fixed desire to jeer at us: these people here—they jeer behind your back. But heavens, I don't see much in them to admire, either. They seem to be built round a gap, a hollow pit. In the middle of their eyes, instead of a man, a sort of bottomless pit. That's Buddhism too. Buddhism seems to me a very conceited, selfish show, a vulgar temple of serenity built over an empty hole in space. No, no, these little darkie people don't impress me, upon actual contact. The place, Ceylon, is a real prison to me, oppressive, and I want to get out. Two weeks to-day, pray God.

I wish I could come to America without meeting the awful "cultured" Americans with their limited self-righteous ideals and their mechanical love-motion and their bullying, detestable negative creed of liberty and democracy. I don't believe either in liberty or democracy. I believe in actual, sacred, inspired authority: divine right of natural kings: I believe in the divine right of natural aristocracy, the right, the sacred duty to wield undisputed authority. Naturally I find myself in diametric opposition to every American—and everybody else, besides

9 Mrs. A. L. Jenkins, a young Australian with whom the Lawrences had become acquainted aboard the *Osterley* between Naples and Colombo.

Americans—whom I come across. Nevertheless, there it stands. Well, so far so good.

Yrs.,

D. H. LAWRENCE.

To LADY CYNTHIA ASQUITH

R.M.S. "Orsova," to Fremantle.
We get there Thursday. Sunday, 30th April, 1922.

Here we are on a ship again—somewhere in a very big blue choppy sea with flying fishes sprinting out of the waves like winged drops, and a Catholic Spanish priest playing Chopin at the piano—very well—and the boat gently rolling.

I didn't like Ceylon—at least I liked looking at it—but not to live in. The East is not for me—the sensuous spiritual voluptuousness, the curious sensitiveness of the naked people, their black bottomless, hopeless eyes—and the heads of elephants and buffaloes poking out of primeval mud—the queer noise of tall metallic palm trees: *ach!*—altogether the tropics have something of the world before the flood—hot dark mud and the life inherent in it: makes me feel rather sick. But wonderful to have known. We saw the Prince of Wales[10] at the Kandy Perahera[10] a lonely little glum white fish he was sitting up there at the Temple of the Tooth with his chin on his hands gazing blankly down on all the swirl of the East, like a sort of Narcissus waiting to commit black suicide. The Perahera wonderful—midnight —huge elephants, great flares of coconut torches, princes like peg-tops swathed round and round with muslin—and then tom-toms and savage music and devil dances—phase after phase— and that lonely little white fish of a Prince[10] up aloft—and the black eyes and black bright sweating bodies of the naked dancers under the torches—and the clanging of great mud-born elephants roaring past—made an enormous impression on me—

[10] Omitted in the English edition of the Huxley *Letters*.

a glimpse into the world before the Flood. I can't quite get back into history. The soft, moist, elephantine prehistoric has sort of swamped in over my known world—and on one drifts.

But you said, not about India, but about us. No, I am not angry—no more of my tirades—the sea seems so big—and the world of elephants and buffaloes seems such a vast twilight—and by sheer or mere proximity with the dark Singhalese one feels the vastness of the blood stream, so dark and hot and from so far off. What does life in particular matter? Why should one care? One doesn't. Yet I don't believe in Buddha—hate him in fact—his rat-hole temples and his rat-hole religion. Better Jesus.

We are going to Australia—Heaven knows why: because it will be cooler, and the sea is wide. Ceylon steams heat and it isn't so much the heat as the chemical decomposition of one's blood by the ultra-violet rays of the sun. Don't know what we'll do in Australia—don't care. The world of idea may be all alike, but the world of physical feeling is very different—one suffers getting adjusted—but that is part of the adventure. I think Frieda feels like me, a bit dazed and indifferent—reckless —I break my heart over England when I am out here. Those natives are *back* of us—in the living sense *lower* than we are. But they're going to swarm over us and suffocate us. We are, have been for five centuries, the growing tip. Now we're going to fall. But you don't catch me going back on my whiteness and Englishness and myself. English in the teeth of all the world, even in the teeth of England. How England deliberately undermines England. You should see India. Between Lloyd George and Rufus Isaacs, etc., we are done—you asked me a year ago who won the war—we've all lost it. But why should we bother, since it's their own souls folk have lost. It is strange and fascinating to wander like Virgil in the shades.

Don't buy *Sea and Sardinia* because I shall have to pay Martin Secker for it. He must send it you. It will amuse you.

I'm glad the boys are well, and that Herbert Asquith likes

reading other people's books. That's better than having to read
one's own: and it's much better to be doing something than
nothing. I merely translate Giovanni Verga—Sicilian—*Mastro
don Gesualdo* and *Novelle Rusticane*—very good—to keep
myself occupied. If your husband would like to read them—
the translations—tell him to ask Curtis Brown.

F. greets you.

D. H. LAWRENCE.

To ELSE JAFFE[1]

"Wyewurk," Thirroul, South Coast, N.S.W.
Australia, 13 June 1922.

Dear Else,

I have been wanting to write to you. The Schweigermutter
says that Friedel[2] is ill with jaundice. I am so sorry, and do hope
it is better by now.

I often think of you here, and wonder what you would think
of this. We're in a very nice place: have got a delightful bunga-
low here about forty miles south of Sydney, right on the shore.
We live mostly with the sea—not much with the land—and
not at all with the people. I don't present any letters of introduction, we don't know a soul on this side of the continent: which
is almost a triumph in itself. For the first time in my life I feel
how lovely it is to know nobody in the whole country: and
nobody can come to the door, except the tradesmen who bring
the bread and meat and so on, and who are very unobtrusive.
One nice thing about these countries is that nobody asks questions. I suppose there have been too many questionable people
here in the past. But it's nice not to have to start explaining
oneself, as one does in Italy.

The people here are awfully nice, casually: thank heaven I
need go no further. The township is just a scatter of bungalows,

1 From *"Not I, But the Wind . . ."*
2 Friedrich Jaffe, Else's son, Frieda Lawrence's nephew.

mostly of wood with corrugated iron roofs, and with some quite good shops: "stores." It lies back from the sea. Nobody wants to be too near the sea here: only we are on the brink. About two miles inland there is a great long hill like a wall, facing the sea and running all down the coast. This is dark greyish with gum-trees, and it has little coal-mines worked into it. The men are mostly coal-miners, so I feel quite at home. The township itself—they never say village here—is all haphazard and new, the streets unpaved, the church built of wood. That part is pleasant—the newness. It feels so free. And though it is midwinter, and the shortest day next week, still every day is as our own summer, and the sun is almost as hot as our June. But the nights are cold.

Australia is a weird, big country. It feels so empty and untrodden. The minute the night begins to go down, even the towns, even Sydney, which is huge, begins to feel unreal, as if it were only a daytime imagination, and in the night it did not exist. That is a queer sensation: as if life here really had never *entered* in: as if it were just sprinkled over, and the land lay untouched. They are terribly afraid of the Japanese. Practically all Australians, and especially Sydney, feel that once there was a fall in England, so that the Powers could not interfere, Japan would at once walk in and occupy the place. They seriously believe this: say it is even the most obvious thing for Japan to do, as a business proposition. Of course Australia would never be able to defend herself. It is queer to find these bogies wherever one goes. But I suppose they *may* materialize.

Labour is very strong and very stupid. Everything except meat is exorbitantly expensive, many things twice as much as in England. And Australian apples are just as cheap in London as in Australia, and sometimes cheaper. It is all very irritating.

This is the most democratic place I have *ever* been in. And the more I see of democracy the more I dislike it. It just brings everything down to the mere vulgar level of wages and prices, electric light and water closets, and nothing else. You *never* knew anything so nothing, nichts, nullus, niente, as the life here. They have good wages, they wear smart boots, and the girls all have silk stockings; they fly around on ponies and in buggies—sort of low one-horse traps—and in motor-cars. They are always vaguely and meaninglessly on the go. And it all seems so empty, so *nothing,* it almost makes you sick. They are healthy, and to my thinking almost imbecile. That's what the life in a new country does to you: it makes you so material, so *outward,* that your real inner life and your inner self die out, and you clatter round like so many mechanical animals. It is very like the Wells story—the fantastic stories. I feel if I lived in Australia for ever I should never open my mouth once to say one word that meant anything. Yet they are very trustful and kind and quite competent in their jobs. There's no need to lock your doors, nobody will come and steal. All the outside life is so easy. But there it ends. There's nothing else. The best society in the country are the shopkeepers—nobody is any better than anybody else, and it really is democratic. But it all feels so slovenly, slipshod, rootless, and empty, it is like a kind of dream. Yet the weird, unawakened country is wonderful and if one could have a dozen people, perhaps, and a big piece of land of one's own—But there, one can't.

There is this for it, that here one doesn't feel the depression and the tension of Europe. Everything is happy-go-lucky, and one couldn't *fret* about anything if one tried. One just doesn't care. And they are all like that. *Au fond* they don't care a straw about anything: except just their little egos. Nothing *really* matters. But they let the *little* things matter sufficiently to keep the whole show going. In a way it's a relief—a relief from the moral and mental and nervous tension of Europe. But to say the least, it's surprising. I never felt such a foreigner to any people in all my life as I do to these. An absolute foreigner, and I haven't one single thing to say to them.

But I am busy doing a novel: with Australia for the setting: a queer show. It goes fairly quickly, so I hope to have it done by August. Then we shall sail via New Zealand and Tahiti for San Francisco, and probably spend the winter in Taos, New Mexico. That is what I think I want to do. Then the next spring come to Europe again. I feel I shall wander for the rest of my days. But I don't care.

I must say this new country has been a surprise to me. Flinders Petrie[3] says new countries are no younger than their parent country. But they are older, more empty, and more devoid of religion or anything that makes for "quality" in life.

I have got a copy of "Aaron's Rod" for you, but am not sure whether I may post it from here or not. Trade relations with Germany don't start till August.

Write to me care of Robert Mountsier, 417 West 118th Street, New York. I wish I had good news for you. Frieda sleeps after her bath.

D. H. LAWRENCE.

If a girl called Ruth Wheelock sends you a little note I gave her to introduce her to you, I think you'd like her. American, was in the consulate in Palermo—we knew her there and in Rome—both like her.

D. H. L.

She's not got any money, unless she earns some or her father gives her some.

To ELSE JAFFE[4]

Taos, New Mexico, U.S.A.
27 September 1922.

My dear Else,

Well, here we are in the Land of the Free and the Home of the Brave. But both freedom and bravery need defining. The Eros book came, and I shall read it as soon as we get breathing

---

3 Sir Flinders Petrie, noted archeologist.
4 From *"Not I, But the Wind . . ."*

space. Even though we are in the desert, in the sleeping land of the Mexican, we gasp on the breath of hurry.

We have got a very charming adobe house on the edge of the Indian Reservation—very smartly furnished with Indian village-made furniture and Mexican and Navajo rugs, and old European pottery.

Behind runs a brook—in front the desert, a level little plain all grey, white-grey sage brush, in yellow flower—and from this plain rise the first Rocky Mountains, heavy and solid. We are seven thousand feet above the sea—in a light, clear air.

The sun by day is hot, night is chilly. At the foot of the sacred Taos Mountain, three miles off, the Indians have their pueblo, like a pile of earth-coloured cube-boxes in a heap; two piles rather, one on one side the stream, one on the other. The stream waters the little valley, and they grow corn and maize, by irrigation. This pueblo owns four square miles of land. They are nearer the Aztec type of Indian—not like Apaches whom I motored last week to see—far over these high, sage-brush deserts and through canyons.

These Indians are soft-spoken, pleasant enough—the young ones come to dance to the drum—very funny and strange. They are Catholics but still keep the old religion, making the weather and shaping the year: all very secret and important to them. They are naturally secretive, and have their backs set against our form of civilization. Yet it rises against them. In the pueblo they have mowing machines and threshing machines, and American schools, and the young men no longer care so much for the sacred dances.

And after all, if we have to go ahead, we must ourselves go ahead. We can go back and pick up some threads—but these Indians are up against a dead wall, even more than we are: but a different wall.

Mabel Sterne is very nice to us—though I hate living on somebody else's property and accepting their kindnesses. She very much wants me to write about here. I don't know if I ever shall. Because though it is so open, so big, free, empty, and even aboriginal—still it has a sort of shutting-out quality, obstinate.

Everything in America goes by *will*. A great negative *will* seems to be turned against all spontaneous life—there seems to be no *feeling* at all—no genuine bowels of compassion and sympathy: all this gripped, iron, *benevolent* will, which in the end is diabolic. How can one write about it, save analytically?

Frieda, like you, always secretly hankered after America and its freedom: Its very freedom *not* to feel. But now she is just beginning to taste the iron ugliness of what it means, to live by will *against* spontaneous inner life, superimposing the individual, egoistic will over the real genuine sacred life. Of course I know you will jeer when I say there is any such thing as sacred spontaneous life, with its pride and its sacred power. I know you too believe in the screwed-up human will dominating life. But I don't. And that's why I think America is neither free nor brave, but a land of tight, iron-clanking little *wills,* everybody trying to put it over everybody else, and a land of men absolutely devoid of the real courage of trust, trust in life's sacred Spontaneity. They can't trust life until they can *control* it. So much for them—cowards! You can have the Land of the Free— as much as I know of it. In the spring I want to come back to Europe.

I send you ten pounds to spend for the children—since you suffer from the exchange. I hope in this little trifle you can profit by it. F. sends her love.

D. H. LAWRENCE.

P.S. If you want winter clothing, or underclothing, for the children or yourself or Alfred, write to my sister, Mrs. L. A. Clarke,⁵ Grosvenor Rd., Ripley near Derby—tell her just what you want, and she will send it. I shall pay her—I have told her you will write—so don't hesitate.

---

5 Ada Lawrence Clarke, wife of W. E. Clarke. The initials given here probably stand for Lettice Ada, the name she had been given at birth. (H. T. M.)

To WILLARD JOHNSON[6]

Taos, New Mexico, Early Autumn, 1922.

Chère Jeunesse,

Many thanks for the Hecht[7] book. I read it through. But I'm sorry, it didn't thrill me a bit, neither the pictures nor the text. It all seems so would-be. Think of the malice, the sheer malice of a Beardsley drawing, the wit and the venom of the mockery. These drawings are so completely without irony, so crass, so strained and so would-be. It isn't that they've got anything to reveal at all. That man's coition with a tree, for example. There's nothing in it but the author's attempt to be startling. Whereas if he wanted to be really wicked, he'd see that even a tree has its own daimon, and a man might lie with the daimon of a tree. Beardsley saw these things. But it takes imagination.

The same with the text. Really, Fantazius Mallare might mutilate himself, like a devotee of one of the early Christian sects, and hang his penis on his nose-end and a testicle under each ear, and definitely testify that way that he'd got such appendages, it wouldn't affect me. The word penis or testicle or vagina doesn't shock me. Why should it? Surely I am man enough to be able to think of my own organs with calm, even with indifference. It isn't the names of things that bother me; nor even ideas about them. I don't keep my passions, or reactions or even sensations *in my head*. They stay down where they belong. And really, Fantazius with his head full of copulation and committing *mental* fornication and sodomy every

6 In the English edition of the Huxley *Letters,* all names which refer to the book under discussion are deleted from this letter. In the American edition they appear as they do here.

7 Ben Hecht. The book was *Fantazius Mallare,* a privately-printed novel with lewd illustrations, in which Hecht satirized authors like Lawrence for their use of sex and psychoanalysis in fiction. With many deletions, some necessary, some merely provocative, this letter was printed, against Lawrence's wish, as a review in *The Laughing Horse,* a college magazine published at the University of California. After the publication of this letter, the magazine was banned by the University.

minute, is just as much a bore as any other tedious individual
with a dominant idea. One wants to say: "Ah, dirty little boy,
leave yourself alone."

Which after all isn't prudery. It's just because one has one's
own genuine sexual experiences, and all these fingerings and
naughty words and shocking little drawings only reveal the
state of mind of a man who has *never* had any sincere, vital
experience in sex; just as a little boy never has, and can't have
had; so he's itching with a feeble curiosity and self-induced
excitement. Which is principally tedious because it shows a
feeble, spunkless sort of state of things.

If Fantazius wasn't a frightened masturbator, he'd know that
sex-contact with another individual meant a whole meeting, a
contact between two alien natures, a grim *rencontre,* half battle
and half delight always, and a sense of renewal and deeper
being afterwards. Fantazius is too feeble and weak-kneed for
the fight, he runs away and chews his fingers and tries to look
important by posing as mad. Being too much of a wet-leg, as
they say in England, nakedly to enter into the battle and
embrace with woman.

The tragedy is, when you've got sex in your head, instead of
down where it belongs, and when you have to go on copulating
with your ears and your nose. It's such a confession of weakness, impotence. Poor Fantazius is sensually, if not technically,
impotent, and the book should have for its sub-title: *Relaxa-
tions for the Impotent.*

But there's the trouble; men have most of them got their sex
in their head nowadays, and nowhere else. They start all their
deeper reactions in their heads, and work themselves from the
top downwards, which of course brings disgust, because you're
only having yourself all the time, no matter what other individual you take as *machine-à-plaisir,* you're only taking yourself all
the time.

Why don't you *jeunesse* let all the pus of festering sex out of your heads, and try to act from the original centres? The old, dark religions understood. "God enters from below," said the Egyptians, and that's right. Why can't you darken your minds, and know that the great gods pulse in the dark, and enter you as darkness through the lower gates. Not through the head. Why don't you seek again the unknown and invisible gods who step sometimes into your arteries, and down the blood vessels to the phallos, to the vagina, and have strange meetings there? There are different dark gods, different passions. Hermes Ithyphallos has more than one road. The god of gods is unknowable, unutterable, but all the more terrible: and from the unutterable god step forth the mysteries of our prompting in different mysterious forms: call it Thoth, or Hermes, or Bacchus, or Horus, or Apollo: different promptings, different mysterious forms. But why don't you leave off your old white festerings in silence, and let a light fall over your mind and heal you? And turn again to the dark gods, which are the dark promptings and passion-motions inside you, and have a reverence for life.[8]

Fantazius seems to me such a poor, impoverished, self-conscious specimen. Why should one be self-conscious and impoverished when one is young and the dark gods are at the gates?

You'll understand if you want to. Otherwise it's your own affair.

D. H. LAWRENCE.

---

[8] This last phrase reads "and have reverence again, and be grateful for life" in the transcription of this letter in Witter Bynner's *Journey With Genius,* New York: John Day Company, 1951.

To BARONIN VON RICHTHOFEN*
Del Monte Ranch, Questa, New Mexico.
5 December, 1922.

My dear Mother-in-Law,

You see, we have flown again, but not far—only twenty-five kilometres, and here we are in an old log-house with five rooms, very primitive, on this big ranch. Behind, the Rocky Mountains, pines and snow-peaks; around us the hills—pine trees, cedars, greasewood, and a small grey bush of the desert. Below, the desert, great and flat like a shadowy lake, very wide. And in the distance more mountains, with small patches of snow—and the sunsets! Now you see the picture.

The Hawk family live five minutes from here, then no houses for four kilometres. Behind, no house for three hundred kilometres or more. Few people, an empty, very beautiful country.

We have hewn down a great balsam pine and cut it to pieces —like a quarry—the gold wood.

We have for companions two young Danes, painters:[1] they will go into a little three-room cabin nearby. Our nearest neighbour, Hawk, is a young man, thirty years old, has a hundred and fifty half-wild animals, a young wife, is nice, not rich.

You have asked about Mabel Dodge: American, rich, only child, from Buffalo on Lake Erie, bankers, forty-two years old, has had three husbands—one Evans (dead), one Dodge (divorced), and one Maurice Sterne (a Jew, Russian, painter, young, also divorced). Now she has an Indian, Tony, a stout chap. She has lived much in Europe—Paris, Nice, Florence— is a little famous in New York and little loved, very intelligent as a woman, another "culture-carrier," likes to play the patroness, hates the white world and loves the Indian out of hate, is very "generous," wants to be "good" and is very wicked, has a

---

* From *"Not I, But the Wind . . ."* as translated there from the German. No subscription is given.
[1] Knud Merrild and Kai Gótzsche.

terrible will-to-power, you know—she wants to be a witch and at the same time a Mary of Bethany at Jesus's feet—a big, white crow, a cooing raven of ill-omen, a little buffalo.

The people in America all want power, but a small, personal base power: bullying. They are all bullies.

Listen, Germany, America is the greatest bully the world has ever seen. Power is proud. But bullying is democratic and base.

Basta, we are still "friends" with Mabel. But do not take this snake to our bosom. You know, these people have only money, nothing else but money, and because all the world wants money, all the money, America has become strong, proud and over-powerful.

If one would only say: "America, your money is sh . . . , go and sh . . .[1a] more"—then America would be a nothing.

To J. M. MURRY

Del Monte Ranch, Questa, New Mexico, U.S.A.
2 Feby., 1923.

Dear Jack,

I got your note just now, via Kot.,[2] about Katherine.[3] Yes, it is something gone out of our lives. We thought of her, I can tell you, at Wellington. Did Ottoline ever send on the card to Katherine I posted from there for her? Yes, I always knew a bond in my heart. Feel a fear where the bond is broken now. Feel as if old moorings were breaking all. What is going to happen to us all? Perhaps it is good for Katherine not to have to see the next phase. We will unite up again when I come to England. It has been a savage enough pilgrimage these last four years. Perhaps K. has taken the only way for her. We keep faith —I always feel death only strengthens that, the faith between those who have it.

[1a] Surely the word "no" has been omitted here in the translation of this letter.
[2] S. S. Koteliansky.
[3] Katherine Mansfield had recently died of tuberculosis.

Still, it makes me afraid. As if worse were coming. I feel like the Sicilians. They always cry for help from their dead. We shall have to cry to ours: we do cry.

I wrote to you to Adelphi Terrace the day after I got your letter, and asked Seltzer to send you *Fantasia of the Unconscious.* I wanted Katherine to read it.

She'll know, though. The dead don't die. They look on and help.

But in America one feels as if *everything* would die, and that is terrible.

I wish it needn't all have been as it has been: I do wish it.

D. H. L.

To M. L. SKINNER

The Miramar, Santa Monica, Cal., 2 Sept., 1923.

Dear Miss Skinner,

I have read *The House of Ellis* carefully: such good stuff in it: but without unity or harmony. I'm afraid as it stands you'd never find a publisher. Yet I hate to think of it all wasted. I like the quality of so much of it. But you have no constructive power. If you like I will take it and re-cast it, and make a book of it. In which case we should have to appear as collaborators, or assume a pseudonym. If you give me a free hand, I'll see if I can't make a complete book out of it. If you'd rather your work remained untouched, I will show it to another publisher: but I am afraid there isn't much chance. You have a real gift—there is real quality in these scenes. But without form, like the world before creation.

I am in California—but don't suppose I shall stay long. Write me care Thomas Seltzer, 5, West 50th St., New York.

If I get this book done, we'll publish it in the spring.[4] And

4 Rewritten by Lawrence, *The House of Ellis* was later published under the title, *The Boy in the Bush*, with Miss Skinner and Lawrence listed as the co-authors.

if you agree to my re-casting this: then I wish you would take up that former novel of yours, about the girl and the convict—and break off where the three run away—keep the first part, and continue as a love story or romance, where the love of the girl is divided between the Irish convict and the young gentleman—make it a tragedy if you like—but let the theme be the conflict between the two *kinds* of love in the heart of the girl: her love for Peter (was that the young man's name?)—and her love for the Irish ex-convict. See if you can't carry that out. Because of course, as you have it, the convict is the more attractive of the two men, but the less amenable. Only all that adventure in the N.W. is not very convincing. Keep the story near Perth—or Albany, if you can.

If you see Mr. Siebenhaar[5] tell him I have hopes of *Max Havelaar* for the spring of next year too.

Best wishes to you all at Leithdale.

Yours very sincerely,

D. H. LAWRENCE.

To MABEL STERNE[6]

Hotel García, Guadalajara, Jal.
17 October, 1923.

Dear Mabel,

I got your letter here to-day—when I arrived from Tepic. Yes, I was pretty angry. But now let us forget it. At least I will forget, forget the bad part. Because also I have some beautiful memories of Taos. That, perhaps, is what makes the sting burn longer.—As for reviling you, when I am angry, I say what I feel. I hope you do the same. When John Evans[7] went round saying, "Mother had to ask the Lawrences to get out," then I felt there

---

5 W. Siebenhaar, translator of *Max Havelaar*, for which Lawrence provided an introduction.

6 From *Lorenzo in Taos*.

7 Son of Mabel Sterne by her first husband.

was nothing to do but to throw the knife back. But now, enough. If it's *got* to be a battle of wills, I'll fight the devil himself, as long as the necessity lasts. But it's not my idea of life.

There, there's an end to the enmity, anyhow.

Frieda is in England, and wants me to go over there. But I don't want to, she'd better come here.

You have striven so hard, and so long, to *compel* life. Can't you now slowly change, and let life slowly drift into you. Surely it is even a greater mystery and preoccupation even than willing, to let the invisible life steal into you and slowly possess you. Not people, or things, or action, or even conscious: but the slow invasion of you by the vast invisible god that lives in the ether. Once you know that, you will never feel "out of work," as you say. And it's only a change of direction. Instead of projecting your will into the ether of the invisible God, let the invisible God interpenetrate into you.—After all, it's not a mere question of washing dishes. It's the soul's own mystery. And one can make a great, great change in all one's flow of life and living, from the power of output to the mystery of intake, without changing one's house or one's husband. "Then shall thy peace be as a river." And when it comes, like a river, then you won't feel out of work or unliving.

People tell me you are divorcing Tony, and there is another young man, and so on. Probably it is not true. I hope it's not. I don't think it is. Tony always has my respect and affection. And when I say in my book: "one cannot go back," it is true, one cannot. But your marriage with Tony may even yet be the rounding of a great curve; since certainly he doesn't merely draw you back, but himself advances perhaps more than you advance, in the essential "onwards."

Yrs,
D. H. LAWRENCE.

P.S.—We rode over the mountains from Tepic and down the barranca and to Matzatlan, and I thought very much of how you and Tony taught F. and me to ride on Granfer and my little Zegua. For that and many things like that, believe me, I am grateful.

D. H. L.

To MABEL STERNE[8]

Hotel García, Guadalajara, Jal., 8 Novem., 1923.

Dear Mabel,

I had your letter from California yesterday. Don't trouble any more. Let the past die and be forgotten.

Don't trouble about the Indians. You can't "save" them: and politics, no matter *what* politics, will only destroy them. I have said many times that you would destroy the Indians. In your lust even for a Saviour's power, you would just destroy them. The same with Collier.[9] He will destroy them. It is his saviour's will to set the claws of his own White egoistic *benevolent* volition into them. Somewhere, the Indians know that you and Collier would, with your salvationist but poisonous white consciousness, destroy them. Remember, Jesus, and The Good, in our sense, in our mystic sense, not just the practical: Jesus, and The Good as you see it, are poison for the Indians. One feels it intensely here in Mexico. Their great saviour Juarez did more to destroy them than all the centuries of Viceroys. Juarez was a pure Indian.—This is really a land of Indians: not merely a pueblo.

I tell you, leave the Indians to their own dark destiny. And leave *yourself* to the same.

I. I shall not *write* that third book: at least not for many years. It's got to be lived out: not thought out.

I also fight to put something through. But it is a long slow, dark, almost invisible fight. Yet, little by little, I win. And unless there comes death, or the unforeseen bad, I shall win.

8 From *Lorenzo in Taos.*

9 John Collier, sociologist, later Commissioner of Indian Affairs throughout the Roosevelt administration.

One day I will come to you and take your submission: when you are ready. Life made you what you are: I understood so much when I was in Buffalo and saw your mother. But life put into you also the germ of something which still you are not, and which you *cannot* be, of yourself, and if you go on in the same way. People, lawyers, politics, enemies, back-biters, friends and pseudo-friends: my dear, it is all Chimæra and nothing. I will take a submission from you one day, since it is still yours to give. But apparently, not yet. I was your enemy. But even saying things against you—and I only said, with emphasis and in many ways, that your will was evil masquerading as good, and I should still say that of your will: even as an enemy I never really forsook you. There, perhaps I have said too much. But don't think, even so, you can make a fool of me.

D. H. L.

Frieda and everybody insist on my going to England. And I, I shall give in once more, in the long fight. I may as well go and settle finally with England. But I shall not stay long. A short time only. And directly or indirectly I shall come back here, this side, Mexico. I fight against the other side: Europe and the White and U. S. Before very long I hope to come and see you again. I'll let you know when I go.

D. H. L.

To BARONIN VON RICHTHOFEN[1]

Hotel García, Guadalajara, Jalisco, Mexico.
10 November, 1923.

My dear Mother-in-Law,

I had the two letters from Frieda at Baden, with the billet-doux from you. Yes, mother-in-law, I believe one has to be seventy before one is full of courage. The young are always half-hearted. Frieda also makes a long, sad nose and says she is writ-

---

[1] From "*Not I, But the Wind . . .*" as translated there from the German.

ing to the moon—Guadalajara is no moon-town, and I am completely on the earth, with solid feet.

But I am coming back, am only waiting for a ship. I shall be in England in December. And in the spring, when the primroses are out, I shall be in Baden. Time goes by faster and faster. Frieda sent me Hartmann von Richthofen's[2] letter. It was nice. But the women have more courage these days than the men—also a letter from Nusch,[3] a little sad but lively. I hope to see her also in the spring. One must spit on one's hands and take firm hold. Don't you think so?

I was at the Barranca, a big, big ravine, and bathed in the hot springs—came home and found the whole of Germany in my room.

I like it here. I don't know how, but it gives me strength, this black country. It is full of man's strength, perhaps not woman's strength, but it is good, like the old German beer-for-the-heroes, for me. Oh, mother-in-law, you are nice and old, and understand, as the first maiden understood, that a man must be more than nice and good, and that heroes are worth more than saints. Frieda doesn't understand that a man must be a hero these days and not only a husband: husband also but more. I must go up and down through the world, I must balance Germany against Mexico and Mexico against Germany. I do not come for peace. The devil, the holy devil, has peace round his neck. I know it well, the courageous old one understands me better than the young one, or at least something in me she understands better. Frieda must always think and write and say and ponder *how* she loves me. It is stupid. I am no Jesus that lies on his mother's lap. I go my way through the world, and if Frieda finds it such hard work to love me, then, dear God, let her love rest, give it holidays. Oh, mother-in-law, you understand, as my mother finally understood, that a man doesn't want, doesn't ask for love from his wife, but for strength, strength, strength. To

2 Cousin of Frieda Lawrence, formerly a member of the Reichstag.
3 Frieda Lawrence's younger sister, Johanna.

fight, to fight, to fight, and to fight again. And one needs courage and strength and weapons. And the stupid woman keeps on saying love, love, love, and writes of love. To the devil with love! Give me strength, battle-strength, weapon-strength, fighting-strength, give me this, you woman!

England is so quiet: writes Frieda. Shame on you that you ask for peace today. I don't want peace. I go around the world fighting. Pfui! Pfui! In the grave I find my peace. First let me fight and win through. Yes, yes, mother-in-law, make me an oak-wreath and bring the town music under the window, when the half-hero returns.

D. H. L.

To MABEL STERNE[4]

110 Heath St., Hampstead, N.W. 3, 9 Jan. 1924.

Dear Mabel,

You certainly are an egoist, and your letters are egoistic, as you say. Soon you must learn to forget yourself. You must learn *not to care,* not to think, and simply to laugh. Poco a poco.

I have heard enough about the place at Fontainebleau[5] where Katherine Mansfield died, to know it is a rotten, false, self-conscious place of people playing a sickly stunt. One doesn't wonder about it *at all.* One knows. Now call into action your common horse-sense, of which you have your share, as I have mine, and use that. Don't go back on your common horse-sense. It is the centaur's way of knowledge. And if we come back into our own, we'll prance in as centaurs, sensible, a bit fierce, and amused. I am sure seriousness is a disease, to-day. It's an awful disease in Murry. So long as there's a bit of a laugh going, things are all right. As soon as this infernal seriousness, like a greasy

4 From *Lorenzo in Taos.*
5 The Fontainebleau Institution run by Gurdjieff about which Mabel Sterne had inquired of Lawrence. A sort of mystic healer, Gurdjieff had become fashionable among a certain group of literary people.

sea, heaves up, everything is lost. And it was so with us at Taos. If only we'd kept up an *honest* laugh. Not a dishonest laugh: but an honest laugh: then the vileness of 1923 need not have been. Now it takes far more courage to dare not to care, and to dare to have a bit of a laugh at *everything,* than to wallow in the deepest seas of seriousness. The thing I admire most about you is your dauntlessness. Be dauntless in this, then. Not any forced will of your own, nor any forced submission, but a certain *real* trust, and the courage *not to care,* and the power to laugh a bit. Do this and we'll have a good time among ourselves. One's got to put a new ripple in the ether. And one can do it only by *not* caring about any of the old things, by going beyond them all with amusement and a bit of jolliness, and having a bit of stark trust inside oneself. Stark trust in a Lord we have no name for, and also stark trust in one another. Instead of a recklessness of defiance and mistrust, a recklessness of trust, like a naked knife.

I find that here in London they all *instinctively* hate me: much more so than in America. But that too, in the end, only makes me laugh. My gods, like the Great God Pan, have a bit of a natural grin on their face. Nous nous entendons.

I am still planning to come west at the end of February or in March, with Frieda, Murry and Brett.[6] I hope you are looking forward to it. But on your honour, Mabel, no seriousness. The seriousness of the Great God Pan, who grins a bit, and when he gets driven too hard, goes fierce. You are one of the very few people in the world at the moment who are capable of this: this fierce recklessness, based on trust, like the recklessness of Pan; trusting deep down to the springs of nature, the sources: and then the laughter.

The old communion was in seriousness and earnestness. The new is in fierceness, daring, knife-like trust, and laughter. Bien entendu.

D. H. L.

6 The Hon. Dorothy Brett, painter.

To J. M. MURRY
> *Frau von Richthofen, Ludwig-Wilhelmstift,*
> *Baden-Baden, 7 Feb., 1924.*

Dear Jack,

We've just got here—all snow on the Black Forest, but down in here only wet.

Europe gives we a *Wehmut,* I tell you.

We stay here two weeks—then back via Paris. I learnt in New York that the income-tax must be paid by March 15th, and I still *have no word* from that miserable Seltzer.

I don't know if you really want to go to Taos. Mabel Luhan writes she is arranging for it. You seemed to me really very unsure. You resent, *au fond,* my going away from Europe. *C'est mon affaire. Je m'en vais.* But you, in this interval decide for yourself, and purely for yourself. Don't think you are doing something for me. I don't want that. Move for yourself alone. Decide for yourself, in your backbone. I don't really want any allegiance or anything of that sort. I don't want any pact. I won't have anything of that sort. If you want to go to America, *bien.* Go without making me responsible.

But if you want to go with Frieda and me and Brett—*encore bien!* One can but try, and I'm willing. But a man like you, if he does anything in the name of, or for the sake of, or because of somebody else, is bound to turn like a crazy snake and bite himself and everybody, on account of it.

Let us clear away all nonsense. I don't *need* you. That is not true. I need nobody. Neither do you need me. If you pretend to need me, you will hate me for it.

Your articles in the *Adelphi* always annoy me. Why care so much about your own fishiness or fleshiness? Why make it so important? Can't you focus yourself outside yourself? Not for ever focused on yourself, *ad nauseam?*

I met ——— ———.[7] Didn't like him.

—————

7 This name is not yet available for publication.

You know I don't care a single straw what you think of me. Realise that, once and for all. But when you get to twisting, I dislike you. And I very much dislike any attempt at an intimacy like the one you had with ——— ———[8] and others. When you start that, I only feel: For God's sake, let me get clear of him.

I don't care what you think of me, I don't care what you say of me, I don't even care what you do against me, as a writer. Trust yourself, then you can expect me to trust you. Leave off being emotional. Leave off twisting. Leave off having any emotion at all. You haven't any genuine ones, except a certain anger. Cut all that would-be sympathetic stuff out. Then know what you're after.

I tell you, if you want to go to America as an unemotional man making an adventure, *bien, allons!* If you want to twist yourself into more knots, don't go with me. That's all. I never had much patience, and I've none now.

D. H. L.

To J. M. MURRY

Del Monte Ranch, Questa, New Mexico.
16 May, 1924.

Dear Jack,

We learn from Brett that you are marrying a girl called Violet le Maistre on the 20th of this month—and I see by the calendar it is already the 16th. If you can settle down with her and be happy I am sure it is the best for you. Better, as you say, than wild-goose-chasing in other continents. I hope you will have a nice place in Dorset, and make friends with your own destiny. I'm sure you can, if you will, take the rest of your life peacefully, with a wife, a home, and probably children. Anyhow, that's what I wish you—an acquiescent, peaceful happiness.

[8] Possibly Gordon Campbell, Irish lawyer. (H. T. M.)

We are out on Frieda's ranch,[9] with three Indians and a Mexican carpenter, building up the log cabin—the 3-room one. It has been neglected for some years. You would like making adobe and so on, and the camp at evening—but I think you'd not feel comfortable in your skin, for long, away from England. It's much better as it is, I'm sure of that. I think by the end of next week the houses will be done. There's a two-room cabin where Mabel can come when she likes, and a one-roomer for Brett. We've got four horses in the clearing—and spring is just here—the wild gooseberries all in flower, and an occasional humming-bird, many blue-jays. But the vibration is so different. England is as unreal as a book one read long ago, *Tom Brown's Schooldays,* or something of that. Often, too, it is trying—one has to bear up hard against it. Then the altitude, about 8,600 ft., tells on one for a time. The sun is setting and the pines are red, the Indians are just starting drumming. All good luck to you.

D. H. L.

To CATHERINE CARSWELL
Del Monte Ranch, Questa, New Mexico.
18 May, 1924.

My dear Catherine,

We have often spoken of you lately. I wonder what you are doing. We had your letter about your cottage and Don's job. That was mean, to take the job back again. You *do* have bad luck.

Did I tell you Mabel Luhan gave Frieda that little ranch—about 160 acres—up here in the skirts of the mountains? We have been up there the last fortnight working like the devil,

9 The ranch, which had formerly belonged to John Evans, son of Mabel Sterne, was about two miles above Del Monte ranch, Questa, where the Lawrences still received their mail. Originally the ranch had been called Flying Heart Ranch but Lawrence changed the name to Lobo. Later the name was again altered, to Kiowa.

with 3 Indians and a Mexican carpenter, building up the 3-room log cabin, which was falling down. We've done all the building, save the chimney—and we've made the adobe bricks for that. I hope in the coming week to finish everything, shingling the roofs of the other cabins too. There are two log cabins, a 3-roomer for us, a 2-roomer Mabel can have when she comes, a little one-roomer for Brett—and a nice log hay-house and corral. We have four horses in the clearing. It is very wild, with the pine-trees coming down the mountain—and the altitude, 8,600 ft., takes a bit of getting used to. But it is also very fine.—Now it is our own, so we can invite you to come. I hope you'll scrape the money together and come for a whole summer, perhaps next year, and try it. Anyway it would make a break, and there is something in looking out on to a new landscape altogether.—I think we shall stay till October, then go down to Mexico, where I must work at my novel. At present I don't write—don't want to—don't care. Things are all far away. I haven't seen a newspaper for two months, and can't bear to think of one. The world is as it is. I am as I am. We don't fit very well.—I never forget that fatal evening at the Café Royal.[1] That is what coming home means to me. Never again, pray the Lord.

We rode down here, Brett and I. Frieda lazy, came in the car. The spring down in the valley is so lovely, the wild plum everywhere white like snow, the cotton-wood trees all tender plumy green, like happy ghosts, and the alfalfa fields a heavy dense green. Such a change, in two weeks. The apple orchards suddenly in bloom. Only the grey desert the same.—Now there is a thunder-storm and I think of my adobes out there at the ranch. We ride back to-morrow.—One doesn't talk any more about being happy—that is child's talk. But I do like

[1] A London party, in February 1924, at which the Lawrences were hosts to the Carswells, Murry, Koteliansky, Brett, Mary Cannan and Mark Gertler, and which ended with Lawrence drunk and ill. It was on this occasion that Murry said, "I love you, Lorenzo, but I won't promise not to betray you."

having the big, unbroken spaces round me. There is something savage, unbreakable in the spirit of place out here—the Indians drumming and yelling at our camp-fire at evening.—But they'll be wiped out too, I expect—schools and education will finish them. But not before the world falls.

Remember me to Don. Save up—and enjoy your cottage meanwhile.

Yours,
D. H. L.

To MABEL STERNE[2]

Lobo, Thursday.

Dear Mabel,

Your letter about "flow." Anyhow, how can one *make* a flow, unless it comes? To me it seems you always want to force it, with your will. You can't just let it be. You want evident signs, and obvious tokens, and all that. On Saturday evening, you can't just let one be still and let the flow be still. You want to "do things" to me, and have me "do things" to you. That isn't flow. I only wanted to sit still and be still on Saturday evening. Must I then exert myself to dance or to provide entertainment. I never ask you to exert yourself. I wish to heaven you would be quiet and let the hours slip by. But you say it's not your nature. You'll say it is your nature to "do things" to people, and have them "do things" to you. That wearies me. Even you apply your *will* to your affection and your flow. And once my own *will* is aroused, it's worse than most people's. But I do assert that, primarily, I *don't* exert any will over people. And I *hate* the electric atmosphere of wills. You'll say it's because I just want my own will to predominate. It's not even that. It's that I want my will only to be a servant to the "flow," the lion that attends Una, the virgin; or the angel with the bright

2 From *Lorenzo in Taos*. The Lawrences had moved up to the Lobo Ranch in May 1924 and stayed through September.

sword, at the gate. That is all I want my will to be. Not a rampaging Lucifer. But in you, even your affection is a subordinate part of your everlasting will, that which is strong in you.

If the problem is beyond solving, it is. Who knows. But there's the problem. How not to arouse these bristling wills of ours—they're in all of us the same—and admit a natural flow. The moment *one* exerts a will, the whole thing rouses in all the rest of us. And hell to pay.

And of course it's so much easier to flow when one is *alone,* and the others are just thought about. As soon as two are together, it requires a great effort not to fall into a combat of wills. Even wrestling with one's material.

As for the apple-blossom picture, the symbolism, the meaning, doesn't get me, so why should I bother about it.

D. H. L.

I know that the only way to life at all, is to accept the invisible flow. And the flow should be manifold, different sorts, not exclusive. As soon as you try to make the flow *exclusive,* you've cut its root. Only one has to guard against false flow—which is *will* in disguise—like Lee Witt[3] or Bynner.[4] Even with Brett, if you'd take your will off her, she'd be all right. But you won't. —It's no good *insisting* on "flow." The minute anybody insists, on anything, the flow is gone. And I *know* when the real flow is gone there is nothing left worth having. And perhaps I have a fatal little germ of hopelessness. Because, of course, your letter stops Frieda's flow, and her will starts up in a fury—as yours about Brett. And what then? Then my will is up in arms, and it's only a fight—useless all round.

---

[3] A one-armed former sheriff and sawmill worker in Taos married to a Buffalo friend of Mabel Sterne.

[4] Witter Bynner, poet.

To MABEL STERNE[7]

Kiowa, Friday Evening.

Dear Mabel,

I found your letter this evening: and here's the answer:

1. Yes, one has to smash up one's old self and get a new one *with* a new skin (slow work).

2. One must kick bunk when one sees it: hence one must be a destructive force. You have hurt yourself, often, by letting the bunk get by and *then* kicking at random, and getting the victims below the belt. You *must* discriminate sufficiently and say: That's *bunk!* Kick it!—not kick in the wrong place.

3. One does talk too much—and one shouldn't. I speak for myself as well. Though I don't think it matters terribly, unless one deliberately makes bad mischief—which happened this summer, in *talk.*

4. About Tony[8]—I'm afraid you and Clarence[9] *caused* him to take a violent prejudice against me, that time. I really have nothing against him: except that it is foolish even at the worst to be swayed too much. About his relation to you, yours to him, I would never venture *seriously* to judge. (You really shouldn't mind the things one says casually—only the things one says really, having considered.) I do think you have a terrible lot of the collective self in you. I do think this helps to split you rather badly in your *private* self. I do think there is a good deal of subtle feminine sort of *épatez le bourgeois* in you: sometimes crude. I think this encroaches into your better relations, with men especially—that is, with Tony. It's a very difficult and tiresome thing, the mass self: and perhaps far stronger than you allow. Always allow for it in yourself: then

---

[7] From *Lorenzo in Taos.*

[8] Tony Luhan, Mabel's Indian husband.

[9] Clarence Thompson, a recent addition to the Luhan ménage, who had reported to Mabel, as purportedly told him by Frieda Lawrence, that Lawrence planned to kill her. While Mabel was receiving these confidences in the middle of the night, Tony left home; it was the Lawrences he said he was fed up with.

you can get your own feet⁹ᵃ of your *own* self, and make your *real* decision. Do, do be careful of your mass self: be very careful to preserve your real, private feelings from your mass feelings. In this instance, your mass feelings will ruin you if you let them. And don't, through a sort of feminine egotism, want Tony to live too much through you. You know how bad that is. It is a pity you ever made Tony jealous of me: it caused a bad confusion in his feelings, which he won't easily be able to straighten out. Because, as you know, he was not naturally jealous of me: his *instinct* knew better.

5. I wish there could be a change. I wish that old built-up self in you, and in the whole world, could give place to a new, alive self. But it's difficult, and *slow*. And perhaps the only thing that will really help one through a great change is discipline, one's own deep, self-discovered discipline, the first "angel with a sword."

To your P.S.—You need have no split between Tony and me: never: if you stick to what is real in your feelings in each direction. Your real feelings in the two directions won't cause any disharmony. But *don't* try to transfer to Tony feelings that don't belong to him: admit all the limitations, simply. And never again try to transfer to me: admit the limitations here too.

Try, above all things, to be still and to contain yourself. You always want to rush into action. Realize that a certain kind of stillness is the most perfect form of action, like a seed can wait. One's action ought to come out of an achieved stillness: not be a mere rushing on.

D. H. L.

⁹ᵃ Undoubtedly this was meant to be "feel."

To ROLF GARDINER
Del Monte Ranch, Questa, New Mexico, U.S.A.
9 Aug., 1924.

Dear Rolf Gardiner,

I thought *Harbottle*[1] poor stuff: snivelling self-pity, exasperatedly smashing a few cheap parlour ornaments, but leaving the house standing stuffy, suburban, sterile, smug, a nice little upholstered nest of essential cowardice. White Fox,[2] forsooth! White rat!

Bah! If ever you edit another paper, take up a hatchet, not a dummy teat of commiseration. What we need is to smash a few big holes in European suburbanity, let in a little real fresh air. Oh, words are action good enough, if they're the right words. But all this blasted snivel of hopelessness and self-pity and "stars"—and "Wind among the trees" and "camp-fires"—and witanagemotery—It's courage we want, fresh air, and not suffused sentiments. Even the stars are stale, that way. If one is going to act, in words, one should go armed to the teeth, and fire carefully at the suburbanians—like Wells, White Fox, Barrie, Jack Squire[3]—even Murry—all the lot. Piff! and down they go!

If it's going to be Youth, then let it be Youth on the warpath, not wandervogeling and piping imitation nature tunes to the taste of a cake of milk chocolate, and pitying itself and "all other unfortunates." To the rubbish heap with all unfortunates. A great *merde!* to all latter-day Joan-of-Arcism. God, God, God, if there *be* any Youth in Europe, let them rally and kick the bottom of all this elderly bunk. Not snivel or feel helpless. What's the good being hopeless, so long as one has a hobnailed boot to kick with? *Down with the Poor in Spirit!* A war! But

---

[1] By John Hargrave, a friend of Gardiner and founder of the Kibbo Kift, later the Social Credit Party. (H. T. M.)

[2] Probably a reference in Harbottle or to Hargrave. (H. T. M.)

[3] J. C. Squire (now Sir John), editor of the *London Mercury*. (H. T. M.)

the Subtlest, most intimate warfare. Smashing the face of what one *knows* is rotten.

Murry said to me last year: "Come, only come, and do what you like with the *Adelphi.*" I came in December. He went green at my first article, and—wouldn't print it. *No, Lorenzo, you'll only make enemies.*—As if that weren't what I want. I hate this slime of all the world's my friend, my half-friend, anyway I'm not going to make an enemy of him.

Well, here's to you and your bygone *Youth.*

D. H. LAWRENCE.

To WILLARD JOHNSON[4]

Just back from the Snake Dance.

One wonders what one came for—what all those people went for. The Hopi country is hideous—a clayey pale-grey desert with death-grey *mesas* sticking up like broken pieces of ancient dry grey bread. And the hell of a lumpy trail for forty miles. Yet car after car lurched and bobbed and ducked across the dismalness, on Sunday afternoon.

The Hopi country is some forty miles across, and three stale *mesas* jut up in its desert. The dance was on the last *mesa,* and on the furthest brim of the last *mesa,* in Hotevilla. The various Hopi villages are like broken edges of bread crust, utterly grey and arid, on top of these *mesas:* and so you pass them: first Walpi: then unseen Chimopova: then Oraibi on the last *mesa:* and beyond Oraibi, on the same *mesa,* but on a still higher level of grey rag-rock, and away at the western brim, is Hotevilla.

The *pueblos* of little grey houses are largely in ruin, dry raggy bits of disheartening ruin. One wonders what dire necessity or what Cain-like stubbornness drove the Hopis to these dismal grey heights and extremities. Anyhow, once they got there, there was evidently no going back. But the *pueblos* are mostly ruin. And even then, very small.

---

4 The date of this letter is probably late August 1924. (H. T. M.)

Hotevilla is a scrap of a place with a plaza no bigger than a
fair-sized back-yard: and the chief house on the square a ruin.
But into this plaza finally three thousand onlookers piled. A
mile from the village was improvised the official camping
ground, like a corral with hundreds of black motor cars. Across
the death-grey desert, bump and lurch, came strings of more
black cars, like a funeral *cortège*. Till everybody had come—
about three thousand bodies.

And all these bodies piled in the oblong plaza, on the roofs,
in the ruined windows, and thick around on the sandy floor,
under the old walls: a great crowd. There were Americans of
all sorts, wild west and tame west, American women in pants,
an extraordinary assortment of female breeches: and at least
two women in skirts, relics of the last era. There were Navajo
women in full skirts and velvet bodices: there were Hopi
women in bright shawls: a negress in a low-cut black blouse and
a black sailor hat: various half-breeds: and all the men to
match. The ruined house had two wide square window-holes:
in the one was forced an apparently naked young lady with a
little black hat on. She laid her naked handsome arm like a
white anaconda along the sill, and posed as Queen Semiramis
seated and waiting. Behind her, the heads of various Americans
to match: perhaps movie people. In the next window-hole, a
poppy-show of Indian women in coloured shawls and glistening
long black fringe above their conventionally demure eyes. Two
windows to the west!

And what had they all come to see?—come so far, over so
weary a way, to camp uncomfortably? To see a little bit of a
snake dance in a plaza no bigger than a back-yard? Light grey-
daubed antelope priests (so called) and a dozen black-daubed
snake-priests (so called). No drums, no pageantry. A hollow
muttering. And then one of the snake-priests hopping slowly
round with the neck of a pale, bird-like snake nipped between
his teeth, while six elder priests dusted the six younger, snake-
adorned priests with prayer feathers on the shoulders, hopping

behind like a children's game. Like a children's game—Old
Roger is dead and is low in his grave! After a few little rounds,
the man set his snake on the sand, and away it steered, towards
the massed spectators sitting around: and after it came a snake
priest with a snake stick, picked it up with a flourish from the
shrinking crowd, and handed it to an antelope priest in the
background. The six young men renewed their snake as the
eagle his youth—sometimes the youngest, a boy of fourteen or
so, had a rattlesnake ornamentally dropping from his teeth,
sometimes a racer, a thin whip snake, sometimes a heavier bull-
snake, which wrapped its long end round his knee like a garter
—till he calmly undid it. More snakes, till the priests at the
back had little armfuls, like armfuls of silk stockings that they
were going to hang on the line to dry.

When all the snakes had had their little ride in a man's
mouth, and had made their little excursion towards the crowd,
they were all gathered, like a real lot of wet silk stockings—say
forty—or thirty—and left to wriggle all together for a minute
in meal, corn-meal, that the women of the *pueblo* had laid
down on the sand of the plaza. Then, hey presto!—they were
snatched up like fallen washing, and the two priests ran away
with them westward, down the *mesa*, to set them free among
the rocks, at the snake-shrine (so called).

And it was over. Navajos began to ride to the sunset, black
motor-cars began to scuttle with their backs to the light. It was
over.

And what had we come to see, all of us? Men with snakes in
their mouths, like a circus? Nice clean snakes, all washed and
cold-creamed by the priests (so called). Like wet pale silk
stockings. Snakes with little bird-like heads, that bit nobody,
but looked more harmless than doves? And funny men with
blackened faces and whitened jaws, like a corpse band?

A show? But it was a tiny little show, for all that distance.

Just a show! The south-west is the great playground of the
white American. The desert isn't good for anything else. But

it does make a fine national playground. And the Indian, with his long hair and his bits of pottery and blankets and clumsy home-made trinkets, he's a wonderful live toy to play with. More fun than keeping rabbits, and just as harmless. Wonderful, really, hopping round with a snake in his mouth. Lots of fun! Oh, the wild west is lots of fun: the Land of Enchantment. Like being right inside the circus-ring: lots of sand, and painted savages jabbering, and snakes and all that. Come on, boys! Lots of fun! The great south-west, the national circus-ground. Come on, boys; we've every bit as much right to it as anybody else. Lots of fun!

As for the hopping Indian with his queer muttering gibberish and his dangling snake—why, he sure is cute! He says he's dancing to make his corn grow. What price irrigation, Jimmy? He says the snakes are emissaries to his rain god, to tell him to send rain to the corn on the Hopi Reservation, so the Hopis will have lots of corn-meal. What price a spell of work on the railway, Jimmy? Get all the corn-meal you want with two dollars a day, anyhow.

But oh, dry up! Let every man have his own religion. And if there wasn't any snake dance we couldn't come to see it. Miss lots of fun. Good old Hopi, he sure is cute with a rattler between his teeth. You sure should see him, boy. If you don't, you miss a lot.

To MABEL STERNE[5]

Del Monte Ranch, Questa, New Mexico.
14 Sept., 1924.

Dear Mabel,

I had your letter about Brill last night.[6] I knew it was very much as he said: that there was a fatal disconnection, and that

5 From *Lorenzo in Taos.*
6 According to Mabel Sterne's account, Dr. Brill had told her she needed to work for her living. "Oh, the unclean compromise and capitulation!" was Mabel Sterne's comment.

it was passing beyond your control. I am glad you are going to put yourself into a doctor's hands. Because you have now to submit to authority, and to a certain measure of control from outside. And except to an authority like a recognized doctor's, you would never have submitted.

The thing to do is to try, try, try to discipline and control yourself. And to remember that, even if all the people in the world go negative and futile, and you yourself have stuck to something which is more than all people or any people, the real thing which is beyond anybody's malevolent reach, then you yourself will never feel negative nor empty. One should discipline oneself never to do things which one's own self disapproves of—and then one can't go to pieces. But it will be hard for you to get over your disintegrative reaction towards people and circumstances—everything. As you say, you went that way so long ago.

We shall be going down to Mexico in October. My chest and throat stay sore, I want to go south. I don't want to go east for the winter: no. For this winter you must fight this thing out more or less by yourself. It is your job.

I don't know if this will reach you—but send it to the club on chance.

D. H. L.

To J. M. MURRY
Del Monte Ranch, Questa, New Mexico, U.S.A.
3 Oct., 1924.

Dear Jack,

We had your letter. I'm glad you have a good time on the Dorset coast, with Violet. But don't you become the "mossy stone"—unless, of course, you want to. And perhaps you will find fulfilment in a baby. Myself, I am not for postponing to the next generation—and so *ad infinitum*. Frieda says every woman hopes her BABY will become the Messiah. It takes a man, not a baby. I'm afraid there'll be no more Son Saviours. One was almost too much, in my opinion.

I'm glad you like the Hopi Dance article. All races have one root, once one gets there. Many stems from one root: the stems never to commingle or "understand" one another. I agree Forster doesn't "understand" his Hindu. And India is to him just negative: because he doesn't go down to the root to meet it. But the *Passage to India* interested me very much. At least the repudiation of our white bunk is genuine, sincere, and pretty thorough, it seems to me. Negative, yes. But King Charles *must* have his head off. Homage to the headsman.

We are leaving here next week. There was a flurry of wild snow in the air yesterday, and the nights are icy. But now, at ten o'clock in the morning, to look across the desert at the mountains you'd think June morning was shining. Frieda is washing the porch: Brett is probably stalking a rabbit with a 22-gun: I am looking out of the kitchen door at the far blue mountains, and the gap, the tiny gate that leads down into the canyon and away to Santa Fe. And in ten days' time we shall be going south—to Mexico. The high thin air gets my chest, bronchially. It's *very* good for the lungs, but fierce for tender bronchi.

We shall never "drop in on one another" again; the ways go wide apart. Sometimes I regret that you didn't take me at what I am, last Christmas: and come here and take a different footing. But apparently you did what was in you: and I what is in me, I do it. As for ———,[5] there is just nothing to say. It is absurd, but there it is. The ultimate son of Moses pining for heavy tablets. I believe the old Moses wouldn't have valued the famous tablets if they hadn't been ponderous, and millstones round everybody's neck. It's just Hebraic. And now the tablets are to be *papier mâché. Pfui! carito!* it's all bunk: heavy, uninspired bunk. *Che lo sia!*—Kangaroo was never ———.[5] Frieda

5 Kot.

was on the wrong track. And now ———⁶ is sodden. *Despedida, despedida Eran fuentes de dolores——*

The country here is very lovely at the moment. Aspens high on the mountains like a fleece of gold. *Ubi est ille Jason?* The scrub oak is dark red, and the wild birds are coming down to the desert. It is time to go south.—Did I tell you my father died on Sept. 10th, the day before my birthday?—The autumn always gets me badly, as it breaks into colours. I want to go south, where there is no autumn, where the cold doesn't crouch over one like a snow-leopard waiting to pounce. The heart of the North is dead, and the fingers of cold are corpse fingers. There is no more hope northwards, and the salt of its inspiration is the tingling of the viaticum on the tongue.

Sounds as if I was imitating an Ossianic lament.

You can get me in Mexico:

> c/o The British Consulate,
> Av. Madero 1,
> Mexico, D.F.

But I want to go south again to Oaxaca, to the Zapotecas and the Maya. *Quien sabe, si se puede!*

Adios!
D. H. L.

To J. M. MURRY

Hotel Francia, Oaxaca, Oax., Mexico.
17 Novem., 1924.

Dear Jack,

I sent you a letter two days ago, and yesterday came the little yellow cry from your liver. You were bound to hate ———,⁶ and he you, after a while: though I don't suppose the hate is mortal, on either side. The *Adelphi* was bound to dwindle: though why not fatten it up a bit. Why in the name of hell

⁶ Kot.

didn't you rouse up a bit, last January, and put a bit of gun-powder in your stuff, and fire a shot or two? But you preferred to be soft, and to go on stirring your own fingers in your own vitals. If it's any good, to you or anybody, all right! But if it's no good, what the hell!—It seems to me, the telephone-book magazine, and the pale yellow *cri de l'âme* are equally out of date. Spunk is what one wants, not introspective sentiment. The last is your vice. You rot your own manhood at the roots, with it. But apparently it's what you want.

The article you wearily mention is the *Snake Dance* article, I suppose. If you really cared about it, I'd tell Curtis Brown to let you have it at the price you can afford to pay. But if you don't really care, what's the good?

Sometimes the American Continent gets on my nerves, and I wish I'd come to Sicily or South Spain for the winter. But as it is, I suppose we shall stay a few months here, since we're moving into a house to-morrow. But if I still feel put out by the vibration of this rather malevolent continent, I'll sail from Vera Cruz and spend my last dollars trying the mushiness of Europe once more, for a while. It's a fool's world, anyhow, and people bore me stiffer and stiffer. Fancy, even a Zapotec Indian, when he becomes governor, is only a fellow in a Sunday suit grinning and scheming. People never, never, never change: that's the calamity. Always the same mush.

But it's no good. Either you go on wheeling a wheelbarrow and lecturing at Cambridge and going softer and softer inside, or you make a hard fight with yourself, pull yourself up, harden yourself, throw your feelings down the drain and face the world as a fighter.—You won't, though.

Yrs.,

D. H. L.

To THE HON. DOROTHY BRETT

Av. Pino Suarez, 43, Oaxaca, Oax.
Monday Morning (1925).[7]

Dear Brett,

Your letter with ———'s[8] enclosed this morning. They make me sick in the pit of my stomach. The cold, insect-like ugliness of it. I shall avoid meeting ———.[9]

If Mexico City is so unpleasant we shall probably stay here an extra week or fortnight, and go straight to Vera Cruz. I don't like the sound of it—you are right, I think, about King.[9a]

And a word about friendship. Friendship between a man and a woman, as a thing of first importance to either, is impossible: and I know it. We are creatures of two halves, spiritual and sensual—and each half is as important as the other. Any relation based on the one half—say the delicate spiritual half alone—*inevitably* brings revulsion and betrayal. It is halfness, or partness, which causes Judas. Your friendship for ———[9b] was spiritual—you dragged sex in and he hated you. He'd have hated you anyhow. The halfness of your friendship I also hate, and between you and me there is no sensual correspondence.

You make the horrid mistake of trying to put your sex into a spiritual relation. Old nuns and saints used to do it, but it soon caused rottenness. Now it is half rotten to start with.

When Maruca *likes* a man and marries him, she is not so wrong. Love is chiefly bunk: an over-exaggeration of the spiritual and individualistic and analytic side. If she likes the man, and he is a man, then better than if she loved him. Each will leave aside some of that hateful *personal* insistence on imaginary perfect satisfaction, which is part of the inevitable bunk of love, and if they meet as mere male and female, *kindly,* in their marriage, they will make roots, not weedy flowers of a love

---

[7] The date of this letter is January 27, 1925. (H. T. M.)
[8] Murry. (H. T. M.)
[9] Unidentified.
[9a] Probably Clinton King, painter. [9b] Probably Murry. (H. T. M.)

match. If ever you can marry a man feeling *kindly* towards him, and knowing he feels kindly to you, do it, and throw love after ————.² If you can marry in a spirit of kindliness, with the criticism and ecstasy both sunk into abeyance, do it. As for ————,² I don't think you have any warm feeling at all for him. I know your Captain ————²: there is a kind of little warm flame that shakes with life in his blue eyes; and that is more worth having than all the high-flown stuff. And he is quite right to leave his door open. Why do you jeer? You're not superior to sex, and you never will be. Only too often you are inferior to it. You like the excitation of sex in the eye, sex in the head. It is an evil and destructive thing. Know from your Captain that a bit of warm flame of life is worth all the spiritualness and delicacy and Christlikeness on this miserable globe. No, Brett. I do *not* want your friendship, till you have a full relation somewhere, a *kindly* relation of both halves, not *in part*, as all your friendships have been. That which is in part is in itself a betrayal. Your "friendship" for me betrays the essential man and male that I am, and makes me ill. Yes, you make me ill, by dragging at one half at the expense of the other half. And I am so much better now you have gone. I refuse any more of this "delicate friendship" business, because it damages one's wholeness.

Nevertheless, I don't feel unkindly to you. In your one half you are loyal enough. But the very halfness makes your loyalty fatal.

So sit under your tree, or by your fire, and try, try, try to get a real kindliness and a wholeness. You were really horrid even with ————²; and no man forgives it you, even on another man's account.

Know, know that this "delicate" halfness *makes* evil. Put away all that Virginal stuff. Don't still go looking for men with strange eyes, who know life from A to Z. Maybe they do, missing

² Unidentified.

out all the rest of the letters, like the meat from the empty eggshell. Look for a little flame of warm kindness. It's more than the Alpha and Omega; and respect the bit of warm kindliness there is in people, even ———² and ———.² And try to be *whole,* not that unreal half thing that all men hate you for, even I. Try and recover your wholeness, that is all. *Then* friendship is possible, in the kindliness of one's heart.

D. H. L.

Remember I think Christ was profoundly, disastrously wrong.

To J. M. MURRY

Av. Pino Suarez, 43, Oaxaca, Oax.

28 Jan., 1925.

Dear Jack,

Brett sent on your letters. That seems to be an absolutely prize sewer-mess, of your old "group."

Mon cher, c'est canaillerie pure et simple. Je m'en fiche— without feeling pious about it.

You remember that charming dinner at the Café Royal that night? You remember saying: I love you, Lorenzo, but I won't promise not to betray you? Well, you CAN'T betray me, and that's all there is to that. *Ergo,* just leave off loving me. Let's wipe off all that Judas-Jesus slime.

Remember, you have betrayed everything and everybody up to now. It may have been your destiny. But in ———³ you met a more ancient Judas than yourself. There are degrees within degrees of initiation into the Judas trick. You're not half-way on yet. Even ———³ is miles ahead of you. It's a case of *sauve-toi.* Judas was a Jew, and you're not quite that, yet.

All I want to say is, don't think you can either love me or

2 Unidentified.
3 Kot.

betray me. Learn that I am not lovable: hence not betrayable.

Frieda and I may come to England in the spring. But I shall not want to see anybody except just my sisters and my agent. Last time was once too many.

One day, perhaps, you and I may meet as men. Up to now, it has been all slush. Best drop that Christ stuff: it's putrescence.

We leave here in a fortnight: where for, I am not quite sure.

Yrs.,

D. H. L.

To A. D. HAWK[5]

Hotel Imperial, Mexico City, March 11, 1925.

Dear Mr. Hawk,

The doctor has made an analysis of blood and so forth, and says I had *much* better come to the ranch, that the sea-voyage will shake me and bring on fever, and England will not be good for me. He insists on our coming to New Mexico: and thank goodness, there is Del Monte to come to. Could you get the apple orchard cottage ready for us? We shall leave (D.V.) next week—perhaps the 17th, when the ship was due to sail—and arrive somewhere about the 21st. I am so glad to be able to come straight to Mrs Hawk and you, and to William and Rachel,[6] and Del Monte. It is really the only home one has got.

Tell Miss Brett. Tell her to prepare for us. We want to have a happy, friendly time, all of us.

Au revoir,

D. H. LAWRENCE.

---

5 From *The Intelligent Heart.*
6 Son and daughter-in-law of A. D. Hawk.

To THE HON. DOROTHY BRETT

Kiowa, Saturday, (1925).[7]

Dear Brett,

There's not much to say—and it's no good saying much.

It's no good our trying to get on together—it won't happen. Myself—I have lost all desire for intense or intimate friendship. Acquaintance is enough. It will be best when we go our separate ways. A life in common is an illusion, when the instinct is always to divide, to separate individuals and set them one against the other. And this seems to be the ruling instinct, unacknowledged. Unite with the one against the other, and it's no good.

Yrs.,

D. H. L.

To M. L. SKINNER

Del Monte Ranch, Questa, New Mexico.

28 August, 1925.

Dear Mollie Skinner,

I sent you a letter yesterday, and last night came yours telling me your brother was dead. He had no luck: one could see in his face that he never would have luck. Perhaps it's really true, lucky in money, unlucky in love. But as a matter of fact, I believe he really never *wanted* to make good. At the bottom of his soul, he preferred to drift penniless through the world. I think if I had to choose, myself, between being a Duke of Portland or having a million sterling and forced to live up to it, I'd rather, far, far rather be a penniless tramp. There is deep inside one a revolt against the fixed thing, fixed society, fixed money, fixed homes, even fixed love. I believe that was what ailed your brother: he couldn't bear the social fixture of everything. It's what ails me, too.

7 Probably mid-April.

And after all he lived his life and had his mates wherever he went. What more does a man want? So many old bourgeois people live on and on, and *can't* die, because they have never been in life at all. Death's not sad, when one has lived.

And that again is what I think about writing a novel: one can live so intensely with one's characters and the experiences one creates or records, it is a life in itself, far better than the vulgar thing people *call* life, jazzing or motoring and so on. No, every day I live I feel more disgust at the thing these Americans call life. Ten times better die penniless on a gold-field.

But be sure of my sympathy.

D. H. LAWRENCE.

To MR. AND MRS. WILLIAM HAWK[8]

S.S. Resolute, "27 Sept." [*1925*].

Dear William & Rachel,

Here it is Sunday afternoon—everybody very bored—nothing happening, except a rather fresh wind, the sea a bit choppy, outdoors just a bit too cold. We get in to Southampton on Wednesday morning, and glad shall I be to see land. There are very few people on board, and most of those are Germans or people from somewhere Russia way, speaking a language never heard before. We've had pretty good weather—went on board last Monday night, and sailed at 1 a.m. Queer to be slipping down the Hudson at midnight, past all the pier lights. It seems now such a long while ago. Though the weather has been pretty good, I had one awful day, blind with a headache. It was when we ran into a warm fog, so suppose it was the old malaria popping up.

I didn't care for New York—it was steamy hot. I had to run about and see people: the two little Seltzer's[9] dangling by a single thread, over the verge of bankruptcy, and nobody a bit

---

8 From *The Intelligent Heart.*
9 Thomas Seltzer, publisher, and his wife Adele.

sorry for them. The new publishers, the Knopfs,[1] are set up in great style, in their offices on Fifth Avenue—deep carpets, and sylphs in a shred of black satin and a shred of brilliant undergarment darting by. But the Knopfs seem really sound and reliable: am afraid the Seltzers had too many "feelings." Adele said dramatically to Frieda: "All I want is to pay OUR debts and DIE." Death is a debt we all pay: the dollars are another matter.

Nina [Witt][2] is as busy as ever re-integrating other people—It was a pleasant house near Washington Square, but of course they were building a huge new 15-storey place next door, so all day long the noise of battle rolled.—The child, Marion Bull, is a handsome girl of eighteen and very nice indeed: trying to go on the stage, and the stagey people being very catty to her. I rather hope she won't go on the stage, it might spoil her.— The boy Harry wasn't yet back in New York.—That woman Mrs Hare[3] sent a car and fetched us to their place on Long Island: beautiful place. But in proudly showing me her bees, she went and got stung just under the eye, and a more extraordinary hostess in an elegant house I never saw, as the afternoon wore on and the swelling swelled and swelled. It was too bad: she was very kind to us.—The nicest thing was when some people motored us out at night to the shore on Long Island, and we made a huge fire of driftwood, and toasted mutton chops, with nothing in sight but sand and the foam in the dark[.]

I lie and think of the ranch: it seems so far away:—these beastly journeys, how I hate them! I'm going to stop it, though, this continual shifting.

How is Miss Wemyss:[4] not still fighting her mother, I hope— like Brett at forty? Send me a line with news of you all:

1 Alfred A. and Blanche Knopf.
2 A girlhood friend of Mabel Sterne, married to Lee Witt of Taos.
3 A Taos acquaintance. (H. T. M.)
4 A cat. We recall that Lady Cynthia Asquith was the daughter of the 11th Earl of Wemyss.

c/o Curtis Brown. 6 Henrietta St.
London. W.C. 2.

I do feel, I don't know what I'm doing on board this ship.
Au revoir & remembrances,

D. H. LAWRENCE.

To JACK CLARKE[5]

Villa Bernarda, Spotorno, Prov. di Genova.
Dec. 19, 1925.

I'm sending you a pound, but it's only ten shillings to you.
I want you to buy something for your Auntie Gertie[6] with the
other ten bob.

Tell your mother I couldn't find a thing for her in that
beastly Savona: except rather lovely cups and plates and things
—and she has enough of those. But if she'd like some, I could
get her a parcel made up.

At last it's raining a bit here: rather nice, the country is so
dry. Our old Giovanni is working away, planting his garden.
One day you'll have to come with your mother to see everything
and *parlare italiano.*

I do hope you get this in time. Write on your Auntie Gertie's
present: *From Bert and Frieda,* and do it respectably, so as not
to shame us, and don't be wessel-brained, or there'll be death
in the pot.

Merry Christmas to you all: don't revel too much. And for
heaven's sake, I hope the green family is better.

Love from your Auntie Frieda and your ever estimable

UNCLE BERT.

What have "those pore collier's boys" been doing lately?

5 From *Early Life of D. H. Lawrence.*
6 Gertrude Cooper, childhood friend and neighbor of Lawrence. Her father,
Thomas Cooper, a checkweighman at the mines and an amateur flutist, was
in large part the model for Aaron in *Aaron's Rod.*

To J. M. MURRY

Villa Bernardo, Spotorno, Pro. di Genova.
4 Jan., 1926.

Dear Jack,

A la guerre comme à la guerre! Make up your mind to change your ways, and call the baby Benvenuto.

My dear Jack, *it's no good!* All you can do now, sanely, is to leave off. *A la vie comme à la vie.* What a man has got to say is never more than relatively important. To kill yourself like Keats, for what you've got to say, is to mix the eggshell in with the omelette. That's Keats' poems to me. The very excess of beauty is the eggshell between one's teeth.

Carino, basta! Carito, deja, deja, la canzon, cheto! Cheto, cheto! Zitto, zitto, zitto! Basta la mossa!

In short, shut up. Throw the *Adelphi* to the devil, throw your own say after it, say good-bye to J. M. M. Filius Meus, *Salvatore di Nessuno se non di se stesso,* and my dear fellow— *give it up!*

As for your humble, he says his say in bits, and pitches it as far from him as he can. And even then it's sometimes a boomerang.

Ach! du lieber Augustin, Augustin, Augustin—I don't care a straw who publishes me and who doesn't, nor where nor how, nor when nor why. I'll contrive, if I can, to get enough money to live on. But I don't take myself seriously, except between 8.0 and 10.0 a.m., and at the stroke of midnight. At other seasons, my say, like any butterfly, may settle where it likes: on the lily of the field or the horsetod in the road: or nowhere. It has departed from me.

My dear chap, people don't want the one-man show of you alone, nor the Punch and Judy show of you and me. Why, oh why, try to ram yourself down people's throats? Offer them a tasty tit-bit, and if they give you five quid, have a drink on it.

No, no! I'm forty, and I want, in a good sense, to enjoy

my life. Saying my say and seeing other people sup it up doesn't amount to a hill o' beans, as far as I go. I want to waste no time over it. That's why I have an agent. I want my own life to live. "This is my body, keep your hands off!"

Earn a bit of money journalistically, and kick your heels. You've perhaps got J. M. M. on the brain even more seriously than J. C.⁷ Don't you remember, we used to talk about having a little ship? The Mediterranean is glittering blue to-day. Bah, that one should be a mountain of mere words! Heave-O! my boy! Get out of it!

D. H. L.

To J. M. MURRY

Villa Bernardo, Spotorno (Genova).
19 Jan., 1926.

Dear Jack,

I would rather you didn't publish my things in the *Adelphi*. As man to man, if ever we were man to man, you and I, I would give them to you willingly. But as writer to writer, I feel it is a sort of self-betrayal. Surely you realise the complete incompatibility of my say with your say. Say your say, *caro!*— and let me say mine. But, for heaven's sake, don't let us pretend to mix them.

Yrs.,
D. H. L.

To WITTER BYNNER

Villa Bernardo, Spotorno, Genova, Italy.
27 Jan., 1926.

Dear Bynner,

*Caravan*⁸ came to-day, and I have read it already, and like it very much. Surely you don't think me an enemy of life?

---

⁷ Jesus Christ.
⁸ A volume of poems by Witter Bynner, published in late 1925. It included a long poem "D. H. Lawrence" and Bynner had sent Lawrence a copy.

My single constancy is love of life! Caro, caro, is it *quite* true?
But it's the only thing to be constant to, I'm with you entirely
there; and against the old. But don't you go and get old just
now. Do you see me merely as a cat? Sometimes a cat, anyhow.
I like these the best of your poems, that I know. They are more
really you. Even serving happiness is no joke! I hope you won't
mind the little sketch of you in *The Plumed Serpent.* I don't
think it's unsympathetic—it only dislikes your spurious sort
of happiness—the spurious side of it. Happiness is a subtle and
aristocratic thing, and you mixed it up with the mob a bit.
Believe me, I'm not the enemy of your happiness: only of the
false money with which you sometimes sought to buy happiness.
You must know what I mean: these poems are very sincere and
really deep in life so you do know. I hope, one day, when I've
shed my fur and claws, and you've acknowledged your own fur
and claws, we may be two men, and two friends truly. I don't
know if I shall come back to America this year: it's a strain.
I might go to Russia. Would you like to go with me? I've even
learned my Russian A B C. Frieda sends her greetings—hope
everything goes well with you.

D. H. LAWRENCE.

To THE HON. DOROTHY BRETT

Ravello, Sunday (Spring, 1926).

Dear Brett,

This is to introduce Miss Williams* and her father. I'll hope
you will do a few walks together.

We leave for Rome early in the morning. I will write from
there. Meanwhile, don't you mope and lie around, it's *infra dig.*
The greatest virtue in life is real courage, that knows how to
face facts and live beyond them. Don't be ————[1]ish, pitying
yourself and caving in. It's despicable. I should have thought,

---

* Unidentified.
[1] Murry. (H. T. M.)

after a dose of that fellow, you'd have had too much desire to be different from him, to follow his sloppy self-indulgent melancholics, absolutely despicable. Rouse up and make a decent thing of your days, no matter what's happened. I do loathe cowardice, and sloppy emotions. My God, did you learn *nothing* from ———,[2] of how NOT to behave? You write the sort of letters he writes! Oh, *basta!* Cut it out! Be something different from that, even to yourself.

D. H. L.

To MABEL STERNE[3]

Villa Bernarda, Spotorno (Genova).
12 April 1926.

My dear Mabel,

I have been back here a week, and in another week we leave this house, for where, I don't quite know. I don't want to come back to America just now—it's so hard and tense. I am weary of that tension, even the tension of the practice of relaxation. My I, my fourth centre, will look after me better than I should ever look after it. Which is all I feel about Gurdjieff. You become perfect in the manipulation of your organism, and the I is in such perfect suspension that if a dog barks the universe is shattered. Perhaps I should say, the I is also so perfectly self-controlled that nothing more ever can happen. Which perhaps is a goal and an end devoutly to be wished.

I do believe in self-discipline. And I don't believe in self-control.

In the end, if you Gurdjieff yourself to the very end, a dog that barks at you will be a dynamo sufficient to explode your universe. When you are final master of yourself, you are nothing, you can't even wag your tail or bark.

But the fact that your I is not your own makes necessary a

2 Murry. (H. T. M.)
3 From *Lorenzo in Taos.*

discipline more patient and flexible and long-lasting than any Gurdjieff's.

I wish you had not written to Edwin Dodge[4] again about the Curonia.[5] Myself, I don't want to go there to stay. An hour would be enough. Since your Duse story, basta! And Edwin Dodge's note to me was very sniffy, as if I were wanting something of him. Heaven forfend! But he was of course quite polite.

I have finished your Memoirs,[6] sent the first part back to Havelock Ellis, will send him the rest to-morrow.

In the first place, why oh why didn't you change the names! My dear Mabel, call in all the copies, keep them under lock and key, and then carefully, scrupulously change the names: at least do that: before you let one page go out of your hands again. Remember, *other people* can be utterly remorseless, if they think you've given them away.

"Memoirs of a Born American"—they are frightfully depressing, leave me with my heart gone way down out of my shoes, so I haven't any heart at all, feel like a disembodied corpse, if you know what that means. At the same time, I should say it's the most serious "confession" that ever came out of America, and perhaps the most heart-destroying revelation of the American life-process that ever has or ever will be produced. It's worse than Oedipus and Medea, and Hamlet and Lear and Macbeth are spinach and eggs in comparison. My dear Mabel, one could shed skyfuls of tears except for the knowledge of the utter futility of shedding even one. The only thing to do is to close down for the time the fountains of emotion, and face life as far as possible emotionless. But you've said a sort of last word—*That's that*—to Jesus' *Consummatun est!* It's not the absolute truth—but then nothing ever is. It's not art, because

---

4 Second husband of Mabel Sterne.
5 Mabel Sterne's villa in Florence.
6 Later published as *Intimate Memories,* Harcourt Brace and Co., New York, 1933.

art always gilds the pill, and this is hemlock in a cup. It seems to me so horribly near the truth, it makes me sick in my solar plexus, like death itself, which finally breaks the solar plexus. My dear Mabel, I do think it was pretty hard lines on all of you, to start with. Life gave America gold and a ghoulish destiny. Heaven help us all! One thing, though, I do think we might learn: if we break, or conquer anyone—like P.,[6a] it's like breaking the floor-joists, you're sure to go through into the cellar, and cripple yourself. It's the broken snake that's the most dangerous. The unbroken slips away into the bushes of life.

Never win over anybody!—there's a motto. I mean never conquer, nor seek to conquer. And never be conquered, except by heaven. And if you don't set your will in opposition to heaven, there's no occasion for conquest there.

But one can't do more than live one's destiny, good or bad, destructive or constructive. One can do much *less,* like B.,[7] and chew substitutes all one's life. Or like E. D.,[8] not have much of a destiny anyhow.

Lord, what a life! It's pouring with rain, and I'm feeling weary to death of struggling with Frieda. I feel like turning to Buddha and crying basta! and sitting under a bho tree.

D. H. L.

To THE HON. DOROTHY BRETT
Pensione Lucchesi, Lungarno Zecca, Firenze.
Friday.[8a]

Dear Brett,

We are here in the most atrocious weather, pouring cold rain all the time. I loathe it. And we are still undecided about Germany. If this weather continues, I shall go. I feel the

6a Unidentified.
7 Probably Brett.
8 Probably Edwin Dodge.
8a The date of this letter is Friday, April 23, 1926. (H. T. M.)

North Pole would be better than Florence, in any more of this weather.

I just got your letter. Why have you let yourself run so low in cash? To get to Santa Fé you need $150.00. The railway is about 93, the Pullman about 40, and food to buy. But see if Mabel won't motor you over. Her Finney Farm is between Boston and New York. If you really get stuck for money, you'll have to borrow from me. I'll enclose a little more to Barmby.*

You'll have no one to meet you in Boston, and I think you must be met by somebody. Usually the Y.W.C.A. representative does it. I hope you got that letter from your father and from the Foreign Office—one can't stand being badgered about. What a curse the world is!

F. and I will be here another week, so write here. Did you get the woolly lamb, sent from Spotorno, and a few little books? Make your preparations carefully before you go. *Ask about being met in Boston.*

D. H. L.

To THE HON. DOROTHY BRETT

*Florence, Sunday, 24th April, 1926.*¹

Dear Brett,

Here is Rachel's¹ᵃ letter—also very depressing! You'll probably find them gone when you arrive. *Don't* go up alone to our ranch; I expressly *don't want* you to go up there *alone*. If you have somebody decent with you, well and good. I am a bit worried about the ranch, anyhow. I feel very strongly it would be better to have some responsible person living there—like Scott Murray.² I almost wish I'd asked Rachel and William if they'd care to live there. I did just hint it, in my letter to them

---

* New York manager of Curtis Brown.
1 The correct date of this letter is April 25, 1926. (H. T. M.)
1ª Mrs. William Hawk, neighbor at the Del Monte ranch.
2 A local handyman in New Mexico.

a week ago. I want you to be very careful and cautiously feel around for what would be the best. Don't blindly dash into anything. But for myself, I definitely feel it would be best to have some good man living permanently up there and making a bit of a living off the place. It would really make it more liveable for all of us and make it more possible ultimately for us to plant a Buddha Bo-tree or a bo-tree of our own, up there, and forgather in its shade. It is what we ought to do ultimately. Meanwhile, we must build up to that. So do think carefully for the future and let us gradually shape the ranch the way it ought to go, for the final best: when we have the bo-tree as well as the pine trees.

It is rather depressing here—vile weather. Florence very crowded, irritable. I don't like it much and don't think I shall stay very long. But another week, anyhow. The two girls leave for London direct on Tuesday—then Frieda and I will have to decide what we do. Mabel writes she will come to Paris in May to see Gourdjieff in Fontainebleau. She thinks salvation lies that way. It may, for her.

If you get stuck for money, let me know. Any expenses incurred for the ranch, I will pay. But be careful and thoughtful, don't do foolish things, and don't buy unnecessary ones. All our means of all sorts are definitely limited.

D. H. L.

I can't stand Francis of Assisi—nor St. Clare—nor St. Catherine. I didn't even like Assisi. They've killed so much of the precious interchange in life: most folks are half dead, maimed, because of those blighters. The indecency of sprinkling good food with ashes and dirtying sensitive mouths!

D. H. L.

To THE HON. DOROTHY BRETT
Villa Mirenda, Scandicci, Firenze, 7 July, 1926.

Dear Brett,

Your letter to-day, saying the hay is cut. That will be wonderful having a haystack, and being able to throw down the bunches of hay to the horses in winter, as I have done at Del Monte. I feel Kiowa is gradually growing into a real self-respecting ranch again. Friedel[3]—he is in Berlin—sent us a photograph of the wagons with Indians and horses: very nice: gave one a wish to be back, too. For some things, I wish I was really there. I would love to see the flowers, and ride up the raspberry canyon, and go along the ditch with a shovel. Then something else, I can't find out what it is, but it is something at the pit of my stomach, holds me away, at least for the moment. It is something connected with America itself, the whole business—yet of course I feel the tree in front of the house is my tree. And even the little aspens by the gate, I feel I have to keep my eye on them.

But I'm awfully sorry you have so much work to do. It would be really better to have Trinidad[4] or somebody. And be sure to tell me how much you spend for *labour,* for the ditch and the hay and those things. And I'll send the money along.

Here it is full summer: hot, quiet, the *cicadas* sing all day long like so many little sewing machines in the leafy trees. The peasant girls and men are all cutting the wheat, with sickles, among the olive trees, and binding it into small, long sheaves. In some places they have already made the wheat stacks, and I hear the thresher away at a big farm. Fruit is in: big apricots, great big figs that they call *fiori,* peaches, plums, the first sweet little pears. But the grapes are green and hard yet. It seems there is a great deal of fruit.

We have met various people: nobody thrilling, but some

---

3 Friedrich Jaffe, Frieda Lawrence's nephew.
4 Tony Luhan's nephew, employed by the Lawrences at the ranch.

quite nice. Lord Berners[5] came out to tea. Do you know him? He was Tyrwhitt, or something like that. He asked us to stay with him in Rome in October, and be motored round to the Etruscan places. We might try a day or two. He was very nice: and apparently rich, too rich: Rolls-Roycey.

We leave here next Monday—the 12th. I am sorry to go, except that the heat is a bit soaked in thunder, and heavy, and I think a little time rather high up in the Black Forest would be fresh and nice. How I should love to breathe the air at the ranch and to taste the well-water! What a pity there is such a strange psychical gulf between America and Europe! One has to undergo a metamorphosis and one can't always bear it. We are due to spend August in England, then in early Sept. come back here. I shall be glad to be back. I haven't done any of my hill-towns yet. I must do them in the autumn. I was so busy with bits of things. Secker and Knopf want me to write another novel, but I'm not going to lay myself waste again in such a hurry. Let the public read the old novels. The Knopfs are in Europe, but don't suppose we shall see them. He says: "It becomes harder and harder to sell good books." Then let him sell bad ones. The way for us to do is to live economically, so we don't need much money—that's how we live here: £300 a year would do me. Then one is independent of them.

How are your headaches? I hope the heat doesn't give you them. Occasionally I get one, an odd stunner.

Remember me to Rachel[6]—also to Betty and Bobby.[7] Is Bobby bad at all, or just a threat? I'm sorry she's not well.

My sisters in England are very depressed about the coal strike: no business doing, more ruin ahead. What a misery!

They've translated *The Plumed Serpent* into Swedish. Hope it'll bite them. How much butter do you get from the cow? Does she run and hide as Susan did. Eggs are abundant here:

5 Formerly of the diplomatic service. Author; composer of operas and ballets.
6 Mrs. William Hawk.
7 Sisters of William Hawk. (H. T. M.)

seven liras a dozen, which is about 26 cents. How are you for money? Let me know. I like the seal to your letter. Where did you find the bird? Does Aaron[8] still have a running eye? And Azul's[8] jaw? The poor creatures! Is Prince[8] a mild lamb with you?

D. H. L.

To ROLF GARDINER

> *c/o Frau von Richthofen, Ludwig-Wilhelmstift,*
> *Baden-Baden, Thursday, July, 1926.*

Dear Rolf Gardiner,

Your letter to-day: as usual, like a bluster in the weather. I am holding my hat on.

But do let us meet. We arrive in London on July 30th—and go to a little flat, 25, Rossetti Garden Mansions, Flood St., Chelsea, S.W. 3. We shall use it as a *pied à terre*. Myself, I have promised to spend some time with my sisters on the Lincs. coast—and to go to Scotland—various things.

I believe we are mutually a bit scared. I of weird movements, and you of me. I don't know why. But if you are in London even for a couple of days after the 30th, do come and see us, and we can talk a little, nervously. No, I shall ask you questions like a doctor of a patient he knows nothing about.

But I should like to come to Yorkshire, I should like even to try to dance a sword-dance with iron-stone miners above Whitby. I should love to be connected with something, with some few people, in something. As far as anything *matters*, I have always been very much alone, and regretted it. But I can't belong to clubs, or societies, or Freemasons, or any other damn thing. So if there is, with you, an activity I *can* belong to, I shall thank my stars. But, of course, I shall be wary beyond words, of committing myself.

8 Probably horses.

Everything needs a beginning, though—and I shall be very glad to abandon my rather meaningless isolation, and join in with some few other men, if I can. If only, in the dirty solution of this world, some new little crystal will begin to form.

Yrs.,

D. H. LAWRENCE.

To EARL BREWSTER[9]

Sutton-on-Sea, Lincs, 30 Aug., 1926.

Dear Earl,

Your letter of 3rd August reaches me to-day—after I'd posted mine to you this morning, to Almora.

I'm awfully sorry you and Achsah are so ill. It sounds to me as if you'd got malaria, though I hope you haven't. What altitude are you? It may be mountain fever, owing to the rarity.

I wish you were here—it is so blowy and blustery and sea-foamy and healthy, so very bracing. I like it. And I'm sad to think you won't see all those sights, Benares, Ajanta Caves, etc. But perhaps you'll be feeling better, and try them . . .

I think you'll be all the better though, for the experience. The best of Eastern thought is surely eternal: but one must maintain a more or less critical attitude. What irritated me in you in the past was a sort of way you had of looking on Buddhism as some sort of easy ether into which you could float away unresisted and unresisting. Believe me, no truth is like that. All truth—and real living is the only truth—has in it the elements of battle and repudiation. *Nothing is wholesale.* The problem of truth is: How can we most deeply live? And the answer is different in every case. And your Buddhism was, in a measure (I don't want to be wholesale either)—a form of sidetracking.

Believe me, you'll be happier, because you'll be truer to your

9 From *D. H. Lawrence: Reminiscences and Correspondence.*

own inner man, after this experience. You've got to get out of the vast lotus-pool of Buddhism on to the little firm island of your own single destiny. Your island can have its own little lotus pool, its own pink lotus. But *you yourself* must never try again to lose yourself in the universal lotus pool: the mud is too awful.

I shall be glad to hear you are safely on the way to Europe. I can promise, almost faithfully, to join you in Syra some time in the winter, if you go there. That is, I want to very much indeed. I am pining to see Athens and Greece.

Curiously, I like England again, now I am up in my own regions. It braces me up: and there seems a queer, odd sort of potentiality in the people, especially the common people. One feels in them some odd, unaccustomed sort of plasm twinkling and nascent. They are not finished. And they have a funny sort of purity and gentleness, and at the same time, unbreakableness, that attracts one.

My best wishes to you and Achsah, and in hopes of meeting soon.

D. H. L.

To ROLF GARDINER
>   *Villa Mirenda, Scandicci, Florence, 3 Dec., 1926.*
Dear Gardiner,

I was glad to get your letter—wondered often about the Baltic meeting—sounds a bit dreary. I think it's hardly worth while trying anything deliberately international—the start at home is so difficult. But the song-tour sounded splendid.

I'm sure you are doing the right thing, with hikes and dances and songs. But somehow it needs a central clue, or it will fizzle away again. There needs a centre of silence, and a heart of darkness—to borrow from Rider Haggard. We'll have to establish some spot on earth, that will be the fissure into the underworld, like the oracle at Delphos, where one can always come to. I will try to do it myself. I will try to come to England and make a place—some quiet house in the country—where one can begin—and from which the hiker, maybe, can branch out. Some place with a big barn and a bit of land—if one has enough money. Don't you think that is what it needs? And then one must set out and learn a deep discipline—and learn dances from all the world, and take whatsoever we can make into our own. And learn music the same; mass music, and canons, and wordless music like the Indians have. And try— keep on trying. It's a thing one has to feel one's way into. And perhaps work a small farm at the same time, to make the living cheap. It's what I want to do. Only I shrink from beginning. It is most difficult to begin. Yet, I feel in my inside, one ought to do it. You are doing the right things, in a skirmishing sort of way. But unless there is a headquarters, there will be no continuing. You yourself will tire. What do you think? If I did come to England to try such a thing, I should depend on you as the organiser of the activities, and the director of activities. About the dances and folk music, you know it all, I know practically nothing. We need only be even two people, to start. I don't believe either in numbers, or haste. But one has to drive one's peg down to the centre of the earth: or one's root: it's the same thing. And there must also be work connected—I mean earning a living—at least earning one's bread.

I'm not coming to England for the *Widowing of Mrs. Holroyd*. I begin to hate journeys—I've journeyed enough. Then my health is always risky. You remember the devil's cold I got coming to England in August. I've always had chest-bronchial troubles and pneumonia after-effects—so have to take care.

How well I can see Hucknall Torkard[1] and the miners! Didn't you go into the church to see the tablet, where Byron's heart is buried? My father used to sing in the Newstead Abbey choir, as a boy. But I've gone many times down Hucknall Long

---

[1] Town near Eastwood, famous for its Byron relics. (H. T. M.)

Lane to Watnall—and I like Watnall Park—it's a great Sunday morning walk. Some of my happiest days I've spent haymaking in the fields just opposite the S. side of Greasley church—bottom of Watnall Hill—adjoining the vicarage: Miriam's father hired those fields. If you're in those parts again, go to Eastwood, where I was born, and lived for my first 21 years. Go to Walker St.—and stand in front of the third house—and look across at Crich on the left, Underwood in front—High Park woods and Annesley on the right: I lived in that house from the age of 6 to 18, and I know that view better than any in the world. Then walk down the fields to the Breach, and in the corner house facing the stile I lived from 1 to 6. And walk up Engine Lane, over the level-crossing at Moorgreen pit, along till you come to the highway (the Alfreton Rd.)—turn to the left, towards Underwood, and go till you come to the lodge gate by the reservoir—go through the gate, and up the drive to the next gate, and continue on the *footpath* just below the drive on the left—on through the wood to Felley Mill (the *White Peacock* farm). When you've crossed the brook, turn to the right through Felley Mill gate, and go up the footpath to Annesley. Or better still, turn to the right, uphill, *before* you descend to the brook, and go on uphill, up the rough deserted pasture—on past Annesley Kennels—long empty—on to Annesley again. That's the country of my heart. From the hills, if you look across at Underwood wood, you'll see a tiny red farm on the edge of the wood. That was Miriam's farm—where I got my first incentive to write. I'll go with you there some day.

I was at my sister's[2] in September, and we drove round—I saw the miners—and pickets—and policemen—it was like a spear through one's heart. I tell you, we'd better buck up and do something for the England to come, for they've pushed the spear through the side of *my* England. If you are in that district, anywhere near Ripley, do go and see my sister, she'd love

[2] Ada.

it. Her husband has a tailor's shop and outlying tailor's trade amongst the colliers. They've "got on," so have a new house and a motor car. But they're nice.

> Mrs. W. E. Clarke,
> "Torestin,"
> Gee St.,
> Ripley (Derby).

Ripley is about 6 miles from Eastwood, by tram-car.

You should do a hike, from Nottingham–Nuttall–Watnall –Moorgreen reservoir–Annesley–Bledworth or Papplewick and across Sherwood Forest, Ollerton, and round perhaps to Newark. And another do., Langley Mill to Ripley, Ripley to Wingfield Manor (one of my favourite ruins), Crich, and then down to Whatstandwell and up again to Alderswasley and so to Bole Hill and Wirksworth and over Via Gellia, or keep on the high ground from Crich and go round Tansley Moor round to Matlock Bridge, or where you like. But it's real England—the hard pith of England. I'll walk it with you one day.

Tell me what you think of *Mrs. Holroyd,* if you see it.

If they give *David* in mid-March, I shall come to England in mid-February. Then I hope to see you properly.

Keep the idea of a *centre* in mind—and look out for a house— not dear, because I don't make much money, but something we might gradually build up.

> Yrs.,
> D. H. LAWRENCE.

"Mrs. Holroyd" was an aunt of mine—she lived in a tiny cottage just up the line from the railway-crossing at Brinsley, near Eastwood. My father was born in the cottage in the quarry hole just by Brinsley level-crossing. But my uncle built the old cottage over again—all spoilt. There's a nice path goes down by the cottage, and up the fields to Coney Grey farm—then round to Eastwood or Moorgreen, as you like.

To DR. TRIGANT BURROW
> Villa Mirenda, Scandicci, Florence, Italy.
> Christmas Day, 1926.

Dear Dr. Burrow,

Many thanks for the paper—*Psychoanalysis in Theory and in Life*. It's the first thing I've read for a long time that isn't out to bully somebody in some way or other. It is true, the essential self is so simple—and nobody lets it be. But I wonder you ever get anybody to listen to you. My experience of people is, as soon as they think themselves clever enough to read a book or hear a lecture, they will only pay attention to some bullying suggestion in which they can take part—or against which they can raise an equally bullying protest. Really one gets sick of people—they can't let be. And I, who loathe sexuality so deeply, am considered a lurid sexuality specialist. *Mi fa male allo stomaco!* But I was really glad to hear a real peaceful word for once. You never thought you were writing a *Noël, Noël!* carol, did you? But sometimes your sentences are like Laocoön snakes, one never knows where the head is, nor the tail.

Tell me some time—it seems rude—what old nation you belong to—England? Wales? surely not Jewish at all (that's not prejudice—only the psychology isn't Jewish).

Best wishes for the New Year.

D. H. LAWRENCE.

To MISS GERTRUDE COOPER[3]
> Villa Mirenda, Jan. 23, 1927.

. . . My God, what a fight for life![4] It's no good trying to understand why these things should be. There's no explanation. One can only do one's best and then live or die. One is between the hammer and the anvil. For myself, I daren't say either have

---

[3] From *Early Life of D. H. Lawrence*.
[4] Gertrude Cooper now lived part of the time with Lawrence's sister Ada and part of the time in tuberculosis sanitoria.

the operation, or don't have it. It worries me too much. You must go way down into yourself, down till you really *feel* which would be right, to have it or not to have it. And then abide by what you feel, in your own still soul, would be the best.

Eh, one wishes things were different. But there's no help for it. One can only do one's best, and then stay brave. Don't weaken or fret—while we live, we must be game. And when we come to die, we'll die game too. Listen to the doctors carefully when they advise you. But when it comes to deciding finally, decide out of your own real self.

The days are already beginning to lengthen, and the narcissus flowers are out in the garden already: but the little white wild ones, down by the stream, aren't out yet, nor the wild crocuses. There are lots of Christmas roses wild, but they are greenish, they don't come really white, so they're not so pretty.

We sat in the sun on the edge of the pine wood and listened to a shepherd playing a tin whistle—very badly. They make the weirdest noises, to call the sheep: grunts from the bottom of the stomach, then wildcat hisses. I suppose it takes a peculiar sound to penetrate a sheep's stupid skull. The leading sheep with the bell was called Laura: "Hoy! Laura! Hoy—a—Hoy! Grunt—squish—squee!" so the shepherd kept on at her. And she, like an old maid, munched a bit, and tripped ahead, the rest trailing after her.

The mountains, the Appenines, are covered with deep snow, and they look very beautiful, sweeping away to the north, the furthest up, at Carrara, glimmering faint and pinkish in the far, far distance. And near at hand, the country lies in the sunshine, all open and rolling, with white buildings like dots here and there, and few people. It is very different from England. One day you must come and really get to know it. On a day like to-day an odd butterfly comes flapping out, and there's a bee now and then. The sun is strong enough. I even saw the tail of a little lizard go whisking down a hole in the wall.

Do you remember in Lynn Croft, when we used to have autograph albums, and put verses and little paintings in them? I can remember Frances[5] chose for somebody's:

"But human bodies are such fools
For all their colleges and schools
That when no *real* ills perplex 'em
They make enough themselves to vex 'em."

And I think that is so true. When one get a job like yours on hand, one thinks what fools people are, grousing and grizzling and making their lives a misery for nothing instead of being thankful they've got off so lightly. . . .

I suppose they're warbling away in Eastwood Congregational Chapel at this moment! Do you remember, how we all used to feel so sugary about the vesper verse: Lord keep us safe this night, secure from all our fears—: Then off out into the dark, with Dicky Pogmore[6] and the Chambers,[7] and all the rest. And how Alan[8] used to love the lumps of mince-pie from the pantry. And Frances did her hair up in brussel-sprouts and made herself a cup of Ovaltine or something of that sort! Sometimes it seems so far off! And sometimes it is like yesterday.

To EARL BREWSTER[9]

Villa Mirenda, Scandicci, Florence, 27 Feb., 1927.

Dear Earl,

Imagine your having to move again! But I'm among the people who like Ravello . . . Will you invite me? Frieda is probably going to Germany about the middle of March. If you and Achsah ask me, I'll come to Ravello for a week or ten days, then we'll go our walking trip. I don't think I shall go to England . . . let them produce *David* as they like. Why should I

5 Sister of Gertrude Cooper.
6 Childhood friend of Lawrence.
7 The family of Jessie Chambers, the Miriam of *Sons and Lovers.*
8 Alan Chambers, brother of Jessie.
9 From *D. H. Lawrence: Reminiscences and Correspondence.*

mix myself up with them personally! I hate the very thought of them all.

Or should we meet in Rome and look at those Etruscan tombs? If I asked Lord X—,[1] he'd motor us to them all and have extra permits. . . . I simply *can't* stand people at close quarters. Better tramp it our two selves. What do you think?

I do think it's awfully important to be honest: with oneself. I don't see how one can even begin to be honest with other people. And as I hate lying, I keep to myself as much as possible. You and I are at the *âge dangereuse* for men: when the whole rhythm of the psyche changes: when one no longer has an easy flow outwards: and when one rebels at a good many things. It is as well to know the thing is physiological: though that doesn't nullify the psychological reality. One resents bitterly a certain swindle about modern life, and especially a sex swindle. One is swindled out of one's proper sex life, a great deal. But it is nobody's individual fault: fault of the age; our own fault as well. The only thing is to wait: and to take the next wave as it rises. Pazienza!

I feel in you a terrible exasperation. One has to go through with it. I try to keep the *Middle* of me harmonious to the middle of the *Middle* of the universe. Outwardly I know I'm in a bad temper, and let it go at that. I stick to what I told you, and put a phallus, a lingam you call it, in each one of my pictures somewhere. And I paint no picture that won't shock people's castrated social spirituality. I do this out of positive belief, that the phallus is a great sacred image: it represents a deep, deep life which has been denied in us, and still is denied. Women deny it horribly, with a grinning travesty of sex. But pazienza! pazienza! One can still believe. And with the lingam, and the belief in the mystery behind it, goes beauty. Oh, I am with you there. But as for life, one can only be patient—which by nature I am not. I think men ought to be able to be honest, to a suffi-

[1] Lord Berners.

cient point, with one another. I've never succeeded yet. Vedremo! And meanwhile one has to preserve one's *central* innocence, and not get bittered. O pazienza! But one does need a bit of trust, mutual trust. You have so many defences, and fences. Pazienza! chi va piano va lontano!

arrivederci,
D. H. LAWRENCE.

To MISS PEARN
Villa Mirenda, Scandicci, Florence, 12 April, 1927.
Dear Miss Pearn,

I got back here last night, so have an address once more. I had a very interesting time looking at Etruscan tombs in Tarquinia and in Maremma—and I want to do a few sketches of Etruscan places.

It was nice to hear of you and Mr. Pollinger[2] hauling on the ropes of my old barge—though why you should have so much trouble I don't know.

I enclose Cynthia Asquith's letter. I wish you would tell me your own opinion candidly, about the story, too.

I am in a quandary about my novel, *Lady Chatterley's Lover.* It's what the world would call very improper. But you know it's not really improper—I always labour at the same thing, to make the sex relation valid and precious, instead of shameful. And this novel is the furthest I've gone. To me it is beautiful and tender and frail as the naked self is, and I shrink very much even from having it typed. Probably the typist would want to interfere——Anyhow, Secker wants me to send it him at once. And Barmby writes that Knopf can't possibly publish till next spring, so I must send the MS. to New York '*à la bonne heure'.* I am inclined to do just nothing. What would you say? You and Mr. Pollinger—whom I've never met, have I? I think per-

---

2 Both Miss Pearn and Mr. Pollinger were employed by Curtis Brown.

haps it's a waste to write any more novels. I could probably live by little things. I mean in magazines.

Anyhow, I hope soon to send you some small things.

What about your holiday? My wife's youngest daughter[3] arrives to-day from London—so if you come out here you will see her.

Saluti!

D. H. LAWRENCE.

To EARL BREWSTER[4]

Villa Mirenda, Scandicci, (Firenze).
Thursday, 9 June.

Dear Earl,

Many thanks for the shoes, which came yesterday. They are a great success, and Frieda is very pleased with hers: says they're gothic—nearly as good as that Mr. L.—who said "To me it's Chartres! Chartres!"—over the little old knitted silk tobacco pouch. . . .

M. and B.[5] are in Florence. . . . Really, nothing is worse than these Americans. They've cut out *everything* except personal conceit and clothes. I was in the Uffizi—Ufizzi—Uffizzi??—with them yesterday—"My, look what awful hands she's got!" is all that comes out of B., for Lippo Lippi—they've never even heard of Botticelli—call him Bo'acelli, with the stopped breath instead of the 't'—they don't know what the Renaissance was. Standing in the Piazza Signoria I say—There's that Michelangelo *David*—and they reply: which one is it then?—that one at the end?—meaning the Bandinelli. Then B. discovers that—"that guy's got a stone in his hand, so I guess he's the nut." It's partly affectation, but it's such a complete one that it's effectual.

---

3 Barbara Weekley, later Mrs. Barr.

4 From *D. H. Lawrence: Reminiscences and Correspondence.* The date of this letter is June 9, 1927.

5 Mrs. Christine Hughes and her daughter Mary Christine. (H. T. M.)

They simply *can't see* anything: you might as well ask a dog to look at a picture or a statue. They're stone blind, culturally. All they can do is to call a man "that guy" or a woman "that skirt." M. would *like* to be able to see: but it's too late: the American cataract has closed over her vision, she's blind. B. frankly loathes anything that wants to be looked at—except herself, other girls, clothes and shops. But it's a process of atavism so rapid and so appalling, I could kill them dead. It's pure atavism. They've negated and negated and negated till there's *nothing*— and they themselves are empty vessels with a squirming mass of nerves. God, how loathsome! . . . It's horrible. And it's largely the result of an affectation of "freedom" from old standards, become a fixed habit and a loathsome disease. Because there's the elements of a nice woman in each of them. . . . And I feel I'd rather go and live in a hyena house than go to live in America.

So much for me!

Nevertheless, I think the world must be fought, not retreated from.

Did you get *Mornings in Mexico?* I had my copy.

I began the Etruscan essays: have done Cerveteri and Tarquinia so far. They interest me very much. One can get lovely photographs from Alinari's so one could make a fine book. Perhaps Frieda and I will do a trip to Cortona, Arezzo, Chiusi, Orvieto, Perugia next week or the week after—before we go to Germany—so I could do enough essays—or sketches—sketches of Etruscan Places—for a book. That would keep us here till end of July—then we'd go to Germany. . . .

The time goes by quickly, now the hot weather is here. But I like it like this.

Thank Achsah for her letter. You'll be glad to settle down in R. again—not long now.

I believe it's going to rain!

D. H. L.

To DR. TRIGANT BURROW

Villa Mirenda, Scandicci, Florence.

13 July, 1927.

Dear Trigant Burrow,

You are the most amusing person that writes to me. It is really funny—resistances—that we are all of us all the while existing by resisting—and that the p.-a. doctor and his patient only come to hugs in order to offer a perfect resistance to mother or father or Mrs. Grundy—sublimating one resistance into another resistance—each man his own nonpareil, and spending his life secretly or openly resisting the nonpareil pretensions of all other men—a very true picture of us all, poor dears. All bullies, all being bullied.

What ails me is the absolute frustration of my primeval societal instinct. The hero illusion starts with the individualist illusion, and all resistances ensue. I think societal instinct much deeper than sex instinct—and societal repression much more devastating. There is no repression of the sexual individual comparable to the repression of the societal man in me, by the individual ego, my own and everybody else's. I am weary even of my own individuality, and simply nauseated by other people's. I should very much like to meet somebody who has been through your laboratory, and come societally unrepressed. Is there anybody? If it weren't for money, the peasants here wouldn't be bad. But money is the stake through the bowels of the societal suicide. What a beastly word, *societal!*

This is to say, if you come to Europe, do let me know. I should like to meet you. I love the way you pull the loose legs out of the tripods of the p-a-ytical pythonesses.

Of course, men will *never* agree—can't—in their *"subjective sense perception."* Subjective sense perceptions are individualistic *ab ovo*. But do tell them to try! What a scrimmage among the mental scientists, and a tearing of mental hair!

Mental science, anyhow, can't exist—any more than the goose can lay the golden egg. But keep 'em at it, pretending.

[264]

I think we shall be in Austria—near Villach—for August and in Bavaria—near Munich—for Sept. Are you coming to Europe?—to the p-a-thing in Innsbruck?

Every Jew is a Jehovah, and every Christian is a Jesus, and every scientist is the Logos, and there's never a man about.

I've got bronchials and am in bed for a bit, and furious.

You can convince a man that he lusts after his grandmother —he doesn't mind!—but how are you going to bring him to see that as an individual he's a blown egg!

I'll try and find your paper on the "Genesis and Meaning of Homosexuality"—you should have said "Genesis and Exodus." But I've long wanted to know the meaning—and there you told it in 1917!

D. H. LAWRENCE.

Letters to here will follow on when we move.

To A. HUXLEY

Mirenda, Monday.

Dear Aldous,

Many thanks for *Proper Studies.* I have read 70 pages, with a little astonishment that you are so serious and professorial. You are not your grandfather's *Enkel* for nothing—that funny dry-mindedness and underneath social morality. But you'll say I'm an introvert, and no fit judge. Though I think to make *people* introverts and extraverts is bunk—the words apply, obviously, to the *direction* of the consciousness or the attention, and not to anything in the individual essence. You are an extravert by inheritance far more than *in esse.* You'd have made a much better introvert, had you been allowed. "Did she fall or was she pushed"—Not that I care very much whether people are intro or extra or anything else, so long as they're a bit *simpatico.* But, my dear, don't be dry and formal and exposition all that— What's the odds! I just read Darwin's *Beagle* again—he dried

[265]

himself—and *tant de bruit pour des insectes!*—But I like the book.

We sit here rather vaguely, and I still haven't been to Florence. It's colder, and we warm up in the evening. Frieda, inspired by Maria, has launched into puddings: boiled batter and jam. I do bits of things—darn my underclothes and try to type out poems—old ones. Reggie[6] and Orioli[7] and Scott-Moncrieff[8] and a young Acton[9] came *en quatre*—I poured tea, they poured the rest.

We shall have to be seeing you soon and making plans for Xmas and Cortina: or rather New Year and Cortina. I think we shall go to Florence for Xmas—somewhere where we can eat turkey and be silly—not sit solitary here. Will you be in Florence, too?

I'm reading Beethoven's letters—always in love with somebody when he wasn't really, and wanting contacts when he didn't really—part of the crucifixion into isolate individuality —*poveri noi.*

Love—whatever that is—to all!

D. H. L.

I don't mean I didn't find the 70 pages good—they're very sane and sound and good—only I myself am in a state of despair about the Word either written or spoken seriously. That's why, I suppose, I wrote this, when I wasn't asked—instead of holding my tongue.

---

6 Reginald Turner, minor writer living in Italy. (H. T. M.)

7 Guisèppe ("Pino") Orioli, bookseller in Florence, later published *Lady Chatterley's Lover* for Lawrence.

8 C. K. Scott Moncrieff, translator of Proust.

9 Harold Acton, a minor British writer. (H. T. M.)

To DONALD CARSWELL

Villa Mirenda, Scandicci, Firenze, 5 Dec., 1927.

Dear Don,

Many thanks for the book. We've both read it, and both really interested. It's awfully good sidelights on recent history, and seems to me psychologically very sound. Only you don't allow enough for the emotional side of our reactions—poor Keir Hardie[1]—and if your Lord Overtoun[2] is sarcastic, which surely it is, then most people will take it for praise.

And you do admire a little overmuch English detachment. It often is mere indifference and lack of life. And you are a bit contemptuous of your Scotch: one feels they are miserable specimens, all told, by the time one winds up with Robertson Nicoll.[3] It's because you under-estimate the *vital* quality, and over-estimate the English detached efficiency, which is not very vital.

I got Cath's letter and wrote ———,[4] whom I've utterly forgot. Tiresome, he is, fussing his little affairs round.

Cath's idea of a Burns' book I like very much: I always wanted to do one myself, but am not Scotchy enough. I read just now Lockhart's bit of a life of Burns. Made me spit! Those damned middle-class Lockharts grew lilies of the valley up their ———, to hear them talk. If Cath is condescending to Burns, I disown her. He was quite right, a man's a man for a' that, and it's *not* a bad poem. He means what he says. My word, you can't know Burns unless you can hate the Lockharts and all the estimable bourgeois and upper classes as he really did— the narrow-gutted pigeons. Don't, for God's sake, be mealy-mouthed like them. *I'd* like to write a Burns life. Oh, why doesn't Burns come to life again, and really salt them! I'm all

---

1 James Keir Hardie, Scottish labor leader. (H. T. M.)
2 Unidentified.
3 Sir William Robertson Nicoll, Scottish writer. (H. T. M.)
4 Unidentified.

for Keir Hardie, my boy. Did you ever *know* Sir G. Trevelyan,[5] for example? Pfui! "I'm it, mealy-mouthed it!" No, my boy, don't be on the side of the angels, it's too lowering.

Germany sounds rather fun—but too far, too far. I'm supposed to go up to the snow in January, but am shirking it. See when January comes. The changing is such a bore.—I think we shall go back to the ranch in spring—March or April—I'd like to be away from Europe for a bit.

We too have no news. Nothing goes very well—money dwindles—the govt. takes 20 per cent off what I do get—and Curtis Brown 10 per cent. *Pax!* What does one exist for, but to be made use of, by people with money?

Frieda sends her love with mine—do hope the boy is better— wish something nice would happen all round.

D. H. Lawrence.

To S. S. KOTELIANSKY[6]

Villa Mirenda, Scandicci, Florence, 8 Dec.

My dear Kot,

I was very much distressed to hear about Ghita[7]—but thankful there'll be no ill consequences. I hope by now you've got her safely at the Cave,[7] and she's about well, and all serene. Damn all motor cars: and I hope they've got to pay good substantial damages.

I suppose the Cave is not being abandoned, after all?

About the printing—dear Kot, what *is* the good of beginning with just one? My novel I'm writing all over again, so that's in abeyance. But *how* can you begin the little books with just me? You'd begin and you'd end there. You've just got to *wring* a few

---

5 Sir George Trevelyan, historian, father of George Macaulay Trevelyan. Author of *The Early Life of Charles James Fox* and of a series of books on the American revolution.

6 From *Letters to S. S. Koteliansky*. Postmarked December 8, 1927. Signature not given.

7 Unidentified.

MSS. out of people, if you're going to start. The worst of it is, what people? They've all commercial contracts.

Have you seen the German magazine *Querschnitt?* It's a very good modern-popular sort of magazine. I believe, if one were going to do anything new and popular today, one would have to be quite bold, jump in with two feet, be unconventional, improper at times, print good nude pictures, and give the thing a *kick*. There's absolutely no public for merely "good" stuff: there really isn't. The public wants pictures, and bits of text. But *live* pictures. I'll send you a copy of *Querschnitt*. The good Jehovah has got to be a bit of a devil if he's going to do anything today. You'd far more easily find artists and draughtsmen for a magazine, than writers. Then the text becomes subsidiary—all the better—and you can put in snappy things of all sorts.

If we don't go to the ranch in the spring, I think we really shall go to Ireland.

Can you get from Gertler[8] any explanation of D's[9] curious behaviour? He wrote very warmly in Sept. asking us to go to Egypt. I replied we'd like to, if we could. And since then, not a word from him—only a note from her, saying she hadn't been able to think of journeys—and evidently not badly wanting us. She's a perfect right not to want us—but then in mere politeness he should answer my letter, and say, do we mind putting the thing off. I'm surprised at his lack of manners. But I suppose there was some mischief made somewhere. However, I was polite, and so can they be.

I expect we'll be here for Christmas—weather dull, most other things too.

---

[8] Mark Gertler, painter, long-time friend of the Lawrences.
[9] Bonamy Dobree, Professor of English, Egyptian University, Cairo. (H. T. M.)

To HARWOOD BREWSTER[1]

Villa Mirenda, Scandicci, Firenze, Sunday.

My dear Harwood,

So you have really found another home for a bit—and another of the "beautiful pretentious" sort! Are you saying hurray!—or are you breaking no eggs about it?

How is Capri? Here, for some weeks, it fogged, and I naturally coughed. These last two days there is a wind from the heart of all the icebergs, so unspeakably cold—but the sun fairly warm. I'm pretty well, considering, though a bit cross. I spent yesterday and to-day doing a picture. Which I have just burnt—and it hasn't even made the stove any hotter. How's that for meanness!

We are sitting tight for Christmas and making a Christmas tree for the contadini. As their name is legion, with a few babies over, it's a job, and my spirit is rather faint. I'm afraid I get less altruistic (nice word) as I get older. Still, the tree isn't stolen yet from the pineta, and the toys are still to buy from the Quarant'otto—a famous bazaar place here. So sufficient unto the day is the evil thereof.

Which is the L.'s[2] coming to tea in about five minutes. . . . But one day I think we shall trot down to Capri to see you: if we don't go to Switzerland up to the snow: dreadful thought, on a day like this!

I enclose ten bob for you for Christmas and you are to buy with it exactly what you choose: a bottle of beer, and a pair of corsets for Rose,[3] the darling, for she must be losing her figure by now; a handbag in the shape of a puppy-dog for your Mother (all the rage! when you take your powder-box out of his tummy, he squeaks!)—and for your father, a wigwam. With what is left

[1] From *D. H. Lawrence: Reminiscences and Correspondence.* The date of this letter is December 1927. Harwood was now 15 years old.
[2] The Wilkinsons, neighbors of the Lawrences at the Mirenda.
[3] An old doll of Harwood's.

over, buy yourself a harp, so that you shall not forget your name is Schwannhild!

Tell your father thank you for his letter, but I couldn't see wood for bo-trees. Ask your Mama the reason for this long-drawn-out silence of hers. If the Villa Torricello is her Capri Swansong, tell her I would fain hear a few notes of that truly rare, never-before-heard melody.

Apart from all this there is no particular news—and here are the L's! Leb'wohl, mein Kind! Don't forget me when you're boozing the champagne and devouring the turkey and the pheasants!

D. H. L.

Your uncle in all but name.

To LADY GLENAVY⁴

Châlet Beau Site, Diablerets, Switz.
Feb. 3, 1928.

Dear Beatrice,

Your letter came on here—where we came a fortnight ago, for my wretched chest—bronchials really to wreck a ship. They said—people, even doctors—altitude and snow. But snow's no good for bronchials, makes 'em worse: though the altitude is tonicky after Tuscany, which is relaxing. Well, that's my wail: I cough and pant, but sound worse than I am, maybe. I expect we'll stick it out here till about end of this month—then back to the Villa Mirenda, to wind up there.—There's deep snow here—a certain amount of winter-sport—none for me—and now it's snowing again—tinkle of sledge bells—me sitting on my bed, with a German feather-bolster over my feet—Frieda lying on her bed reading André Gide's *Corydon,* which is a damp little production: and no sound in the white and crumbling world. We've got a flat in this châlet.

---

4 From *The Intelligent Heart.*

Well, there's the mise-en-scène—there's no drama. We still keep the Ireland idea. But we've got to drag our effects out of the Villa Mirenda. And moreover I've got on my conscience a novel I wrote, and which is much too shocking—verbally—for any publisher. Says shit! and fuck! in so many syllables. So if it's going to be published I'll have to do it myself—therefore think of bringing it out this spring privately in Florence—1000 copies, half for England, half for America—at two guineas. So perhaps earn some money, very welcome. But it's a good novel— love, as usual—and very nice too, but says all the things it shouldn't say. If I do that—publish it in Florence—it'll keep me there till end of April. Even so, May is a good time to arrive in Ireland.

We're really due to go back to the ranch in New Mexico—you know about it—owned by Frieda—on the west side of Rocky Mts—altitude nearly 9000 ft—looking over the high plateau to Arizona—four horses, buggy, forest, all that. It's very lovely, and I'd be well there. But it's fearfully far and dear to get there—3 days in train, one in motor-car. Brett looks after it now. But I doubt if I'll go so far. Ireland is much nearer. I'd like to see you all. Lord, how those children have come on! Makes me nervous. Poor old Gordon![5] Soon be a grandfather!

Did you know I painted pictures last year—seven or eight big oils—nudes—some people very shocked—worse than my writing. But I think they're rather lovely and almost holy. I always remember when you scolded me for making Paul in *Sons and Lovers* paint dress-lengths. I agree, after many years—it would be rather boring. I did a picture of the Boccaccio story of the nuns and the gardener—much more fun than batik.

Are there three children? somehow I only had track of Biddy and Paddy: and now they're jazzers and golfers! Dio mio!

Is your hair still the same colour? F is a bit grey, and I found two white hairs in my beard. C'est le premier pas qui coûte.

I'd really like to come to Ireland, and see you all, and Liam

5 Gordon Campbell, Lord Glenavy.

O'Flaherty[6]—and Dublin—and go to the west, I hope it wouldn't always rain, and I wouldn't have a political aspect, and be shot or arrested. But I'd like to come, and I think we will once the Mirenda is wound up—in April—and that novel more or less off my hands. Somehow I can form no picture at all of Ireland—much more easily of Ecuador or Manchuria. But I think a country which doesn't really exist and doesn't assert its non-existence violently any more—as Italy does—must be rather a relief. Geographically nowhere, as you say. Suppose one painted nudes in Ireland—not tough stucco John[7] ones— would we be thrown in the Castle dungeons? Do the policemen wear orange trousers and goose-feathers: no, orange is Belfast: green: green and pink policemen, and money made of glass, and all motor-cars pale pink by law? And a state harpist at every street corner—and runes all over the house-fronts—and the pavements with poems let in in little white pebbles—and lordly gentlemen in bright collars of gold, like Malachi, and two-edged swords, forcing every civilian to pronounce six words in Erse before he passes on. That's how I imagine it, so don't disappoint me. And in some streets no walking allowed, forced to dance a jig from end to end. And ladies at night walking with their white bosoms lit up with a necklace of tiny electric lights. And nuns in scarlet, and priests in lemon colour. Oh Ireland! and Gordon in a leopard-skin!

Never mind! au revoir,

D. H. LAWRENCE.

To MARTIN SECKER

Diablerets, Monday, 5 March, 1928.

Dear Secker,

I posted off the MS. of the novel to Pollinger[8] to-day— changed the title to: *John Thomas and Lady Jane:*[9] which I

6 Irish novelist.
7 Augustus John. (H. T. M.)
8 Of the Curtis Brown office.
9 *Lady Chatterley's Lover.*

hope you like, as it's much more suitable than the other. I don't at all know how much you'll react to the book, probably you'll hate it. Aldous Huxley and Maria liked it very much—so they said. ———¹ went into a fearful rage over it—a moral rage. They're the only people who have read it so far.

Then the expurgations—I did a fair amount of blanking out and changing, then I sort of got colour-blind, and didn't know any more what was supposed to be proper and what not. So you must consider it. Don't all in a rush be scared and want to pull whole sections out. Just consider a bit patiently, in detail, what is *possible* and what isn't. I know it's not easy to judge. And then if there are little bits you can leave out without making obvious gaps, then I'm willing you should leave them out. But if you want any substantial alterations made, then consider the thing carefully, in detail, and mark it carefully in blue pencil, and send me the pages you want changed, and I'll do my best. I think we ought to manage to make it feasible.

I leave in the morning for Milan, where I meet Frieda. I do hope I shan't get any cold or anything going down, for I'm a good bit better now. This evening it's trying to rain—warm spring rain on sudden snow. Just as well to descend for a bit.

Well, I hope you won't hate the novel—though you easily may. It's a bit of a revolution in itself—a bit of a bomb.

D. H. L.

To A. AND M. HUXLEY
Villa Mirenda, Scandicci, Firenze, 9 March.
Dear Aldous and Maria,

To-day I lunched with Orioli, and we took the MS. of the novel to the printer: great moment. Juliette, who read the MS. and was *very* cross, morally so, suggested rather savagely I should call it: *John Thomas and Lady Jane.* Many a true word

¹ Juliette Huxley (wife of Julian Huxley).

spoken in spite, so I promptly called it that. Remains to be seen if Secker and Knopf will stand it.—Afterwards, Juliette was *almost* reconciled to the novel: but she thought: *what* if Anthony were 16, and read it!—What indeed! However, to-morrow night I shall have a specimen page from the printer—and by Monday I may hear what Curtis Brown and Secker think of their expurgated *(sic)* MS. I'm prepared for anything—but shall go ahead here.—Saw Douglas[4] to-day—but nothing new about him, still thinking of Jerusalem and preferring Chianti.

We wound up very nicely in Diablerets. Juliette and her mother and Mademoiselle all looked after me like angels, and we made a paradise[5] with a woollen serpent! Juliette brought it to the station for a last word of advice—me as paradise-manufacturer—and nearly died of shame because Mademoiselle stood like an easel holding it for me to see—on the platform—and I cocked my eye—and all the station peeped and peeped at Juliette's Adam and Eve nude in lisle thread and pink wool!

Tomorrow F.'s elder sister[6] due to come.—House full of violets and anemones. Wilks[7] depart at end of month.

Disgustedly!

D. H. L.

To WITTER BYNNER

Villa Mirenda, Scandicci, Florence.

13 March, 1928.

Dear Bynner,

I sniffed the red herring in your last letter a long time: then at last decide it's a live sprat. I mean about *The Plumed Serpent* and "the hero." On the whole, I think you're right. The hero is obsolete, and the leader of men is a back number. After all, at the back of the hero is the militant ideal: and the

---

4 Norman Douglas.
5 An embroidery.
6 Else Jaffe.
7 The Wilkinsons, neighbors at the Mirenda.

militant ideal, or the ideal militant seems to me also a cold egg. We're sort of sick of all forms of militarism and militantism, and *Miles* is a name no more, for a man. On the whole I agree with you, the leader-cum-follower relationship is a bore. And the new relationship will be some sort of tenderness, sensitive, between men and men and men and women, and not the one up one down, lead on I follow, *ich dien* sort of business. So you see I'm becoming a lamb at last, and you'll even find it hard to take umbrage at me. Do you think?

But still, *in a way,* one has to fight, but not in the O Glory! sort of way. I feel one still has to fight for the phallic reality, as against the non-phallic cerebration unrealities. I suppose the phallic consciousness is part of the whole consciousness which is your aim. To me it's a vital part.

So I wrote my novel, which I want to call *John Thomas and Lady Jane*. But that I have to submerge into a subtitle, and call it *Lady Chatterley's Lover*. But I am printing here in Florence an unexpurgated edition of this tender and phallic novel, far too good for the public. The expurgated will come in the autumn. But this, the full fine flower with pistil and stamens standing, I hope to have ready by May 15th.—1000 copies, of which 500 for America, at ten dollars a copy. I shall send you a few little order-forms, and *do* please send a few out for me, to the right people. You can reach a lot of the right sort of people in the Universities. I shall mail direct from Florence, as soon as the book is ready: a good book. And why should the red flower have its pistil nipped out, before it is allowed to appear? So I shall trust you in this.

We are in this house till May 6th, then I don't know where. I want to come to New Mexico—perhaps even earn a little money this way to come with.

Tante belle cose!

D. H. LAWRENCE.

To MRS. HAMILTON EAMES

Villa Mirenda, Scandicci, Florence.
15 March, 1928.

Dear Marian,

I've not yet sent you the promised book: but that was because I didn't have a nice one. Now I'm correcting proofs of my *Collected Poems,* and that seems very suitable. So as soon as I get copies, I'll write in one and send it you.

I was glad to hear you are gaily and hopefully embarked with a husband. Imagine Emma Eames[8] being in the family! I do hope your husband will put out a few brave blossoms. The world badly needs a few courageous artists. The present lot have their tails sadly between their legs. When your husband writes, see that it's chirpy and defiant.

I'm going to send you a few order-forms for my new novel, which I'm printing here in Florence. It's a tender phallic novel: now you're married you'll understand it. I have to publish it here, as it's too phallic for the gross public. So if you can, give the leaflets to a few people who might like to buy the book. It's worth it.

And some time this year I do hope we'll be in New York *en route* to New Mexico, then we'll drink a pink and cheerful draught from the soda fountain, for our mutual healths together.

Sincerely,
D. H. LAWRENCE.

Make your mother[8a] buy my novel: good for her, after so much behaviourism.

---

8 Famous opera singer.
8a Nina Witt, an early friend of Mabel Sterne in Buffalo and a Taos acquaintance of the Lawrences.

To JULIETTE HUXLEY
> *Villa Mirenda, Scandicci, Florence.*
> *17 April, 1928.*

Dear Juliette,

Why do you say I laugh at you? I may laugh at some things about you. I laugh at you when you say, "What if Anthony were sixteen, and read this novel!" He'd be too bored at 16: but at twenty, of course, he *should* read it. Was your mind a sexual blank at sixteen? Is anybody's? And what ails the mind in that respect is that it has nothing to go on, it grinds away in abstraction. So I laugh at you and shall go on laughing when you say: What if Anthony were 16, and read your novel! What, indeed! But of course I don't laugh at *you,* nor at your mother either. For absurdities I laugh at everybody, including myself: and why not? But at the essential person I don't laugh. And of course, you ought to know it, and not have those silly misgivings.

I've been having a tussle with my novel: publishers, agents, etc., in London holding up hands of pious horror (because it may affect *their pockets),* and trying to make me feel disastrously in the wrong. Now the Knopfs write from New York they like it very much, and hope to be able to get it into shape to offer to the public. I doubt they can't.[8b] But it's nice of them.

I'm in the midst of the proofs—hope to finish them this week. But I still haven't chosen the cover paper. The orders came in very nicely from England. Are you risking a copy, or not?

It's been nasty weather—not really nice since we came back. But to-day looks promising. To-morrow Lady Colefax is due to come to tea. I'm busy finishing off my pictures—think I shall send them to Dorothy Warren[9] for her to exhibit in her gallery

---

[8b] This is as it appears in the Huxley *Letters* but probably Lawrence meant to write "I doubt they can."

[9] Owner of the Warren Gallery in London, niece of Lady Ottoline Morrell.

in Maddox St.—she wants to. But don't go and see them—you'd only be in a rage as you were that morning in les Aroles.

We want to leave this house on the 30th—so we've not much longer. I may stay in Florence to see my book out on the 15th, then to Switzerland, to cure. I think we'll go to Vermala Montana, above Sierre (or is it Sion?)—because it's a flat plateau and I can walk without gasping. My chest is so-so—but I'm better really.

Anyhow, we'll see you during the summer—perhaps August. Remember me to Julian, and I hope the book goes gaily, and he'll feel nice and chirpy doing it: and not try to do too many other things. Frieda has actually written too. How are the children? Is Anthony at school?

D. H. L.

I suppose your mother is back in her Neuchâtel. Remember me to her when you write.

To HELEN W. BRAMBLE

Villa Mirenda, Scandicci, Florence.
17 April, 1928.

Dear Miss Bramble,

Many thanks for your letter and the copies of letters about the *Escaped Cock*. But what a lovely little anthology! I am delighted to have them. Now I know I've committed the unpardonable sin, I feel all right. I always was so afraid I might be saved: like ten dollars in the bank. No more fear of that! But, oh, I do so want to know how many souls were *lost* through my maleficence: and the editor's. The more the merrier! Do you think Carrie J. Hill,[1] who has nothing but sympathy in her dear old heart "for us both"—one at a time, my dear—might be able to tell me? No wonder *The Forum* looks red, fiery and Mephistophelian. Let it be more so. Long live the cloven hoof!

---

[1] One of the letter-writers.

Of course you may have lost a few subscriptions *pro tem.*
But, believe me, those lost souls will either come back or send
delegates. You won't lose in the long run. Deadness is what loses
in the long run. Anything that makes 'em wriggle becomes at
last indispensable. *Vive le gai coq, et le coq gai!*

I hope Carrie Hill will read my novel—and that it will fall
into the hands of the son of nineteen, and that he'll read it
aloud to the gaudy end before a stunned and aghast parent can
stop him. Oh, what a lot of hypocrites!

So I enclose a few order forms, and please send one to George
Williamson, Litchfield, Mich.,[2] and to Carrie dear, and a few
others: I might even get them to lose their souls, instead of
saving 'em: which would be *so* much more becoming.

Your sincere "traitor and enemy of the human race,"

D. H. LAWRENCE.

To LADY OTTOLINE MORRELL
Villa Mirenda, Scandicci, Florence.
24 May, 1928.

My dear Ottoline[3]

I'm most grieved to think you've had such a time and so
much pain with that mysterious illness: worse even than I
thought. It puzzles me terribly why these things should come.
But do you know what I think? I think it's because one isn't
just vulgarly selfish enough, vulgarly *physically* selfish, self-
keeping and self-preserving. One wastes one's common flesh too
much: then these microbes, which are the pure incarnation of
invisible selfishness, pounce on one.

You ask me, do I feel things very much?—and I do. And
that's why I too am ill. The hurts, and the bitterness sink in,
however much one may reject them with one's spirit. They sink

2 Evidently another of the letter-writers.
3 Because of the angry response of Lady Ottoline to her portrait in *Women in
Love,* she and Lawrence had been estranged for some ten years previous to 1928.

in, and there they lie, inside one, wasting one. What is the matter with us is primarily chagrin. Then the microbes pounce. One ought to be tough and selfish: and one is never tough enough, and never selfish in the proper self-preserving way. Then one is laid low.

I've been in bed again this last week, but not bad, a touch of 'flu. And it's no good going to Switzerland to be bitter cold. It's even cold here.

Yes, I'm sad about Garsington,[4] very sad that it has gone. While you still had it I always felt in some way I still had it. If only one could have two lives: the first, in which to make one's mistakes, which seem as if they *had* to be made; and the second in which to profit by them. If it could only be so, what a lovely Garsington we could all have, and no bitterness at the end of it!

But don't say you feel you're not important in life. You've been an important influence in lots of lives, as you have in mine: through being fundamentally generous, and through being Ottoline. After all, there's only one Ottoline. And she has moved one's imagination. It doesn't matter what sort of vision comes out of a man's imagination, his vision of Ottoline. Any more than a photograph of me is me, or even "like" me. The so-called portraits of Ottoline can't possibly be Ottoline— no one knows that better than an artist. But Ottoline has moved men's imagination, deeply, and that's perhaps the most a woman can do. And in the world to-day, full of women, how rare to fine one that can move the imagination! No, I wish, and wish deeply, there could be Ottoline again and Garsington again, and we could start afresh.

But we can start afresh anyhow, in a quieter, gentler way.

I'm doing the last proofs of my novel now, so in about a week I expect we shall leave. I hope the book won't shock you—but I'm sure it won't. You will understand what I'm trying to do:

4 The Morrells' place in Oxfordshire.

the full natural *rapprochement* of a man and a woman; and the re-entry into life of a bit of the old phallic awareness and the old phallic insouciance.

I do hope you are feeling a bit better each day. I'm a lot better really; only this bit of 'flu put me back.

Frieda sends her love and her sympathy with mine.

D. H. LAWRENCE.

To H. AND C. CROSBY

Villa Mirenda, Scandicci (Florence).

Friday, 26 May, 1928.

Dear Harry Crosby and Caresse,

My wife went to Florence yesterday and brought the Queen of Naples' snuff-box and three pieces of gold, from Orioli, to my utter amazement.[5] But *cari miei,* it won't do. I am sure you're not Croesuses to that extent: and anyhow, what right have I to receive these things? For heaven's sake, you embarrass me! I hope to heaven you're quite, quite rich, for if you're not, I shall feel really bad about it. Here I am, quite uneasy in my skin. Gold rolls *mir zur Füssen?* Gold—I feel almost wicked with it!

The *wagon-lit* man was a knave, and tried to bully Orioli out of 200 liras, but only got 100. I wonder very much that he delivered the goods. Why, oh why, did you send them! I considered myself paid in excess before, so now where am I?

But I shall buy some snuff and put it in the snuff-box and take it as my grandfather did: and offer worthy souls a pinch and a sneeze, with little finger lifted.

But at present I feel rather worried—for the first time I know what *embarras de richesse* means. Perhaps one day we can square it somehow.

Meanwhile very many thanks—but in future I shall tell you the price of my pen to a centime, and not a button more.

D. H. LAWRENCE.

5 Gifts from the Crosbys.

To A. AND M. HUXLEY
Kesselmatte, Gsteig b. Gstaad, 31 July, 1928.

Dear Aldous and Maria,

I should have written before, but have been under the altitude—felt perfectly wretched, and made design for my tombstone in Gsteig churchyard, with suitable inscription: "Departed this life, etc., etc.—*He was fed up!*" However, last Friday—or Thursday afternoon, I forget which—I decided to live a little longer—and to-day I walked down to the village, and what is much worse, up again. It's like climbing to the Diablerets glacier. However, here I am, with a crick in my neck I admit, and Achsah[6] *et famille* will be drippingly arriving to tea just now. The sun is sharply hot, the wind quite cool. But the sun sort of dissolves one's corpuscles. I daren't try another sun-bath, not for a minute. So I rather envy you your red colour all over—or pansy-bronze or calceolaria or burnt-monkey-musk, whatever it is—and I would willingly dangle myself before a shark if I could swim in the deep sea and sit in the southern sun naked and undiminished. In fact, if I don't actually sit on a muck-heap and scrape myself with a tin lid, it's because I haven't the energy.

I suppose all the ordered copies of *Lady Jane* are in England: so the booksellers have hastily written to say we must take back their copies at once, they couldn't handle the *Lady,* and I must cancel their orders, and will we remove the offence at once. That is in all 114 copies we have to fetch back. Of course, these children of God haven't paid.—Then there are rumours that the police are going to raid the shops: I suppose people hope they will. At the same time, the first batch has arrived safely at its various destinations in America.

I believe I have lost most of my friends in the escapade, but this is a small loss, alas! I never had any. Richard Aldington writes he gets a great kick out of it, and it's a feather in the cap

6 Achsah (Mrs. Earl) Brewster.

of the XX century. It's a fool's cap anyhow, why should I put a feather in it. An American young man writes: But oh, your friends, Lorenzo! By their reactions shall you know them!—I shan't, because they'll keep them severely dark. I have unkindly set my foot down, and won't either give it or lend it to the ————'s[7] and of course, buying is beyond their idea.

I see the white flutter of our spotless friends away down on the high-road—poor dears, such a climb! Heaven is not reached in a single bound! No indeed, ————[8], it isn't, and it was an American who first registered the fact.

Well, I feel there's not much of me left. What little there is gives you the Easter Kiss and hopes we'll crow in chorus once more, one day, like risen Easter eggs.

D. H. L.

To A. STIEGLITZ
Kesselmatte, Gsteig b. Gstaad (Bern), Switzerland.
15 August, 1928.

Dear Stieglitz,

Many thanks for sending that cable to Florence. I'm glad you liked *Lady C.* She seems to have exploded like a bomb among most of my English friends, and they're still suffering from shell-shock. But they're coming round already: some few already feeling it was good for 'em. Give them time. There are rumours of suppression in England, and rumours of ban in America. But I can't help it. I've shot my shot, anyhow: I shot an arrow into the air tee-de-dum!

Don't be alarmed about the pictures—they're quite good. Anyhow, they *contain* something—which is more than you can say of most moderns, which are all excellent rind of the fruit, but no fruit. And because a picture has subject-matter it is not therefore less a picture. Besides, what's a deformed guitar and

---

7 Probably the Brewsters. (H. T. M.)
8 Probably Earl (Brewster).

a shred of newspaper but subject-matter? There's the greatest lot of bunk talked about modern painting ever. If a picture is to hit deep into the senses, which is its business, it must hit down to the soul and up into the mind—that is, it has to mean something to the co-ordinating soul and the co-ordinating spirit which are central in man's consciousness: and the meaning has to come through direct sense impression. I know what I'm about. As for their space composition and their mass-reaction and their arabesques, if that isn't all *literary* and idea-concept, what is? Such a lot of canary cages, and never a bird in one of 'em? What, I ask you, is Roger Fry?*—a literary gentleman, or a painter? My God, look at his pictures! The pen is mightier than the palette in his case.

But I'm not really keen on exhibiting, so don't go to any trouble. Dorothy Warren is supposed to be showing my things in London in first half of October—that is, if I don't go and stop her—which leaves the pictures free for November. But as I say, I don't really care whether the canvases come to New York or not. Only if you show me, at least have a look at Hon. Dorothy Brett's things and see if you don't like them.

I want to come to America in late autumn anyhow, to go to the ranch. So I hope we shall meet. How *did* O'Keefe[1] take the book?

Sincerely,

D. H. LAWRENCE.

To ADA LAWRENCE CLARKE[2]

Switzerland, Sept. 10, 1928.

My God—these mincing young females all mincing together in a female bunch, they little know what a terrible thing they're preparing for themselves later, when this mincing young female

* Painter and art critic.
1 Georgia O'Keefe, painter, wife of Alfred Stieglitz.
2 From *Early Life of D. H. Lawrence.*

business wears itself out. Are *all* young Englishwomen instinctively homosexual? Looks like it, to me. Of course, I'm only
speaking of the instincts, not of any practice. But that instinct
sends a man's feelings recoiling to the ultimate pole. My God!
what a ghastly mess "purity" is leading to! Poor Bertie,[3] I
sympathise with him—a prisoner already. I think it is *quite*
wrong for young children to have so many hours schooling.
Three hours in the morning would be quite enough, up to the
age of eight. But I suppose one has to do as the world does, else
be exceptional. As for myself, I take my stand on exception. . . .
We leave on the 17th for Baden Baden. I don't think I shall
come to England. The thought of it depresses me. Frieda will
come to England for ten days or a fortnight. I want her to see
my picture show. Dorothy Warren opens it either on the 5th
or the 9th of Oct. The first two days will be by invitation only.
I can have her send you a card if you wish—but I'd advise you
not to go—you won't like the things. Best leave 'em alone.—
But the show will be open to the public till the end of October.
. . . The cows have now all come down from the high Alps—
summer is over—time to go.

D. H. LAWRENCE.

To A. HUXLEY

La Vigie, Port-Cros (Var), Sunday.[6]

Dear Aldous,

I have read *Point Counter Point* with a heart sinking through
my boot-soles and a rising admiration. I do think you've shown
the truth, perhaps the last truth, about you and your generation, with really fine courage. It seems to me it would take ten
times the courage to write *P. Counter P.* that it took to write
Lady C.: and if the public knew *what* it was reading, it would
throw a hundred stones at you, to one at me. I do think that art
has to reveal the palpitating moment or the state of man as it

---

3 Ada's younger son.
6 The date of this letter is October or November 1928.

is. And I think you do that, terribly. But what a moment! and what a state! if you can only palpitate to murder, suicide, and rape, in their various degrees—and you state plainly that it is so—*caro*, however are we going to live through the days? Preparing still another murder, suicide, and rape? But it becomes of a phantasmal boredom and produces ultimately inertia, inertia, inertia and final atrophy of the feelings. Till, I suppose, comes a final super-war, and murder, suicide, rape sweeps away the vast bulk of mankind. It is as you say—intellectual appreciation does not amount to so much, it's what you thrill to. And if murder, suicide, rape is what you thrill to, and nothing else, then it's your destiny—you can't change it *mentally*. You live by what you thrill to, and there's the end of it. Still for all that it's a *perverse* courage which makes the man accept the slow suicide of inertia and sterility: the perverseness of a perverse child.—It's amazing how men are like that. Richard Aldington[7] is exactly the same inside, murder, suicide, rape—with a desire to *be* raped very strong—same thing really —just like you—only he doesn't face it, and gilds his perverseness. It makes me feel ill, I've had more hemorrhage here and been in bed this week. *Sporca miseria*. If I don't find some solid spot to climb out of, in this bog, I'm done. I can't stand murder, suicide, rape—especially rape: and especially being raped. Why do men only thrill to a woman who'll rape them?[8] All I want to do to your Lucy is smack her across the mouth, your Rampion is the most boring character in the book—a gas-bag. Your attempt at intellectual sympathy!—It's all rather disgusting, and I feel like a badger that has its hole on Wimbledon Common and trying not to be caught. Well, *caro*, I feel like saying good-bye to you—but one will have to go on saying good-bye for years.

D. H. L.

[7] Aldington's name is deleted in the English edition of the Huxley *Letters*.
[8] "and s— on their face" is the end of this sentence in the American edition of the Huxley *Letters*.

To MORRIS L. ERNST

La Vigie, Ile de Port-Cros, Var, France.
10 Novem., 1928.

I have finished reading *To the Pure.*[9] I find it a curious, interesting, pertinent book, curiously moving. As the work of lawyers rather than literary men, it conveys an impression that no truly literary work would achieve. I look out with those unemotional lawyer's eyes, and have a queer experience. I am left feeling puzzled, uneasy, and a little frightened, as if I had been watching a great unchained ape fumbling through his hairs for something—he doesn't quite know what—which he will squash if he gets it. I see that weird and horrible animal, Social Man, devoid of real individuality or personality, fumbling gropingly and menacingly for something he is afraid of, but he doesn't know what it is. It is a lawyer's vision, not an artist's—but it is the result of experience in dealing with the Social Man. The book, in its queer muddle—for legal precision is artistic muddle—creates the weird reactionary of the ageless censor-animal curiously and vividly. It leaves one feeling breathless, and makes one realise the necessity of keeping a chain on the beast. For censorship is one of the lower and debasing activities of social man—that is obvious.

Myself, I believe censorship helps nobody; and hurts many. But the book has brought it home to me much more grimly than before. Our civilisation cannot afford to let the censor-moron loose. The censor-moron does not really hate anything but the living and growing human consciousness. It is our developing and extending consciousness that he threatens—and our consciousness in its newest, most sensitive activity, its vital growth. To arrest or circumscribe the vital consciousness is to produce morons, and nothing but a moron would wish to do it.

No, the book is a good book—and the very effect of muddle

[9] By Morris Ernst.

which it has on me conveys most vividly the feeling of the groping atavistic working of the ageless censor, furtive, under-hand, mean.

Print this letter if you like—or any bit of it. I believe in the living extending consciousness of man. I believe the conscious-ness of man has now to embrace the emotions and passions of sex, and the deep effects of human physical contact. This is the glimmering edge of our awareness and our field of understand-ing, in the endless business of knowing ourselves. And no censor must or shall or even can really interfere.

Sincerely,
D. H. LAWRENCE.

To BARONESS VON RICHTHOFEN[4]

Ile De Port-Cros, Var, Wednesday.

My dear Mother-in-Law:

I am glad you are better. You have been too brave. You know, you are heavy on your feet now, you are no longer a young, light thing. You must not walk so far. I remember with grief the "Fisch Kultur," a mad excursion and you insisted doing it. No, no, you must go gently and wisely. To force things is not for you.

Tomorrow we leave here. Thank the Lord, the weather is good, blue sky, blue quiet sea, and so warm. But I have enough. I would never like to stay more than a month on a little island. But as an experience it was nice. I think we will only go as far as Bandol, a little place on the coast, half an hour from Toulon. But there we are on the main line, and only an hour from Marseille. And we can think where we really want a house—neither of us knows what we want.

They write from Florence it rains and rains and rains; awful. Thank God, we aren't there. My book of stories came with the

---

4 From *"Not I, But the Wind . . ."* as translated there from the German. The date of this letter is November 14, 1928. (H. T. M.)

Inselalmanach and Möricke. You know I have not broken with Insel? They pay me fifty pounds instead of thirty-five and Else* can translate when she wants to. That's good.

I send you five pounds, if you want more tell me. It is my money and I give it you with pleasure, but please pay the ten marks for Frieda's dress.

The Brewsters are in Capri again. They say it is the best place in the world. Good, when you know it!

Keep still and quiet inside yourself, then your legs will go without pain.

D. H. L.

To J. D. CHAMBERS

Ile de Port-Cros, Var, France, 14 Novem., 1928.

Dear David,

I hardly recognised you as J.D.—and you must be a man now, instead of a thin little lad with very fair hair. Ugh, what a gap in time! it makes me feel scared.

Whatever I forget, I shall never forget the Haggs[1]—I loved it so. I loved to come to you all, it really was a new life began in me there. The water-pippin by the door—those maiden-blush roses that Flower would lean over and eat and trip floundering round.—And stewed figs for tea in winter, and in August green stewed apples. Do you still have them? Tell your mother I never forget, no matter where life carries us.—And does she still blush if somebody comes and finds her in a dirty white apron? Or doesn't she wear work-aprons any more? Oh, I'd love to be nineteen again, and coming up through the Warren and catching the first glimpse of the buildings. Then I'd sit on the sofa under the window, and we'd crowd round the little table to tea, in that tiny little kitchen I was so at home in.

Son' tempi passati, cari miei! quanto cari, non saprete mai!—

---

* Else Jaffe, Frieda Lawrence's sister, who was Lawrence's German translator.
1 Greasley Haggs, below Willey Farm where the Chambers family lived. David Chambers was a brother of Jessie, the Miriam of *Sons and Lovers.*

To CHARLES WILSON [*1928*]

I could never tell you in English how much it all meant to me, how I still feel about it.

If there is anything I can ever do for you, do tell me.— Because whatever else I am, I am somewhere still the same Bert who rushed with such joy to the Haggs.

Ever,

D. H. LAWRENCE.

The best address is: c/o Curtis Brown, Ltd., 6, Henrietta Street, Covent Garden, W.C.2.

To CHARLES WILSON

Hôtel Beau Rivage, Bandol, Var., 28 Dec., 1928.

Dear Charles Wilson,

Many thanks for the calendar and the greeting. Here are three scraps of a sort of poetry, which will perhaps do as a "message." I've done a book of such poems—really they are *pensées*—which I shall publish later—but you may as well start in with these three bits.[2]

I hope you got your copy of *Lady Chatterley*. It was finally sent from Florence, so if it doesn't arrive it is lost.

I wonder when we shall come to England. I read with shame of the miners' "Hampers" and the "Fund." It's a nice thing to make them live on charity and crumbs of cake, when what they want is manly independence. The whole scheme of things is unjust and rotten, and money is just a disease upon humanity. It's time there was an *enormous* revolution—not to instal soviets, but to give life itself a chance. What's the good of an industrial system piling up rubbish, while nobody lives. We want a revolution not in the name of money or work or any of that, but of life—and let money and work be as casual in human

---

2 The poems were "O! Start A Revolution!", "For God's Sake—," and "It's Either You Fight or You Die." Lawrence sent them as a "New Year's Greeting to the Willington Men, for 1929."

life as they are in a bird's life, damn it all. Oh, it's time the whole thing was changed, absolutely. And the men will have to do it—you've got to smash money and this beastly *possessive* spirit. I get more revolutionary every minute, but for *life's* sake. The dead materialism of Marx socialism and soviets seems to me no better than what we've got. What we want is life and *trust;* men trusting men, and making living a free thing, not a a thing to be *earned.* But if men trusted men, we could soon have a new world, and send this one to the devil.

There's more message—perhaps too strong for you. But the beastliness of the show, the *injustice*—just see the rich English down here on the Riviera, *thousands* of them—nauseates me. Men can't stand injustice.

Happy New Year.

D. H. LAWRENCE.

To LADY OTTOLINE MORRELL
Hôtel Beau Rivage, Bandol, Var, France.
28 Dec., 1928.

My dear Ottoline,

I was glad to hear from you again, and very glad to know you are better. Aldous also wrote that you were really wonderfully well, after that bad time. As for me, it's *poco á poco,* but I'm really getting better all the time.

We have been down on this coast since October, and I must say it has suited me well, it's a good winter climate. I didn't know Katherine had been here—wonder where she stayed.[3] But I think in a fortnight we shall move on to Spain. From here it's not so very far. We've got to find somewhere to live, now we've given up the Florence house. Frieda gets fidgety, being without a house. But she doesn't really know *where* she wants one. Where does one want to live, finally?

---

3 Actually Katherine Mansfield had been in Bandol when Lawrence had persuaded her and Murry to come to Cornwall.

About *Lady C.*—you mustn't think I advocate perpetual sex. Far from it. Nothing nauseates me more than promiscuous sex in and out of season. But I want, with *Lady C.,* to make an *adjustment in consciousness* to the basic physical realities. I realise that one of the reasons why the common people often keep—or kept—the good *natural glow* of life, just warm life, longer than educated people, was because it was still possible for them to say ——4! or ——4 without either a shudder or a sensation. If a man had been able to say to you when you were young and in love: an' if tha ——4, an' if tha ——4, I' glad, I shouldna want a woman who couldna ——4 nor ——4—surely it would have been a liberation to you, and it would have helped to keep your heart warm. Think of poor Swift's insane *But* of horror at the end of every verse of that poem to Celia. But Celia ——!4—you see the very fact that it should horrify him, and simply devastate his consciousness, is all wrong, and a bitter shame to poor Celia. It's just the awful and truly unnecessary *recoil* from these things that I would like to break. It's a question of conscious acceptance and adjustment—only that. God forbid that I should be taken as urging loose sex activity. There is a brief time for sex, and a long time when sex is out of place. But when it is out of place as an activity there still should be the large and quiet space in the consciousness where it lives quiescent. Old people can have a lovely quiescent sort of sex, like apples, leaving the young quite free for *their* sort.

It's such a pity preachers have always dinned in: Go thou and do likewise! That's not the point. The point is: It is so, let it be so, with a generous heart.

Well, forgive all this, but I don't want you to misunderstand me, because I always count on your sympathy somewhere.

4 The text used here follows the text in the Huxley *Letters* where these exci-sions had been required both by English and American law. Although the law is now rather less strict on this score, the deleted words cannot be supplied without reference to the original letter which is not available to the Editor.

Frieda sends her love, and one day I hope we'll have a few quiet chats and laughs together—there's still time for that.

D. H. LAWRENCE.

To LADY OTTOLINE MORRELL
Hôtel Beau Rivage, Bandol, Var., 5 Feby., 1929.

My dear Ottoline,

Aldous and Maria were here for ten days or so—neither of them very well, run down. Aldous with liver, and Maria going very thin and not eating enough. I think the *Counter-Point* book sort of got between them—she found it hard to forgive the death of the child—which one can well understand. But, as I say, there's more than one self to everybody, and the Aldous that writes those novels is only one little Aldous amongst others—probably much nicer—that don't write novels—I mean it's only one of his little selves that writes the book and makes the child die, it's not *all* himself. No, I don't like his books: even if I admire a sort of desperate courage of repulsion and repudiation in them. But again, I feel only half a man writes the books—a sort of precocious adolescent. There is surely much more of a man in the actual Aldous. They went on in the car to Italy, and yesterday came a desperate post card saying they had broken down at Albenga, near Savona, and having to stay in a very bad hotel, very cold, and the wind bitter. I hope they're out of it by now. To-day was a beautiful, beautiful day—all bright royal sunshine, and no wind, so one just sat out and felt the brightness. But mostly there has been a very cold wind. It's a cold winter here too, but nearly always clear.

I'm so sad you have such bad health. Aldous thought you so much better. But if you have those blinding headaches, my word, I sympathise. I never really had headaches until I was ill eighteen months ago—but now I have a holy terror of them. Thank goodness mine are better now. What do you think yours come from? I believe they often arise from a condition of weakness, that one doesn't take sufficient account of. Are you sure you eat enough? Do you drink a little burgundy? Since I am here, and can eat, and drink wine again, I am surprised how the headaches don't come. One just has to build up resistance—that seems to me the only way.

And I agree with you, people are most exhausting. I like them all right at a little distance, if they will leave me alone—but I don't want to talk to them any more. I find I can still sit on a bench and be quite happy, just seeing the sea twinkle and the fisher people potter with their lobster pots. What is there to say any more, to ordinary people at least? It is lovely to be alone, especially when the sun shines. I think you should winter abroad, in some quiet place like this where you see the sun rise behind the sea at dawn, and every day different, and every day, somehow, the spangle and glitter of the sea is a different spangle and glitter. I watch the dawn every day as I lie in bed. And now the sun has moved such a long way, and rises behind the queer, tressy, shaking eucalyptus tree.

But I want to go soon, now. Frieda has not been contented here in a hotel—she wanted a house. But I liked the hotel—warm and no effort. Then lately they have been making a great fuss over *Lady C.* Scotland Yard holding it up—visiting my agents—sort of threatening criminal proceedings—and holding up my mail—and actually confiscating two copies, MS. copies of my poems, *Pansies,* which I sent to my agent Curtis Brown—saying the poems were indecent and obscene—which they're not—and putting me to a lot of trouble. I don't mind when I'm well, but one gets run down. And those dirty *canaille* to be calling me obscene! Really, why does one write! Or why does one write the things I write! I suppose it's destiny, but on the whole, an unkind one. Those precious young people who are supposed to admire one so much never stand up and give one a bit of backing. I believe they'd see me thrown into prison for life, and never lift a finger. What a spunkless world!

I was glad to hear of Bertie Russell. Perhaps he and his Dora will do something, after all—better than his donning away in Cambridge.

I had such a silly, funny little letter from E. M. Forster, telling me *à propos* of nothing that he admires me but doesn't read me. Do you ever see him?

Did I tell you my pictures are going to be reproduced and put in a book—in colour—at 10 guineas a copy? I wrote a long foreword on painting in relation to life—good, I think, really.

Don't you think it's nonsense when Murry says that my world is not the ordinary man's world and that I am a sort of animal with a sixth sense. Seems to me more likely he's a sort of animal with only four senses—the real sense of touch missing. They all seem determined to make a freak of me—to save their own short-failings, and make them "normal."

I wanted to go to Spain, but now it's upset—and Frieda doesn't want me to go. So I don't know what we shall do. I can even be arrested if I come to England—under the Post Office laws—oh, la la! I feel like wandering away somewhere—south—south—perhaps to Africa. But I shall let you know.

I do most sincerely hope you'll be better, for I know so well what it is to fight with pain and struggle on from day to day. What I feel is that you are physically too weak, you need building up, you need to build up resistance. I'm sure you are in some way exhausted, and can't recuperate. Tell the doctors to find a way of nourishing you and fortifying you.

Remember me to Philip[5]—Aldous says he is busy editing memoirs for a book, which I'm sure he'll like doing.

We have got a copy of *Sergeant Grishka*[6]—good in its way, but so depressing and—sort of Jewish: not quite true.

I do hope you'll be better and feel stronger.

Love from us both,

D. H. LAWRENCE.

[5] Philip Morrell, Lady Ottoline's husband.
[6] *The Case of Sergeant Grischa* by Arnold Zweig.

To J. M. MURRY

Hôtel Principe Alfonso, Palma de Mallorca, Spain.

20 May, 1929.

Dear Jack,

Your letter came on here—I had your other one, too, with photographs of the children—felt so distressed about your wife.

But you see, my dear chap, leaving aside all my impatience and "don't care," I know well that we "missed it," as you put it. I don't understand you, your workings are beyond me. And you don't get me. You said in your review of my poems: "this is not life, life is not like that." And you have the same attitude to the real me. Life is not like that—*ergo,* there is no such animal. Hence my "don't care." I am tired of being told there is no such animal, by animals who are merely different. If I am a giraffe, and the ordinary Englishmen who write about me and say they know me are nice well-behaved dogs, there it is, the animals are different. And the me that you say you love is not me, but an idol of your own imagination. Believe me, you don't love me. The animal that I am you instinctively dislike—just as all the Lynds[7] and Squires[8] and Eliots[9] and Goulds[9a] instinctively dislike it—and you all say there's no such animal, or if there is there ought not to be—so why not stick to your position? If I am the only man in your life, it is not because I am I, but merely because I provided the speck of dust on which you formed your crystal of an imaginary man. We don't know one another—if you knew *how* little we know one another! And let's not pretend. By pretending a bit, we had some jolly times, in the past. But we all had to pretend a bit—and we could none of us keep it up. Believe me, we belong to different worlds, different ways of consciousness, you and I, and the best we can

7 Robert Lynd, who had reviewed *The Rainbow* disapprovingly.
8 J. C. Squire, editor of the *London Mercury.*
9 T. S. Eliot.
9a Gerald Gould, who had reviewed *The Rainbow* disparagingly.

do is to let one another alone, for ever and ever. We are a dissonance.

My health is a great nuisance, but by no means as bad as all that, and I have no idea of passing out. We want to leave next week for a short tour in Spain—then go north. So don't think of coming to Mallorca. It is no good our meeting—even when we are immortal spirits, we shall dwell in different Hades. Why not accept it. But I do hope your wife is getting better and the children are well and gay.

D. H. L.

To EARL AND ACHSAH BREWSTER[2]

Hotel Principe Alfonso, Palma de Mallorca, Spain.
2 June 1929.

Dear Earl and Achsah,

Well, what a budget!—Harwood falling over a cliff and spraining her ankle (though I want to know *which* precepts of her mother's bore her up from more serious damage)—and a distant cousin who should be dead coming out of an earthquake to claim the family inheritance—and no home once more—and an all-pervading uncertainty. No, it won't do. Achsah, my dear, you must come to a few decisions *all on your own.* Earl is out of the running *pro tem,* and I seriously think Buddha and deep breathing are rather a bane, both of them. Now Earl will never fit properly into a normal environment, so it's no use counting on him. As for Harwood being a doctor—if she *wants* to, let her—and if she's going to, then it's high time she began some regular work in preparation, at some regular school or college. If it's not going to be America, let it be England. But for God's sake do *something* about it—another year has gone by, she's going to be seventeen, and the muddle only deepens. Achsah, it is now up to you. This is a question of environment

---

[2] From *D. H. Lawrence: Reminiscences and Correspondence.*

and adaptation to the western world. Earl has more or less destroyed his adaptation and dislocated himself from the western environment.... He doesn't want to adapt. Neither do I, beyond a certain point. But up to a point, one must.... Let her (Harwood) be a doctor if she wants to; and in that case, start out at once with some proper schooling in a school, in England or America.

Yes, I like R.N.[3] all right—but I didn't know he called himself my disciple. I certainly don't call myself his master. I know almost nothing of him, and he knows almost nothing of me—and I feel we're as different as chalk and cheese. But people must have their little fancies.

We keep lingering on here. Now we say we will sail to Marseille on June 11th. It is very pleasant here, we know people, the island is extremely calm and lazy, one wastes no energy, and I think it has been good for me. So far, it isn't at all too hot—but one feels it may begin to be so. It's an excellent climate, no rain, practically, and nearly always sunny. If we come to Italy just now, we shall probably go to the Lago di Garda. Frieda has a great idea that that's where she wants to be. I don't feel any particular urge, but I liked it when we were there before. And I certainly think July and August would be too hot here. We could come back in the winter if we wished.

That little book of poetry *Pansies* should be out this month. I will have a copy sent to you.

... We think ... we might sell the ranch. It's too far off.

No more news—I do hope Harwood's ankle is better, and that you are all cheerful. Love from both.

D. H. L.

---

[3] Robert Nichols, poet, whom Lawrence had visited in hospital in 1915 and written about to Lady Ottoline. The Lawrences had just met him again in Mallorca.

To HARWOOD BREWSTER[4]

Hotel Löwen, Lichtenthal, Baden-Baden.
15 Aug., 1929.

Dear Harwood,

Here we are—I'm back in your room, and the sun is shining in almost hot, the garden is very green and pretty, it's almost tea-time, and we're just off to Geroldsan to tea—that village where we walked, do you remember, and came back in the bus. So now you see the whole picture. Frieda's bunch of birthday roses stands on my table and the pink petals fall on your letter— it was a lovely bunch of roses. We thought of you on your birthday, last year at Gsteig. . . . Not once have I seen Achsah's white wings fluttering down the Lichtenthaler Allee this year, nor up the steps to the Trinkallee: though almost. I see her ghost sitting at a little table in the corner sipping the hot water at a penny a time, and feeling so good after it: though I declare it is indigestible. Baden is very green and leafy this year, and the geraniums are very red, and the people are very fat, and the frocks are very weird, some with flouncing flat tails like beavers, some with pointed raggledy tagglendies all getting mixed up with their legs. I suppose you sport the latter sort. We don't go much to the Musik—I'm rather worse at walking, than better— though the doctor says, as far as lung goes, I am very much healed up, but my asthma, which seems to go to my legs, is not much better. So I cough, to the general annoyance or cold commiseration of a nervous universe. And I suppose, cough I shall —though perhaps one day I shall leave it behind, I suppose.

We had quite a nice party on Sunday night—peach Bowle made with champagne and Ganwinkelheimer; large blue trout, ducks, and fat meringues. But I forget, perhaps you still think with horror of the fleshpots.

I suppose you have seen in the newspapers what a dreadful man I am, and what fearsome pictures I paint. When the magis-

---

4 From *D. H. Lawrence: Reminiscences and Correspondence.*

trate said that perhaps even children had seen them, I half hoped you would rise up and chirp: Yes Sir! Please Sir! And I thought them so pretty! But alas, you weren't in court to bear witness.

Well, my dear, so now you're seventeen and going to be a doctor, so hurry up and cure my asthma, for you've only got half an Uncle David instead of a whole one. And I send you a quid, since it seems your fate to receive a paltry quid. And write me about your school, and your plans, and the future.

love.

D. H. L.

We shall be here another week or perhaps more—then we want to go to Italy to find a house to live in. Achsah, what are your plans? I wrote to Earl.

To RHYS DAVIES

Hôtel Löwen, Lichtenthal, Baden-Baden.
24 Aug., 1929.

Dear Davies,

Your letter this morning—and what a dismal picture of the Welsh countryside! Do you think people are going to die away into a sort of mushroom state, or, when they get low enough, will a new sort of life come in and make them tackle their conditions? Only God knows. But I loathe this mushroomy, fishy apathy. What's the good of despair unless it's lurid!

I'm worried about your novels. The problem is, would the big, bloated public swallow you anyhow, at this state of affairs? If Gollancz doesn't come across, then come to terms pretty quick with the Mandrake for one of your books: ask for at least £150 down, *on receipt of manuscript.* They ought to give it you at once. And urge that they publish before Christmas. It seems to me, that if you catch them on the rise of the wave, the Mandrake ought to serve your purpose very well. They have aroused a certain interest—and there is a big public waiting to get anything which they think is not orthodox, does not come via the "good" publishers. There is the enormous "proper" public, of Heinemann or Gollancz. But I believe the "improper" public is almost as big, if not bigger, so long as they are fairly safe. For men like you and me the "proper" public is already a dead horse—certainly so, in my case. But then I am amazed to realise how huge, and how much more potent the improper public is. And it is on this the Mandrake will draw. And they may have a run of real success—I would risk them, if I were you. But I don't think they'll have a long run. Stephenson is another sort of mushroom—he grows too fast. And the big publishers, after a while, will quash them. But for the moment they may just be your ticket. That's how it looks to me. I'd gladly write any sort of foreword for you—but better not. In the first place because of the police, in the second, it's not really good for your reputation. But if you or Stephenson think of any way in which I could be of use, let me know. I could certainly do a review.

I want Charlie Lahr[5] to start a little fortnightly rag called *The Squib,* or something like that—just to rag them all, to get at them and lampoon them, make fun of them, jeer at them and altogether have a good time. We would have a little thing of about ten pages, not much bigger than this note-paper in size, and we'd all have *noms de plume*—I'd be David Dolittle—and sell it at anything up to sixpence—do a few numbers just for fun, and if it got really started, put it on a money basis—a business basis. For the beginning we'd find the money between us—costs ought to be very slight—I'd stand a few quid. The trouble is a good editor. Would you like to try it?—perhaps with Mrs. Lahr to help. We want short little peppery things, pansies, tiny articles. I'm sure you'd be good at squibs. Your idea of the lily-white policemen of London fainting with shock

5 London book-seller.

at the sight of one of my nudes would make an A1 squib. The thing to do would be to seize on the ridiculous points in politics—literature and newspapers—and people—and just ridicule them—watch the press and the books and just get a laugh out of them.

We leave here to-morrow for Bavaria, and I'm glad. Baden is quite lovely in its way, and everybody quite nice, in their way, yet one feels that the Germans, underneath, *aren't nice*. And these huge German women sitting round one like mountains that would never even know if they sat *on* one—I'm sure their bottoms would be too tough for my poor pinching—they simply give me the horrors. I want to go somewhere where the women are a bit *smaller:* and where their hats don't sit so menacingly on their heads. You can get me in Bavaria

> c/o Dr. Max Mohr,[6]
> "Wolfsgrube,"
> Rottach-am-Tegernsee,
> Oberbayern.

But I shall send an address.

In Sept. we want to go down to Italy to look for a house—and let's hope the gods will guide us.

Tell your mother and sister I'm very glad they stick up for me. They are quite right, I'm quite a nice person, really. God knows why I should have so much mud poured over me.

The poor young man of the faggots and peas (what a good pansy there is there!); *have* you seen any of his stories or poems? And *what* are they like?

If you get much more boost in the Welsh papers you'll soon be able to pose as the national bard, and wear a crown of leaks—or is it written leeks? *porri.*

D. H. L.

6 German physician and dramatist.

To A. HUXLEY

Kaffee Angermaier, Rottach-am-Tegernsee,
Oberbayern. 5 Sept.[7]

Dear Aldous,

Had your letter—also Maria's—glad all goes gaily. Here we've been so-so. On Sunday Frieda had a bone-setter from a neighbouring village—a farmer. He felt her foot, said: *Na! 's ist 'raus!*—shoved with his thumbs, a little click. *Fertig!* he said, and so it was. It was really funny. The bone was off the centre, resting on the side of the socket. He just pushed it back, the whole thing took a minute. But he said if it had gone a few more months it would have been too late, as the socket fills in to fit itself up to the displaced bone.—And I had paid 12 guineas to the Park Lane specialist, ————:[8] and four guineas to the masseuse in Baden: and there is still the bill of the long-bearded *Herr Medizinabrat* ————[8] to pay—also a sort of specialist. *Voilà les médecins!* I call it monstrous. If she hadn't come here she'd have limped all her life, and now already she goes quite normal, only a little bit of stiffness. *"Ach!* wear it off like a rusty key!" said the man.

The next is, I've been in bed all week feeling a wreck—and two doctors, *freundlich,* descended on me. One is a new, very modern one, who was a *Pfarrer*—a priest—and has a *Klinik* in München and does wonders, chiefly with diet and breathing. He wasn't the ordinary *Artz* at all—says that in a few weeks, with diet and a bit of breathing, I ought to be well. He says that we are all undergoing a great change in our animal man— that includes woman, of course. But especially men between 42 and 49 are in a state of change. The new animal man will be different from the old—and already demands different food

[7] The date of this letter is Sept. 5, 1929.
[8] Unidentified.

and different rhythms—but he is given only old food and old rhythms, and so gets poisoned. He says mine is partly poison from unwanted food—and I know that's true. Especially heavy German food is poison to me. He says, go back to simple food. The Roman legions conquered the world on millet porridge— he says he gets amazing results by substituting millet porridge for bread and potatoes, etc. Then as much raw food as possible —fruit, salads, etc.—no coffee, but tea if you like it—no vinegar or strong acid—otherwise pretty well anything plain—roast beef and so on—beer—a little wine—but no cake and pastry— and no rich sauces. The great thing is, if you can, to live mainly on the good, rather solid porridges—millet, oatmeal, barley— then raw fruits and vegetables—then yaourt and sour milk and light cheese—and nuts. He says my asthma comes from the vagus nerve, which controls the expansion of the blood-vessels—and the vagus nerve is in a constant state of reaction, from the stomach's recoil from constant food which it *doesn't really want,* and consequent constant poisoning. He says this causes my cough, in a large measure, and I believe him. He says much more important than climate is not to be poisoned by wrong food. And any food you feel you don't really want is wrong.

Now I feel that this, on the whole, is true. I feel I don't want most of the food I eat, merely because it is the kind of food it is: even the bread.—So now for a new diet and a new man—I write it out in detail because I think it applies a good deal to Maria, and also to you, as well as to me.

We wanted to leave about 15th. Motor to Innsbruck—then to Verona—then perhaps to Venice for a few days to meet Dorothy Warren and settle about the pictures—then finally Florence, to cast round for a house. But this doctor threatens not to let me go till I am better—so we may be detained here a bit. Anyhow, I feel this is the right track, doctor or no doctor.

So heaven knows when we shall see you—we'll have to leave it on the knees of the gods.

Grüsse!

D. H. L.

To MABEL STERNE*

Villa Beau Soleil, Bandol
Var, France, 6 Jan., 1930.

Dear Mabel,

Ida[1] says she has written you about our coming to Taos in the spring. I think, if I felt safe about it, I have the energy to get up and start, and I feel that once I got there, I should begin to be well again. Europe is slowly killing me, I feel.

Ida seems pretty well. She goes around here with various friends of ours, and seems to enjoy herself all right. In fact I think she's really in a healthier state of mind than when I saw her last in New Mexico. We talk and make plans: plans of coming back to the ranch and having places near one another— and perhaps having a sort of old school, like the Greek philosophers, talks in a garden—that is, under the pine-trees. I feel I might perhaps get going with a few young people, building up a new unit of life out there, making a new concept of life. Who knows! We have always talked of it. My being ill so long has made me realise perhaps I had better talk to the young and try to make a bit of a new thing with them, and not bother much more about my own personal life. Perhaps now I should submit, and be a teacher. I have fought so against it.

For my own part, though I am perhaps *more* irascible, being more easily irritable, not being well, still, I think I am more inwardly tolerant and companionable. Who knows! Anyhow, people's little oddities don't frighten me any more: even their badnesses. I think we might get on easily together. Frieda is

* From *Lorenzo in Taos.*
1 Ida Rauh, former actress and previous wife of Max Eastman.

suspicious, but I think even she is weary of the old watchful and hostile attitude, and doesn't care very much when people affront her a bit. So many of our feelings are illusion. We don't *really* have them. I think we might all be a great soothing and support to one another. I do really. I think we might even trust one another, sufficiently. It would be very good to have a real togetherness.

I wish we could start afresh with this year. You have never really trusted *anybody,* and you have never felt any real togetherness with anybody. Perhaps we might begin, and then do our best. We are too much cut off: I am too much cut off.

I hope you are feeling well, and fairly serene. I had your story. Of course it was *all* about yourself: just yourself. But I suppose, while you remain alone, you cannot escape yourself.

Well, here's to the spring, and a little new hope.

D. H. L.

To MRS. H. CROSBY

Beau Soleil, Bandol, Var., 20 Jan., '30.

Dear Caresse,

Thank you for the dream book. Harry[2] had a real poetic gift—if only he hadn't tried to disintegrate himself so! This disintegrating spirit, and the tangled sound of it, makes my soul weary to death.

I shall be interested to read the diary later, if you wish me to—or what of it you wish me to. And if I could write a suitable foreword, I'd be glad to. But for the next two months, I'm not allowed to do *anything.* The doctor came from England and said I must lie in bed for two months, and do *nothing* and see no people—absolute rest. Oh, dear! and Harry was really so well, physically. And my nerves are so healthy, but my chest lets me down. So there we are. Life and death in all of us!

---

[2] Harry Crosby, who had recently committed suicide.

Did *Chariot of the Sun* ever appear? I have never seen a copy. I should like very much to have one, if the book exists.

And is it possible for you to send me a couple of imperfect copies of *Escaped Cock,* as you once suggested? I should be glad.

Oh, yes—don't you try to recover yourself too soon—it is much better to be a little blind and stunned for a time longer, and not make efforts to see or to feel. Work is the best, and a certain numbness, a merciful numbness. It was too dreadful a blow—and it was wrong.

D. H. L.

To G. ORIOLI[3]

Villa Beau Soleil, Bandol, France.
Jan. 30, 1930.

Dear Pino,

Douglas said you were ill, but he didn't say how or what. I do hope it isn't bad. I expect you got yourself thoroughly upset Christmassing at Nice and Menton. When you were here I knew from your voice that you were knocking yourself up. Why are you so silly? Why do you think you want to razzle and drink like Douglas? It doesn't agree with you—and you are only miserable. Remember that by family you are born moral, and so you'll always be miserable when you go off the hooks. You'll merely kill yourself if you try to live up to Douglas' festive standards. You're not made that way.

There's a preach!—and all the time, here I'm in bed too. The doctor says I must stay in bed for two months['] absolute rest—no work—no seeing people—then perhaps go to the ranch.—Frieda's daughter Barbara is here—her sister has just gone away. My sisters come in about a fortnight.

---

[3] From *The Intelligent Heart.*

The Huxleys are in England, as *Point Counter Point* is being made into a play—first night tomorrow—and Aldous seems to be enjoying himself, figuring among the actors and actresses, and being *It*.

Ask Carletto[4] to send me a line to say how you are.

D. H. L.

To M. HUXLEY

Ad Astra, Vence. Wed.

Dear Maria,

Your letter came on—a good letter, made me understand about the play very well. I'm afraid the public wants to be made to feel it is all on the side of the angels. But I hope the run will be longer than you think, and make a bit of money anyhow.

Here I came at last, as I was getting so feeble and so thin. It isn't a sanatorium, really—an hotel where a nurse takes your temperature and two doctors look at you once a week—for the rest, just an hotel. They examined me with X-rays and all that. It is as I say—the lung has moved very little since Mexico, in five years. But the broncs are awful, and they have inflamed my lower man, the *ventre* and the liver. I suppose that's why I've gone so thin—I daren't tell you my weight—but I've lost a lot this winter, can't understand why. Of course they can do nothing for me—food, the food is good, but it's hotel food— they say milk is bad for my liver, and it's true. They don't say rest all the time—I go down to lunch, down two flights of steep stairs, alas—and I'm going to practise walking again. I think they are right and the English doctor wrong. A certain amount of movement is better. I've got a good balcony and lovely view— and the air is much better than Bandol. If ever you want to live in these parts, try a place like Vence.—Frieda is in the Nouvel

4 In Orioli's employ.

Hôtel in Vence—she goes back to the Beau Soleil Saturday—her daughter Barbara is there. They will pack up and go to a little house in Cagnes, which the di Chiaras⁵ are giving up. Then they'll come on the bus, about 20 minutes, to see me.—It's dull here—only French people convalescing and nothing in my line. But I'm feeling more chirpy, and shall try to get *on my legs*. It would be fun to see you, end of this month. When I hope I can walk a bit. I wish we could have been somewhere to have a good time like Diablerets. Or I wish I could sail away to somewhere really thrilling—perhaps we shall go to the ranch. What I want is to be thoroughly cheered up somehow—not this rest-cure business.

Well, it all sounds very egoistic—that's the worst of being sick. The mimosa is all out, in clouds—like Australia, and the almond blossom very lovely, especially around Bandol. Today was a marvellous day—I sat in the garden. Perhaps we might have a few jolly days, if you came down—just jolly, like Diablerets.

D. H. L.

To M. HUXLEY

*Ad Astra, Vence, Friday.*⁵ᵃ

Dear Maria,

The two parcels came now—very luxurious. Frieda trying them all—very extravagant of you to send so much. And Coréine and the Browning book. It's interesting, the Browning, yet somehow humiliating—bourgeois. The bourgeois at its highest level makes one squirm a bit.

I am rather worse here—such bad nights, and cough, and heart, and pain decidedly worse here—and miserable. Seems

---

⁵ Old friends from Capri. Mrs. di Chiara was an American.
⁵ᵃ The date of this letter is February 1930. Lawrence died March 2, 1930.

to me like *grippe,* but they say not. It's not a good place—
shan't stay long—I'm better in a house—I'm miserable.

Frieda has Barbey[6] with her—and Ida Rauh. When do you
think of coming?

D. H. L.

This place no good.

---

[6] Frieda Lawrence's daughter Barbara.

INDEX

INDEX